The Tangsas of Arunachal Pradesh

By the Same Author

— Indigenous Knowledge and Human Development: A Study in North East India.

About the Authors

Dr. Indira Barua, M.A., Ph.D. (1975) joined as a faculty member in the Department of Anthropology, Dibrugarh University and retired from the services in 2011. During her 25 years of service in the University she was involved in both academic and research activities and was the members of various academic and administrative bodies of the University. After retirement she continued her academic career as a UGC Emeritus Fellow for two years. Her publications include three books and two edited books on North East India covering the colourful tribes of this region. She has published scientific research papers in National and International Journals and her publications were duly recognized by various International bodies and were selected in their special volumes. She had attended seminars and conferences of various countries and was also invited to deliver talks. She supervised several research scholars for Ph.D. Degree and continued her research activities. She is the life member of many professional bodies.

Her research covers broad areas, e.g. ethnographic study, social demography and child care and development, Indigenous knowledge and various social problems.

Dr. Deepanjana Dutta Das, M.Sc., Ph.D. started her academic carrier in D.H.S.K. College, Dibrugarh and later on she joined Dibrugarh University as a Faculty Member. She served the University for two decades in different capacities till 2015. Besides the literary contributions, mostly written in Assamese, she has jointly edited two books and several research papers in various journals. She is also the life member of several professional associations. Her areas of special interest and publications include the field of Physical Anthropology, human biology, Anthropological demography, growth and nutrition.

THE TANGSAS OF ARUNACHAL PRADESH
A Socio-Demographic Profile

Indira Barua
Deepanjana D. Das

CONCEPT PUBLISHING COMPANY PVT. LTD.
NEW DELHI-110059

ISBN-13: 978-93-88937-70-2

First Published 2021

Published and Printed by

Since 1974

Concept Publishing Company Pvt. Ltd.
A/15-16, Commercial Block, Mohan Garden,
New Delhi-110059 (INDIA)
T : 91 11 25351460, 91 11 25351794
E : publishing@conceptpub.com; *W* : www.conceptpub.com

Cataloging in Publication Data--Courtesy: D.K. Agencies (P) Ltd. <docinfo@dkagencies.com>

Barua, Indira, author.
The Tangsas of Arunachal Pradesh : a socio-demographic profile / Indira Barua, Deepanjana D. Das.
pages cm
Study conducted among the Tangsas of Changlang District of Arunachal Pradesh, India.
Includes bibliographical references and index.
ISBN 9789388937702

1. Tangsa (Indic people)—India—Arunachal Pradesh—Social conditions. 2. Tangsa (Indic people)—India—Arunachal Pradesh—Economic conditions. 3. Tangsa (Indic people)—Social life and customs. 4. Changlang (India : District)—Social life and customs. I. Das, Deepanjana Dutta, author. II. Title.

LCC DS432.T33B37 2021 | DDC 305.8954054163 23

Preface and Acknowledgements

The present study concentrates with a very relevant and challenging topic i.e., "Social Demography". Demographic study is the statistical study of population composition, distribution and trends. Though the term Population Studies is more popular, yet the word "Demography" is used under wider field. In recent years, social demography enjoys a high status within the social science, which developed in tandem over the course of the 20th century. Its major focus is the impact of social and cultural factors on the demographic features of society. Simply it looks at the life around individuals and characteristics, such as age, gender, race, sexual orientation, religion, income, marital status, birth rate, death rate, average size of family, education, individual history etc. It is basically grouping of people by those characteristics. Therefore demography and culture have had a long but ambivalent relationship. Cultural influences are widely recognized as important for demographic outcome, but are often 'back grounded' in demographic research.

Broadly defined as the study of population composition and change, social demography encompasses a variety of substantive sub-areas. Thematically, an important focus of the Social Demography programme is how gender, age, race, family origin and historical or cultural contexts shape individual's lives and opportunities. Methodologically, social demographers typically use quantitative research methods, including the analysis of survey data, but are increasingly incorporating ethnographic and other qualitative approaches into their research.

The major focus is the impact of social and cultural factors on demographic feature of society, such as pattern of marriage and child bearing, the age structure of the population, life expectancy and so forth. Social demographers believe that social processes and structure regulate demographic process. Migration and influence of migration play its role in demographic features. Social demographers typically use qualitative research method, including the analysis of survey data, but are increasing incorporating ethnographic and other qualitative approach into their research. Social demography may *oe* applied both at micro and macro level.

Micro demography is the narrow view of population studies. The researches include the study of fertility, mortality, distribution, migration etc., individual family or group of a particular area or community. Macro demography includes the interrelation between population and social, economic and cultural condition of a country and their effects on population growth.

Anthropological demography particularly uses anthropological theory and methods to provide a better understanding of demographic phenomenon in current and past populations. It lies at the interaction of demography and socio-cultural anthropology with their efforts to understand population process, mainly fertility, migration and mortality. Both the disciplines share one research subject, mainly human population, though they focus on complementary aspects.

North East India is a paradise of diversity in terms of its natural habitat as well as in the variation of population with regards to language, culture and habitual pattern. Each has its own unique characteristics, but in broader level reflects homogenous nature, which are the characteristics of the population of North East India. North East occupies a strategic importance since early days and become a museum of races. The "Unity in Diversity" is the motto among the population of North East India. In such a situation every group may be considered as a unit to understand the socio-demographic profile. With this aim and objective the present study was carried on among the Tangsas of Changlang District of Arunachal Pradesh. Intensive investigation has been made among the two major groups of Tangsas, i.e., the Lungsangs and the Mukloms to understand and project the basic socio-demographic profile of the Tangsas covering six villages.

The present study is the outcome with a Financial Assistance from Indian Council of Social Science Research (ICSSR), New Delhi. We wish to take this opportunity to express our sincere thanks to ICSSR for granting the Financial Assistance without which it would not have been possible to complete this work. The responsibility for any unintentional factual error or any erroneous views which might have entered into the text is, however, entirely ours. We wish to avail this opportunity to express our thanks to all the members of the Tangsa Community of Arunachal Pradesh and Assam for their untiring help in providing the valuable information of their society.

Lastly but not the least we thank all the Project Fellows, namely Ms. Bobby Dutta, Khomeng Khemrang, Ms. Rakhi Rani Das for collection of field data.

Dr. (Mrs.) Indira Barua
and
Dr. (Mrs.) Deepanjana Dutta Das

Contents

List of Tables

1
Introduction

The present study aims to obtain certain significant socio-demographic features of the Tangsas of Arunachal Pradesh. Social demography, no doubt plays an important role in understanding the demographic situation of a community or a geographical locality. The significance of the study is that scholars' working in such area is to give specific attention to correlate demographic variables with that of social variables.

Demography is the study of human population primarily with respect to their size, composition and growth. The term demography comes from two Greek words, '*demos*' means people and '*graphia*' means to draw or write. Thus literally speaking, demography is concerned with writing about the people. The term was first used by Prof. A. Grilland in 1855 and since then the term has been gaining attention amongst the biological workers in this field. Treating demography, as a part of Anthropology, *Oxford University Dictionary* mentions, "Demography is that part of Anthropology, which treats of the statistics of birth, death, disease etc." Distribution of age, sex, birth, death and migration are the basic components of the demographic analysis of a population. Hauser and Duncan (1959) define demography as "the study of size, territorial distribution and composition of population, changes therein and the components of such changes, which may be identified as natality, mortality, territorial movement (migration) and social mobility (changes of status). From this definition, one can see that demography concerns with the static as well as dynamic aspects of human population. Bogue gave another important definition of demography in 1969. According to him, "Demography is the mathematical study of size, composition and special distribution of human populations and of changes overtime in these aspects through the operation of the five processes of fertility, mortality, marriage, migration and social mobility."

The social demography may be put under two sections, i.e. macro-demography and micro-demography. The former includes studies of systems, cultures and societies on a large scale, and the latter studies the individual and the family as a unit of society. Bogue mentions, "It is the study of the growth, distribution and redistribution of the population within a community, economic area or other local area. This includes both numerical and compositional aspects and is performed by using meaningful sub-divisions of community or local areas." The different aspects of the social demography are size of population, organization of population, i.e. age, sex, marital status, educational level, religion, caste, race, health etc. It also includes population distribution, i.e. the geographic, social, economic and demographic and residence (rural-urban).

Fertility is an important field of demographic study. In biology, fertility refers to the total reproductive performance or total number of live birth of a woman in her life. It comes from a Latin word "*fertile*" meaning to bear. So, fertility means to conceive and bear the offsprig, while mortality refers to the number of death of a population. Fertility causes addition of a population through birth whereas mortality brings declination through death. Thus, the study of fertility and mortality are fundamental determinants of population, growth and decline. Population growth is becoming a global concern as it shows a steady increase over time with the advancement of medical science and technology and socio-cultural development. Fertility is the major positive components of population dynamics.

Nag (1976), Benedict (1972) and others have pointed out that several biological and socio-cultural factors affecting human population. It varies from population to population and may also vary within a population. It is called differential fertility. In North East India different population are found to be in different stages of cultural development and thus provide ample scope for investigating this demographic aspect in different population groups of this part of the country.

Some of the important biological and socio-cultural factors affecting fertility are as follows:

(i) ***Biological factors:*** Biological factors, particularly, age at menarche and age at menopause play a vital role in the fertility performance. Menarche exposes a woman to possible child bearing. In fact, in many societies, age at menarche determines the age at marriage. Women with the early onset of menarche are more fecund than one's with late age at menarche leading to early pregnancy and earlier birth for a given exposure to the risk of conception cited by Bhasin and Nag (2002). Studies of Bhasin and Nag (2002) reveals that relatively late onset of menarche seems to lower fertility and impact of relatively early onset on fertility seems to be not exactly clear.

(ii) ***Social and cultural factors:*** Organization of population is the most important determinant of social and cultural factors. The characteristics include, age at marriage, type of marriage, family size and type, educational level, occupational status etc. Social customs, religious beliefs, deep-rooted values also affect fertility. Rural-urban residence also differentiates fertility.

(iii) ***Health and health related factors:*** Hygienic condition, diseases, food habits, also reflect demographic situation. As health condition go on improving and with that fecundity also increases and death rate comes down, more particularly in developing and underdeveloped countries. The health status affects the demographic scenario which on the other hand is the outcome of many biological and social factors.

The above discussion gives us an idea that biological and socio-cultural factors are equally responsible in a demographic study.

Present Study

The present study has been confined among the Tangsas. The Tangsas are mostly concentrated in the three districts of Arunachal Pradesh, i.e. the Changlang, the Tirap and the Lohit. For the purpose of present study, six Tangsa villages of Arunachal Pradesh have been selected for intensive study. Out of these six villages, 3 villages are inhabited by the Lungchang Tangsas and the other 3 villages are populated by the Muklom Tangsas.

Arunachal Pradesh

Arunachal Pradesh which translates to "Land of dawn-lit mountain" is the largest among the North East Indian states, commonly known as "seven sisters" states. It comprises territory which was included under the erstwhile North East Frontier Agency popularly referred as NEFA (from the British Colonial era). The beginning of the North East Frontier Agency went back to the British rulers in India who also constituted a similar administrative set-up under almost an identical nomenclature of North-West Frontier Agency at the extreme North-West of undivided India.

NEFA was renamed as Arunachal Pradesh on 20th January, 1972 and the area became the Indian Union Territory of Arunachal Pradesh, and, in 1987 it became an Indian state. Table 1.1 shows the name of States, Capitals, Population, Literacy, Area and Population density of the "Seven Sisters of North East India".

Table 1.1: North East States, Capitals, Population, Literacy, Area and Population Density

States	*Capital*	*Population*	*Literacy %*	*Area (sq. km)*	*Population density (/km^2)*
Arunachal Pradesh	Itanagar	1,383,727	63.38	83,743	17
Assam	Dispur	31,205,390	72.19	78,438	397
Manipur	Imphal	2,570,390	79.21	22,327	122
Meghalaya	Shillong	2,966,889	74.43	22,429	132
Mizoam	Aizwal	10,97,206	91.33	21,081	52
Nagaland	Kohima	19,78,502	79.55	16,579	119
Tripura	Agartala	36,73,917	87.22	10,486	350

Source: Census of India, 2011.

The territory of Arunachal Pradesh is spread along the south face of the eastern Himalayas immediately below the water divide between Tibet on the one hand and India on the other. Most of the Arunachal Pradesh is covered by the Himalayas. However, part of Lohit, Changlang and Tirap are covered by the Patkai hills, Kangto, Nyegi, Kangsang, the main Gorichan peak and the Eastern Gorichan peak are some of the highest peaks in this region of the Himalayas. The land is mostly mountainous with the Himalayan ranges running North-south. These divide the state into five river valleys: Kameng, Subansiri, Siang, Lohit and Tirap. All these rivers and rivulets of the areas are fed by snow from the Himalayas. The mightiest of these rivers is the Siang, known as Tsanpa in Tibet, which becomes the Brahmaputra after it is joined by the Dibong and the Lohit in the plains of Assam.

The Himalayan ranges that extend up to Arunachal Pradesh to separate it from Tibet. The ranges extend towards Nagaland and form a boundary between India and Burma in Changlang and Tirap district acting as natural barrier called Patkai Bum Hills. They are comparatively low Mountain than the greatest Himalayas.

It has over 2000 km of border with Bhutan, China, Myanmar and Bangladesh and is connected to the rest of India by a narrow 20 km wide corridor of land towards the west. North East India is one of the most ethnically and a linguistically diverse region in Asia, each state has distinct cultures and traditions of its own.

From times immemorial, India's North East has been the meeting point of many communities, faiths and cultures. It is a place renowned for its magical beauty and bewildering diversity. North East India is the home for more than 166 separate tribes speaking a wide range of languages. Some groups have migrated over the centuries from places as far as South-East Asia; they retain their cultural traditions and values, but are beginning to adapt to contemporary lifestyles. Its jungles are dense, its rivers are powerful and rain and thunderstorms sweep across the hills, village and plains during the annual monsoons.

The states are famous for their scenic beauty. The states also have many other tourists' attractions. The seven states of North East India with their capitals and land area in sq. km has been presented in Table 1.1. Of these, Sikkim became an Indian protectorate in 1947 and a full state in 1975. It is surrounded by Nepal, Bhutan, China, Myanmar and Bangladesh. However, they share only 21 km common border with the rest of India *via* the Chicken's Neck.

The Land

Arunachal Pradesh is situated in the easternmost part of India (Map 1.1). It is known as the "Land of the Rising Sun". It is the largest state in the North Eastern region of the Indian subcontinent covering an area of 83,743 sq. km (32,346 sq. miles). It is the least density populated country. Arunachal Pradesh is situated between 26.28° and 29.30° North Latitudes and 91.29°E and 97.30°E Longitudes and has an area of 83,743 sq. km (32,333 sq. miles). A mountainous territory, which is properly brought under formal administration since independence, its former name was the North East Frontier Agency (NEFA). Strategically, Arunachal Pradesh holds an important position as it shares its border with the Republic of China on its North, the State of Assam in its South, Myanmar on its East and the Royal Kingdom of Bhutan on the West (Table 1.2).

The North East is a true frontier region. No other region of India has international border as extensive as that of North East India.

As per 2011 Census there were 16 districts in Arunachal Pradesh. But the process of creating new districts is going on, and as per 2016 report, there are now 20 districts (Table 1.3) in Arunachal Pradesh.

Most part of Arunachal Pradesh is mountainous, consisting of high ridges, variously aligned, and separating deep valleys. It rises to the north, culminating in crests of the Great Himalaya. The highest peak of Arunachal Pradesh is the Kangto situated in the west of the Chinese border. The

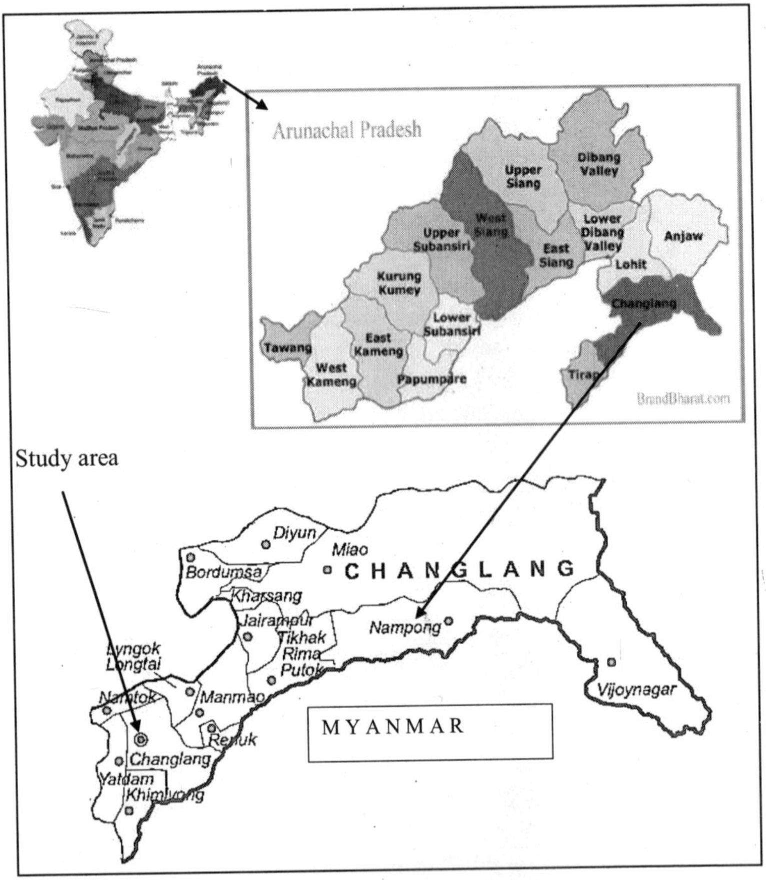

Fig. 1.1: Maps

Table 1.2: State-wise Length of International Border of North East Region in km

States	Bangladesh	Bhutan	China	Myanmar	Nepal	Total
Arunachal Pradesh	0	217	1080	520	0	1817
Assam	263	267	0	0	0	530
Manipur	0	0	0	398	0	398
Meghalaya	443	0	0	0	0	443
Mizoram	318	0	0	510	0	828
Nagaland	0	0	0	215	0	215
Sikkim	0	32	220.35	0	97.80	350.15
Tripura	856	0	0	0	0	856
Total	**1880**	**516**	**1300.35**	**1643**	**97.80**	**5437.15**

Source: Ministry of Development, North East Region.

Table 1.3: Number of Districts in Arunachal Pradesh

Sl. No.	*Districts*	*District Head-quarters*	*Population*	*Area (km^2)*	*Population density (/km^2)*
1.	Tawang	Tawang Town	49,950	2,085	19
2.	West Kameng	Bomdila	87,013	7,422	10
3.	East Kameng	Seppa	78,413	4,134	14
4.	Papum Pare	Yupia	1,76,385	2,875	42
5.	Kurung Kumey	Koloriang	89,717	8,818	10
6.**	Kra Daadi	Jamin	–	–	–
7.	Lower Subansiri	Ziro	82,839	3,460	24
8.	Upper Subansiri	Daporijho	83,205	7,032	8
9.	West Siang	Along	1,12,272	8,325	22
10.	East Siang	Pasighat	9,90,919	4005	12
11.**	Central Siang	Pangin	–	–	–
12.	Upper Siang	Yingkiong	33,146	6,188	5
13.	Lower Dibang Valley	Roing	53,986	3,900	14
14.	Upper Dibang Valley	Anini	7,948	9,129	1
15.	Anjaw	Hawai	21,089	6,190	3
16.	Lohit	Tezu	1,45,538	2,402	13
17.**	Namsai	Namsai	–	–	–
18.	**Changlang**	**Changlang**	**1,47,951**	**4,662**	**27**
19.	Tirap	Khonsa	111,997	2362	42
20.**	Longding	Longding	–	–	–

(** marks for carved out of the district mentioned just above)

Note: As of 2016, Arunachal Pradesh comprises of 20 districts. The most of them are inhabited by various tribal groups.

Brahmaputra river is the main river known as the Siang in Arunachal Pradesh and its main tributaries are Tirap, Lohit (Zayu Qu), Subansiri, Kameng and Bharali.

The climate of Arunachal Pradesh dominated by the Himalayan system varies with altitude. The climate is hot and humid at the lower altitudes and in the valleys covered by swampy dense forest particularly in the Eastern section.

The average temperature of Arunachal Pradesh ranges from 15°C to 21°C and 22°C to 30°C during winter and monsoon, respectively. The rainfall of Arunachal Pradesh is the heaviest in the country. The average annual rainfall is more than 300 mm. The pre-monsoon rain begins towards the end of March lasting for 4 months (May to September). The months of June and July begin with maximum amount of rainfall in this area.

Nature has been exceedingly kind and has endowed this beautiful state with diverse forests and magnificent wildlife. The richness of the flora and fauna presents a panorama of biological diversity including about 5000 plant species, 85 terrestrial mammals, over 500 species of birds and a large species of butterflies, insects, reptiles etc.

The vegetation of Arunachal Pradesh falls under four broad climatic categories and can be classified in five broad forest types, like tropical forests, sub-tropical forests, pine forests, temperate forests and alpine forests. Varieties of bamboo and grasses are also found.

Fauna and Flora

The Arunachal Pradesh is rich with flora and fauna. There are as many as 25 species of mammals included in Schedule-1 of the Wildlife (Protection) Act, 1972.

The large herbivorous of the foot-hills and adjoining plains are the elephant (*Elephas maximus*), gaur (*Bos gaurus*) and the wild buffalo (*Bubalus bufalis*).

Four major cats of Arunachal Pradesh are tigers (*Panthera tigris*), leopards (*Panthera pardus*), clouded leopards (*Neofelis nebulosa*) and snow leopards (*Panthera uncia*). The golden cats, leopard cats and the marbled cats are also found here.

Seven species of primates, i.e. hoolock gibbon, slow loris, Assamese macaque, rhesus macaque, pig-tailed macaque, stump tailed macaque and cappel langur also found in the forests of the state. Three goat antelopes, i.e. serow, goral and takin are found. The highly endangered hispid hare (*Capralagus hispiclus*) is also found in low grassy areas of the state.

Several Rodents (squirrel, porcupine and rats), lively mongoose, linsang, shrew and bat species are also found. On higher elevations, animals like goral, Himalayan black bear, red *panda* are found. Over 500 bird species inhabit Arunachal Pradesh including some endangered and endemic ones, like white winged wood duck, Sclater's Monal, Temmincks Tragopan, black necked crane, Mishmi wren and Bengal Storican.

The 'Mithun' (*Bos frontails*) exists both in wild and semi-domesticated form. This animal has religious significance and intimate relation with socio-cultural life of the people.

Arunachal Pradesh is also the happy home of Indian Hornbills, which is also the State Bird. The white winged wood duck, a rare endangered species, has been sheltered in Namdapha National Park. Namdapha Sanctuary was upgraded to the status of National Park in 1983.

This is the richest state for pheasants, with some ten species. The state also abounds in a variety of reptiles, amphibians, Pisces and innumerable species of butterflies, moths, beetles and other insects.

There are two National Parks and nine Wildlife Sanctuaries in the state managed by the forest department.

The varied forest types of eastern Himalaya exhibit an enormous floristic diversity. Apart from large number of timber species, there are innumerable varieties and kinds of orchids, medicinal plants, ferns, bamboos, canes wild relative of large number of our cultivated plants and even plants of biological curiosities, such as parasites, saprophytes etc. are found. Other important groups of plants are Rhododendrous, Hedychiums and Oaks, etc. Because of diverse types of orchids available in Arunachal Pradesh, it is referred as "Orchid Paradise". Out of about a thousand species of orchids in India, over 600 are to be found in Arunachal alone.

The People

According to the 2011 Census (provisional), the total population of Arunachal Pradesh was 1,382,611 compared to 8,64,558 in the 1991 Census scattered over 12 towns and 3649 villages. The number of males is 7,20,232 and the number of females is 6,62,379. The percentage of the total population of the state/union territory in the total population of North East India is 3.03; while out of total population of India is 0.11. The population density was 13.0 per sq. km, the lowest of any state or territory in India. As against decadal growth rate of 21.34 per cent at the national level, the population of the state has increased by 26.03 per cent in this decade compared (2001-2011) to past decade (1991- 2001). The density of Arunachal Pradesh in current decade is 43 per sq. mile. The sex-ratio of Arunachal Pradesh is 901 females to 1000 males is lower than the national average of 933. Most of the populations of Arunachal Pradesh are tribal peoples, related to the Tibetans and the peoples of Myanmar. There are 82 tribes and sub-tribes, of which the main ones in the west are the Nissi (Nishi or Dafla), the Sulung, the Sherdukpen, the Aka, the Monpa, the Apa Tani and the Hill Miri. The largest tribal group is that of the Adi (formerly Abor), who occupy the central part of Arunachal Pradesh, while the Mishmi dominate the North Eastern hill country and the Wancho, the Nocte and the Tangsa are centred in the South-east of the state, around the district of Tirap (which neighbours Nagaland). Between them, the tribal peoples speak over 50 distinct languages and dialects (mostly of the Tibeto-Burmese branch of the Sino-Tibetan linguistic family), making English (the official language of the state), Hindi, Bengali and Assamese the main means of inter-communication.

Relatively large percentage of population of Arunachal are nature worshippers (indigenous religion) and follow their own distinct traditional institutions like the Nyeder Namlo by the Nishi, the Rangfrah by the Tangsa and Nocte, Medar Melo by the Apatanis, the Kargu Gamgi by the Galo and Donyi-Polo Dere by the Adi under the umbrella of indigenous religion the Donyi-Polo. A smaller number of Arunachali people have traditionally identified as Hindus, although the number of animist traditions are increasing. Although influenced by Buddhism, most of the tribal peoples are animists, venerating natural and elemental deities or spirits and often practicing ritual animal sacrifices (notably of the *mithun*, a semi-domesticated gaur or wild boar). Near the Chinese border some adhere to Tibetan Buddhism particularly in the district of Twang, west Kameng and isolated region adjacent to Tibet. Theravada Buddhism is practiced by groups living near the Burmese border (13%). Around 19 per cent of the population is followers of the Christian faith.

Literacy has risen in official figures to 66.95 per cent in 2011 from 54.74 per cent in 2001. The literate population is said to number 7,89,943. The number of literate males is 4,54,532 (73.69%) and number of literate females is 3,35,411 (59.57%). Arunachal Pradesh is one of the linguistically richest and most diverse regions in all of Asia being home to at least 30 and possibly as many as 50 distinct languages in addition to innumerable dialects and sub-dialects thereof. The vast majority of languages; indigenous to modern day Arunachal Pradesh belong to the Paleao-Mongoloid with Tibeto-Burman groups of language family. The majority of these in turn belong to a single branch of Tibeto-Burman, namely Aabhu Thanyi language.

Most of these communities are ethnically similar, having derived from an original common stock but their geographical isolation from each other has brought amongst them certain distinctive characteristics in language, dress and customs. The major festivals celebrated by different tribes of Arunachal Pradesh are Mopin, Solung, Nyokum, Losar, Si-Donyi, Dree, Reh, Sipong, Yong, Chalu-Loker, Tamladu, Sarok, Moh/Mol, Kshyat-Sowai, Sangken, Oriya, Nichido etc. (Singh, 1995).

The tribes of Arunachal Pradesh have highly ordered and organized system of functioning in their villages. All matters relating to the community as a whole are decided at the village level. The socio-administrative structure of the society, as evolved over a period of centuries, recognizes democratic participation right down to the level of villages.

Economy

Arunachal Pradesh is rich in natural resources and as a result lots of scopes are there to utilize it and develop the state. Several steps have been taken from time to time to improve their economy. Their economy is primarily based on agriculture. About 80 per cent of the state population is engaged in agricultural activities. The important food crops of the state are paddy, maize, pulses, wheat etc. The major cash crops are jute, cotton, rubber, tea, fruits etc. The Arunachal Pradesh Mineral Development and Trading Corporation Limited was established in 1991 to develop mineral reserves, notably in the South-east, at the Namchik-Namphuk coal mine. The state is also reckoned to have petroleum resources of some 1.5 m metric tons and significant reserves of natural gas in addition to deposits including dolomite, limestone, graphite, marble, mica, iron, copper, lead and zinc.

By the end of the 1990s there were 18 medium-sized industries and 3,368 small industrial enterprises registered in Arunachal Pradesh apart from a cement plant, a fruit processing plant and citronella-oil distillery. Activities including agro-processing such as timber, rice and oil milling, manufacturing soap and candles, sericulture and handicrafts (there were 88 craft and weaving training centres in the state).

Most of the population is engaged in agriculture, often on a subsistence basis, but increasingly commercial. Many depended on *jhum* (shifting or slash-and-burn) cultivation in which trees and undergrowth are burned and cleared for planting for a few seasons, before the farmer moves to a new area. However, this has accounted for much of the deforestation in the state and other methods are becoming more prevalent. The main crop is rice, grown on valley bottoms and on some terraced slopes maize, millets, pulses, potatoes, wheat and mustard are the other important crops. About 62 per cent of the total area of the state is under forests coverage.

The government has established a number of cottage industries, training-*cum*-production centres, where local boys and girls are trained in various crafts to enable them to earn their livelihood by practicing these crafts. The craft centres are also helping the people in finding markets for their products.

Of late, the state is initiating far reaching and comprehensive strides for a rapid industrial development in the towns of Arunachal Pradesh. At present, there are nearly 1616 industrial estates which play a vital role in Arunachal's economy.

Textile and weaving serve the cultural identity and economic benefit. In Arunachal Pradesh weaving is the occupation of the womenfolk who have a beautiful sense of colour combination. The favourite colours are black, yellow, dark blue, green, scarlet and madder. The designs are basically geometrical type varying from a formal arrangement of lines and bands to elaborate pattern of diamonds and lozenges.

It is not known when the people of Arunachal Pradesh learned the art of weaving. According to one of the legends, the art of weaving was learnt in a dream from the goddess *Podi Barbi*. A Galo song narrates a full story of how the cotton is grown, plucked, spun and how it is woven with cotton yarn in a loom. The song, which is sung with the dance by the village girls, narrates that in the olden days when the cotton was not grown and the people had not enough clothes, they started the cultivation of cotton. Thus, weaving among the people of Arunachal Pradesh is as old as the story itself. The people knew of clothes as a means of protecting themselves against rigours of the climate. The women of this area are good weavers and they have a good colour choice and artistic designs of their own.

The colour and design have their symbolic meaning among some tribes of Arunachal Pradesh. The use of certain kinds of clothes and ornaments is often associated with a family's social position and achievements in the fields of hospitality and war. The motifs, designs and patterns, however, are quite complex and their symbolic meaning and usages are rather significant. The elaborate processes of spinning, dying and finally weaving remind us of the rich discoveries of the women who were supposed to weave respective clothes for their families.

Arunachal Pradesh has a vibrant craft tradition and every tribe excels in craftsmanship. Cane and bamboo is an important craft of this area, and the workmanship is of a very high order. Many tribesmen make their own hats, which are often extremely decorative, adorned with the beaks and feathers of birds or with tufts of hair dyed red. They also make varieties of baskets, bags and other containers. There is a wide range of cane belts, woven and plain, and in northern Subansiri, tribes have even elaborately woven brassieres of cane and fibre.

When we look to the Administrative procedure, we find that various measures were taken by the British administration while dealing with Arunachal Pradesh. It was realized by the British rulers in India that the territories under tribal occupation had specific problems which needed special administrative approach. It was considered necessary to form these regions into specially Non-Regulation Tract to be administered by simpler codes directly by the Deputy Commissioners. Such divisions were made for proper administration. The year 1912-13 marked further progress in the history of frontier administration of the province.

During 1914-15 steps were taken to demarcate areas of administrative units:

(i) The Central and Eastern Sections
(ii) The Lakhimpur Frontier Tract
(iii) The Western Section

The first two sections were placed under one Political Officer with headquarters at Sadiya and the western section under another Political Officer with headquarters at Charduar. In 1919, the title of Western section was changed to Balipara Frontier Tract and Central and Eastern section to Sadiya Frontier Tract.

In the year 1943, a new administrative division, called Tirap Frontier Tract was created out of the some areas of Lakhimpur Frontier Tract and the Sadiya Frontier Tract with its headquarters at Margherita. The Balipara Frontier Tract was again divided into the Se-la-sub-Agency and the Subansiri Areas in 1946. After Independence, in 1948, the remaining portion of the Sadiya Frontier Tract was further divided into two divisions, the Abor Hills and the Mishmi Hills. The Frontier Tracts were again renamed in 1954 as Kameng Frontier Divisions, Siang Frontier Division, Lohit Frontier Division, Tirap Frontier Division and Tuensang Frontier Division under the North East Frontier Agency.

In 1964, the above frontier divisions were redesigned as districts. On 1st December, 1965, the erstwhile North East Frontier Agency was divided into 5 districts, i.e. (i) Kameng, (ii) Subansiri, (iii) Siang, (iv) Lohit, and (v) Tirap. Subsequently, the number of districts increased as each of five districts was bifurcated into a number of districts; minimum 2 new districts were formed from each earlier district.

Tirap is one of the important districts of Arunachal Pradesh. As already mentioned it has a history of its own. Tirap Frontier Tract was formed by curving out some areas of Lakhimpur and Sadiya in 1943. After Independence, it was renamed as the Tirap Frontier Division under the North East Frontier Area. Finally in 1965, Tirap Frontier Division was recognized as Tirap District. In November 1987, the erstwhile Tirap district was divided into two districts—Tirap and Changlang districts.

Changlang District

The present study has been confined among the Tangsas of Changlang district. It is located in the South-eastern part of Arunachal Pradesh. The district lies within the Latitude of 27.74 N and Longitudes 96.64 E and altitude from sea level 200-4500 metres. There are total 13 circles, 4 Blocks and 4 sub-divisions in Changlang district. The area of this district is 4662 sq. km. It is bounded in the East and South by International boundary Myanmar. It is bounded in the North by inter-district boundary, i.e. Lohit district and South-West by Tirap district. The West is bounded by interstate boundary, i.e. Assam.

Changlang district is the abode of Tangsas, the Singpho, the Nocte and many other tribal communities. It is located in the South-eastern part of Arunachal Pradesh. The word Changlang is a generic term. This word has been derived from Lungchang words. In Lungchang dialect "Chang" and "Lung" means a kind of plant which is used as fish poison. Thus, there is a common view that the name Changlang is derived from the local spelt as Changlang. The word Changlangkan means a hill top where people discovered the poisonous herb which is used for poisoning fish in the river. The altitude of Changlang district Headquarter is 1903.5 feet.

The Changlang became a district on 14th November, 1987, establishing Changlang town as its administrative headquarter. The Tangsas occupy the largest group of tribal population. Other major tribes of the district are the Singphos, the Tutsa and the Yobins (but not yet recognized as ST of Arunachal Pradesh). According to 2011 Census, total population of the district is 1,48,226. The number of male is 76,948 and the number of female is 71,278. Out of these the Tangsas constitute 38,760, the Singphos 16,982 and the Tutsas 5,844 (half of their population live in Tirap district of Arunachal Pradesh). The district has a population density of 32 persons per sq. km (83 sq. mile). Its population growth rate over the decades 2001-2011 was 17.96 per cent. The Changlang has a sex-ratio of 914 females for every 1000 males. The literacy rate is 61.9 per cent.

The district is largely in the Great Patkai Mountain ranges (with the altitude of 200–1800 metres). The average annual rainfall is above 200 mm. The daily maximum temperature is 31°C and the minimum is 8°C. Most of the landmass of the district is featuring undulated rugged maintains covered by evergreen thick forest. There is a narrow strip of the plains of Nao-Dihing and Burhi-Dihing, the tributaries of Brahmaputra River in the north and eastern part wherein Miao. Jairampur, Nampong, Kharsang and Bordumsa circles are located.

Namdapha National Park and Deomali peak is located in the Changlang district of Arunachal Pradesh. There are also two passes, namely Chankan pass and Pangsu pass in the Changlang district which have acclaimed national and international recognition. The historic

Stillwell road which was constructed by the American during Second World War also runs via Changlang district. The Jairampur Second World War Cemetery is also located in the Jairampur-Nampong road in the Changlang district.

The mountain range has got numerous passes which facilitated migration of Hindus, the Buddhist and other communities to South East Asia in ancient times. In medieval period the Taishans, the Tangsas, the Tutsas, the Singphos, the Khamptis and a host of communities used these passes to enter into the Indian territory to make this land permanent home. Thus, Changlang today is home to several tribes and communities who add varying colour and beauty to our culture and heritage, (Rao 2006).

Changlang district is very rich with coal and oil, the two important mineral resources of the area. In olden times gold was extracted from the sands of Burhi Dihing and other rivers with the help of Burmese gold washers. Salt was also manufactured from the saline springs and wells especially by the Tangsas, the Tutsas and the Noctes. Salt manufactured by these people was marketed in the plains of Assam and also in Myanmar.

Changlang district headquarters is about 149 km away from the Dibrugarh. There is no direct bus communication in between Dibrugarh and Changlang district. For means of road communication with outside of Changlang there are buses running under Arunachal Pradesh State Transport Corporation from Changlang to other parts of Arunachal Pradesh or Changlang district and Assam. There are some private means of communication like Tata Sumos.

The only road connecting Changlang with Assam is the Changlang-Margherita road, which is only about 44 km away from Margherita. There are also roads connecting Changlang with Manmao circle and Tirap district. But the condition of the road is not very good. So, Changlang-Margherita road is generally used for communication to outside the Changlang.

The day-to-day necessary materials are supplied by truck from Margherita or Tinsukia towns of Assam.

For communication from Changlang town to other villages there is Auto rickshaws. Besides, some people have used their own vehicles like bike, car etc. The conditions of the roads are not so good as compared to Assam. The roads are zigzag and running up and down.

In Changlang circle there are a number of Primary Schools and Anganwadi Centres at every village level. As per 7th AISES Survey 2003 conducted by NCERT there are total 131 Primary schools, 22 Upper Primary schools, 8 Secondary and 7 Higher Secondary schools. There is only 1 Degree College. A total 169 educational institutes are there in Changlang district.

The region is extremely rich in respect of flora and fauna. The Patkai hills are thickly wooded with coniferous and non-coniferous trees and variety of shrubs. This region contains a variety of valuable plants and trees like *hollong, mekai, hollock, champa, sam, gand-soroi, nahar jutuli, lali kadam, barpat, khokon, uriam*, rubber, *markai-sal*, cinnamon, agar, pine, *simolu, onyenga, pipul, sal mugra, poma, amra, banson*, and many others. Several species of plants and trees are useful to manufacture medicines, perfumery and incense items. The local population greatly depends on the rich stock of tubers, foliage, flowers, fruits and economy is based largely on the forest products. But, now the people of Changlang have started taking interest in tea plantation. Several tea estates have come up by replacing thickly wooded forests in the district.

This region is equally richer in fauna which comprise tiger, leopard, black panther, clouded leopard, cat, civet cat, elephant, rhinoceros, buffalo, *mithun*, black bear, red bear, boar, jackal, wild dog, swamp deer, spotted deer, antelope, barking deer, musk deer, porcupine, terrapin otter, *langur*, drill ape, monkey, flying squirrel etc. Variety of birds, e. g. great Indian hornbill, *tragopan*, ducks, teals, Asiatic goosander, Imperial pigeon, parrot, *parkeet*, doves, mynah, *bhimraj,* shrike, sunbird, snipe kingfisher, woodpecker, *ravan*, blackbird, fowl, bird of paradise, *highjar*, goshawk etc. are widely noticed in the area. Varieties of fishes are also present in the waters of all rivers.

Agriculture

The agricultural conditions of the Changlang district reflect more or less the overall scenario of Arunachal Pradesh. Soil of the district is fertile and can yield both food as well as cash crops in large scale. The soil can be divided into alluvial plains, river valleys, sedimentary hills and metamorphites. The people of Changlang district mostly depend on agriculture. They practice both shifting or *jhum* cultivation and wet rice cultivation. But now a day's wet rice cultivation is increasing and *jhum* rice cultivation is practiced on side by side. Rice, maize, *kochu* (arum), *bankhe*, chilies, watermelon, seasonal vegetable and mustard are the major crops grown here. Now-a-days the people of Changlang have started taking interest in tea plantations. Several tea estates have come up in the district.

The religious and socio-cultural ceremonies and rituals of the tribes of this area are closely linked with the process of cultivation. Most of the festivals are especially related with the process of pre-and post-harvesting of *jhum* and wet paddy cultivation. Also there are some festivals which are celebrated at the individual family level too.

Introducing the People

A. The Tangsas

It has already been mentioned that the present study has been entirely confined among the Tangsas of Arunachal Pradesh. Now, an effort is made to give a brief introduction of the Tangsas indicating their origin and history, settlement pattern and certain aspects of their social system. The Tangsas are divided into several sub-tribes which are again divided into various exogamous clans. Each sub-tribe has their own dialect and some uniqueness in socio-cultural spheres. So, an emphasis has been made to project their uniqueness in the sub-tribe level also.

Tangsa is a tribe, inhabiting the sub-Himalayan region of Arunachal Pradesh towards the south-east. The Tangsas inhabit the eastern hills in Changlang district along the Indo-Mayanmar border. The main concentration of the Tangsas is in the valley of the Tirap River and the Namchik "extending from the Patkai range in the south to the border of State of Assam in the north" (Chowdhury, 1973:254). Since no written records are available, it is indeed difficult to find the year of their migration. The Tangsas are one of the major tribes inhabiting the central part of the Changlang district of Arunachal Pradesh of North East India. They are a distinct ethnic group with their own identity. The community is recognized as a scheduled tribe of Arunachal Pradesh.

The various sub-tribes labelled to day as Tangsa are trans-Patkai tribes, who trace their origin in the highlands of Burma in the south as their ancestral homeland. They are very rich in oral literature and interpret their own route of migration in the sub-tribe level. Dutta remarks, "The oral historical traditions prevalent among various sections suggest migrations that must have taken place only within the last few centuries" (Dutta, 1959:36). Different groups moved out at different times in search of *jhum* land or pushed out by feuds with other groups in the ancestral habitat.

The scholars refer or analyse the word 'Tangsa' from different angles. The common interpretation is that the word 'Tangsa' is the amalgams of two local words, i.e. *Tang* (hills) and *Sa* (people). Thus, the literal meaning of the word 'Tangsa' is Hill people. It has also been mentioned that the word 'Tang' means up-stair posterity and *'Sa'* means son of *Tang* or children of *Tang*, so called Tangsa. Similarly, the word 'Tang' refers three conjugative meanings: (i) Tang means up-stair, (ii) Tang means conqueror, and (iii) Tang means Hill people. Thus, the word carries a significant interpretation. Dutta (1959:1) says "the Tangsas are a large tribe comprising a number of sub-tribes". As different sub-tribes and clans migrated in different batches at various times, nobody could get a chance to become the sole leader of the tribe, whom may be considered as the master of Tangsa tribe. Majority of scholars including Dutta state that Tangsa means "hill people". The people are conservative and sentimental to their identity. They could preserve their oral literature and historical narrative in such a way that it still helps to understand their migration and tradition.

The Tangsas consist of a number of sub-tribes, each speaking a distincts dialect, but have close affinities with each other. Each sub-tribe has a number of exogamous clans. As all the tribes did not migrate together, each tribe has their own version of migration. There are also differences of opinion about the number of sub-tribes of Tangsas. Though, it was mentioned about the number of sub-tribes as 32, yet all scholars are in opinion that only 15 could be traced distinctly. But all agree that the Tangsas are divided into several sub-tribes. Dutta (1959:1) remarks, "The Tangsas are a large tribe comprising a number of sub-tribes." (1991). On the other hand a literate informant gave a different meaning to the term. According to him, *Tang* stands for sacrifice and *Sa* for small. That is groups, which made ritual sacrifice for small things, such as pigs and cattle including buffalo. Those tribal people who practiced only animal sacrifice were called as Tangsa even in their ancestral habitat in Burma (Myanmar). There are certain other tribes collectively referred as *Pangsa*, who had migrated to their new habitat much later than Tangsa. The word *Pangsa* means *Pang* left behind, *Sa* means younger. It was reported that this group of tribes sacrificed human being beside the animal sacrifice in their original habitat. They continued the same practice in the new habitat also. It was reported by Baveja (1961:79) that though at one time the Tangsas were head-hunters, yet during his visit to Changlang, he could not find any sign of it. Singh mentioned that next to Tangsa communities are called *Pangsa* or *Pangwa*. As there is reference of term *Pangsa*, it is considered that interpretation of the migration of this group later on to the new habitat is remembered by a section of Tangsas. But for all practical purposes, the *Pangsa* group is all subsumed under Tangsa in the administrative level as well as among the common people. Regarding the human sacrifice it was reported that in 1942, William Walker, a British political officer at Sadiya, brought a halt to the barbarous act. And after that, there was no incidence of human sacrifice reported from this area.

The *Tangsa-Pangsa* terminology no doubt confirms their migration in different stages. According to Baveja, the village chief could not tell as to when this people had come to this part of the country. All he could say was "we came long back from Burma border. Our brothers, the Kachens are still there." Without written record, it was difficult to find out the year of migration to Tirap. Baveja personally felt, it could not have been later than the last part of Ahom rule in Assam as their contacts across the border are still fresh.

According to conservative Tangsas, the main Tangsa group include Muklom (or Muklum), Lungchang, Tikhak, Have and the Ponthai (Bhagabati, 1991). These groups were believed to migrate to this area long back, whereas the *Pangsa* segment includes Mosang, Morang, Kimsing, Ron-Rang, Yogli, Lungri (Longri), Sanke, and the Longphi. The Tangsa-Pangsa amalgam, broadly referred to as the Tangsas, is thus an assembly of some 15 named tribal units, or sub-tribes each of which is also a dialect group (Bhagabati, 1991). Each of these units or sub-tribes were meaningful social universe, each possessing most of the characteristics of the tribe, such as cultural and linguistic homogeneity, territorial contiguity, a common pattern of social organization though not organized as single political unit under any sort of centralized leadership or chief. According to 1981 Census, the total population of the tribe is 16,475 grouped into 32 sub-tribes of which only 15 groups of the Tangsas could be identified by the Anthropological Survey of India in 1985 (Singh, 1994). As per 2001 Census, the total population in Arunachal Pradesh is 10,91,117 persons. Out of this, the Tangsas constitute 38,760 populations in Changlang district (Kenglang, 2004). Thus, though their oral history mentioned about 32 sub-tribes, yet in practical purposes only 15 sub-tribes were identified.

For the present project, two major sub-tribes of Tangsas, i.e. the Lungchangs and the Mukloms have been considered. There were no differences of opinion that they belong to the original Tangsa group.

Migration

The history and migration of the Tangsas from their origin to the different parts of South-East Asia is a long process. The Tangsas had passed through various phases of migration and encountered diverse types of problems enrooted. So, they took various precautionary measures while settling in a particular area. This is one of the reasons why most of the Tangsa villages were located on the hills. This they did due to security and strategic reasons. The Tangsas had used several routes of migration and all the sub-tribes did not move together. They migrated from one place to another and lived in a number of places before making Changlang district as their home. The Tangsa oral historical literature strongly testified to the fact that they originally belonged to the South-East Asian countries. Rao (2006) mentions that the Tangsa have their original home in Burma hill called Masoi Sinarapum in the Hukong valley. As different sub-tribes have their own interpretation regarding migration, it is difficult to accept one single view.

When the people feel necessary to shift to a new place, first they are to consult with members of village council. While shifting they consider mainly on two aspects, i.e. (a) Topography and (b) Safety from natural calamities and epidemic. They carefully select the site and ensured that it is not easily accessible to the rival groups or enemies. Once settled, they evolve their own mechanism for functioning of the village society. The Tangsas do not like the interference from neighbouring villages. Once the village site is selected, they select the ritual place, which is considered as utmost necessary. In most cases, selection of the village site is such that, the boundaries are marked through natural streams, rivers and hillock. Any encroachments of boundary by force are not allowed. But under certain circumstances; they may go for erecting boundary for a short period of time. In case of dispute on the village boundary it is normally decided by the council of nearby villages. As they follow the rules with heart, there are hardly any controversies of the village boundary. The villagers maintain a cordial relation. Co-operation and mutual understanding is reflected in community feast, rituals, hunting and many communal activities.

Earlier, the Tangsas were wrongly referred to as the Naga group of people. But that confusion was rectified in 1956, and since then they have been known by the name Tangsa. But there are instances, where they still referred as Tangsa Naga and put name plate in their home, mentioning prominently as 'Tangsa Naga'. In the Tangsa village situated in Assam, it was possible to trace several such cases. The Patkai range and Namkin range may be considered as major routes of migration which were used by various tribes for migration to North East India.

Ethnically, the Tangsas belong to the Mongoloid racial group of Tibeto-Burman linguistic family. Here, an effort has been made to describe the history and migration of the Lungchangs and the Muklom Tangsas. It is believed that it would at least give an understanding of the migration of Tangsas as a whole.

B. The Lungchangs

The Lungchangs constitute one of the major sub-tribe of the Tangsas. They belong to the *Tangwa* division of the Tangsas. The name is a combination of two words–*Tang* means stone and *chang* means birth. Thus, the name indicates that "people who are born or have originated from stone". They trace their migration from Hukong valley of Burma and reached Changlang following the course of Tirap River. Barua (1991) also considers Burma as the original homeland of the Lungchangs, but could not definitely tell about the exact place of their origin. Rao (2006) worked among the Tangsas and tried to come to a definite conclusion about the migration of the Lungchangs with the help of local leaders. Ultimately, it was concluded that Lungchangs originally belonged to place called Tangsung Lungchang, located on the mountain range called Masoi Sinarapum in the Hukong valley of Burma (Rao, 2006: 95). History is full of examples, where we find that due to strong pressure of powerful tribes, the people of those areas moved towards the Patkai ranges in the west. It is a confirmed fact that the powerful kingdom established by Kublai Khan compelled large scale migration from the Hukong valley. Frequent raids of several warrior tribes of Mongolia, China, and Lower Burma were another cause of large scale migration from that area.

It was mentioned by some of the villagers or the oral histories that persist among the Lungchangs indicate that they started to move to find a place where the first rays of sun falls. They noticed that a mountain located in the west, where the first rays of sun falls and thought that they were deprived of the sun rays and in order to reach that place they moved towards that hill. But to their surprise, they again found that another hill located in the west, received the first sunlight. Thus, their movement continued until they reached the Changlang beyond which they did not notice any new hills, which was showered with first rays of sun-light. It was also assumed that due to cold and wet climatic condition, they started their movement towards west. The history and migration is not so smooth. Because, most of the Mongoloid tribes of North East India took the same route of migration and thus inter tribal rivalry caused much trouble. Historical evidence revealed that the Tai Ahoms who followed the same route under the leadership of Sukapha had to fight with Tangsas even in the Hukong valley. During the reign of Suhenpha (1488-1493 C.E.) the hostility between the Ahoms and the Tangsas renewed. After some initial defeat, the Ahoms succeeded in defeating the Tangsas (Gait, 1992:80-81). From that point of time, the Tangsas avoided the direct confrontation with the Ahoms and settled in a comparatively safe place. They purposefully started moving towards the northern slopes of the Patkai hills in the Tirap valley and avoided the north-westerly route leading to the Brahmaputra valley. They started to enter the Tirap valley through Okhutohap and Pangsa passes in different batches. The movement of the Lungchangs and other Tangsas is slow compared to other tribes like the Khamtis, the Singphos and the Kacharis. After settling different places, considering diverse factors, ultimately one batch of the Lungchangs crossed over to the north of Tirap River at Ngasai and gradually reached the top of Changlang Changkan to settle down permanently. Thus, the Changlang village emerged as a strong political centre on the northern side of the Tirap valley. And the Lungchangs, who settled first in the village, earned the title of *Kengnya* (early settlers). They considered Changlang as favourable place to stay because the hill top settlement had given them an opportunity to keep a watch of the enemy. It also received sunlight in the morning, earlier than other villages. Slowly they got the opportunity of mixing with the local people living in the plains of Brahmaputra valley. From that original settlement, they started to move in different directions and established several new villages.

The movement of Lungchang from their original habitat continued. It was mentioned that in the vicinity of Jangsung-Lungchang there was another Lungchang village called Vapai-keng. The Langchang of this village also migrated to the Tirap valley following the first batch of Lungchangs who settled at Changlang-Changkan. Perhaps the same factors behind every migration, i.e. adverse socio-economic and political condition disturb law and order and inter-tribal rivalry or enmity forced the people to migrate from that spot. In the process of searching for fresh areas for the settlement, several new villages came into existence. The Rangkatu was the first village of the latter groups of Tangsas, who migrated from their settlement. And in course of development several new villages emerged.

The Lungchangs Tangsa has been divided into several exogamous clans. The Lungchangs earlier used to act as middle man between the Assamese and the Lungri, Tutsa, Mukloms in the course of trade in iron implements, salt and cloths. At present also they initiate to contract marriage alliances with other Tangsa sub-groups, Adis, Nepalis and Assamese. As they are more exposed to outside world than the other sub-tribes of Tangsas they are in a position to interact with other communities, professional and businessman, in a more comfortable way.

C. The Mukloms

The Mukloms constitute one of the major sub-tribe of the Tangsas. Like the Lungchangs, they are also very rich in their oral literature, which is handed down from one generation to another. This helped them to trace their origin and migration. The Muklom Tangsas are distributed in about 20 villages of Changlang district (Rao, 2006:118). The Mukloms trace their descent from a legendry brother and sister who survived the natural calamity due to blessing of *Lord Rang Frah.* The total population of the Mukloms recorded in 1971 was around 2200 (Singh, 1995:345-360).

The Muklom oral literature provides valuable in history of the migration and settlement of this sub-tribe. It has already been mentioned that each sub-tribe had their independent version of origin and movement. But, it has been revealed that independent account is recorded not only in the sub-tribe level but in the village level also. This has confirmed that they have migrated in different batches in different time period and established their settlement accordingly. From various interpretations, it is assumed that the Mukloms might have arrived in India in different batches, during the medieval period.

It is commonly believed that the original home of the Mukloms was in Molom Solom, a place located in the east, when sun rises on the earth. The population pressures ultimately compelled them to move in several directions. Generally, the members of the same clan moved together. It was reported by Rao (2006:118) that the Mukloms migrated to Changlang district and initially settled in Longshang village. Later on it became a big Muklom settlement and the people started to move out of the village. They established new Muklom settlement in the nearby areas, i.e. Waphang, Thamlom and Khimyong.

For the present study, we have selected the New Thamlom village, and according to the villagers they came from Thamlom. And much later, when the population grew, the Mukloms started to establish new villages. A new village Kothungkung was established from it also, they moved outward and Yanman, Saching and Chingsa villages were established.

In the present project, the village Yanman is one of our selected villages. As each village have their own oral tradition, it is difficult to put down in writing any definite place of origin for the Muklom Tangsas. It was also interpreted that during their migration they stopped at a place called Moklum, wherefrom they migrated to different direction. It was mentioned by Rao (2006:122) the Mukoms of Yanman trace their origin from Salkhong-ko-wang (point of rising sun). From various interpretations it may be assumed that different sub-tribes of the Tangsas moved in search of suitable place, where they would be showered with sun-light. The search for cultivable land and safety and security of their own tribe no doubt play a major role in the migration and selection of new settlement.

The Muklom Tangsa has been divided into several exogamous clans. Though each sub-tribe has its own distinctiveness in certain spheres, yet the Tangsa as a whole projects some general characteristics which give them a distinct tribal identity. A brief description of the socio-cultural life of the Tangsas has been described in this chapter.

Physical Features

The Tangsas belong to the Mongoloid racial group. They are medium statured, generally with a well-built body. Their height varies from 5ft to 5.6ft in both the cases of men and women. The complexion of these people is fair with a slight yellowish tinge. The Mongolian or epicanthic fold is present in the eyes of both men and women, particularly in the case of children.

Language

Every group of sub-tribes of Tangsas speaks different languages belonging to the Tibeto-Burman group of language. Some additions and omissions of prefixes are present in the language of these sub-tribes belonging to the Tangsa tribe. They do not have any script of their own. They use Assamese and English script for the purpose of writing.

Religion

The Tangsas are the believers of Supreme Being who is invisible, but created and cares for the world. He lives in the sky and bestows his blessings on mankind. The religion of the Tangsas is a replication of the Buddhists, the Hindus and other indigenous communities and tribes.

Tangsa religion, like all other tribal religion is based on a belief in spirits and deities. That is why the Tangsas perform the magico-religious rituals for the malicious spirits. They believe that the spirits should always be propitiated by offerings and sacrifices, because they are quick to take offence and bring harm to mankind.

Priests perform all religious ceremonies. He can consults omen about harvesting, hunting, fishing etc. The profession of a priest is not hereditary. Anyone who has sufficient knowledge about the procedure and paraphernalia of the craft may aspire to this position. At present the Tangsas are influenced by a new religious faith, i.e. *Rang fra* whom they worship as supreme being.

Festivals

The Tangsa festivals revolve around the process of cultivation, especially the *jhum* and wet paddy cultivation. Ceremonies and celebrations start right from identification of a plot of land (for cultivation) to the completion of harvesting of crops. The ceremonies, religious rites, cultural events, and festivals are like linked to each other and every stage of the progress of an agricultural season. Everybody has its own time schedule to organize and celebrate any festival and cultural events. Normally, the dates of a festival are fixed in such a way that everyone has got leisure time to celebrate the festival. The names and dates of festival differ from one village to another. The mode of cultivation of crops decides the nature of festivals celebrated by the villagers. Their festivals are celebrated both in community and individual family level. The Tangsas festivals hold ceremonies, perform rituals and also offer sacrifices to invoke different spirits, gods, goddesses and the Supreme Being Lord Rang to obtain greater production, peace, prosperity and happiness.

The Tangsas have distinct social system, which is reflected in the family and marriage system. The uniqueness of each sub-tribe is also noticeable.

Objectives of the Study

The specific aims and objectives of the present study are:

- To project the socio-cultural life of the Tangsas; and
- To examine certain aspects of demographic situation of the Tangsas.

The study aims to obtain an integrated picture of the socio-demographic features of the Tangsas where utmost care is given to correlate demographic variables with variables of the social system.

To fulfil these major objectives certain important parameters have been identified to project the socio-demographic picture of the Tangsas:

(i) Composition of population constitutes the most important denominator of demographic study. A study of age and sex composition no doubt provides us the trend of population growth among the Tangsas.

(ii) Ethnographic present indicates the demographic situation. To project the ethnography of the Tangsas, the family system, marriage pattern, religious life and economic condition of the Tangsas has been described.

(iii) Ethnographic accounts reveal that age and sex composition influences the social organization and life of the people. Sex preference, age at marriage, marriage prohibition is important aspects of population demography. Socio-cultural beliefs and practices also determine various aspects of population structure. These aspects have been considered in the present project.

(iv) An attempt has been made to observe the impact of biological factors, i.e. age at menarche, age at marriage, the reproductive performance of women. Though outwardly biological, the influence of socio-cultural aspects is easily desirable.

(v) Fertility and mortality are the two major factors that can influence directly the size of a population and structure. Fertility is the addition of a population through birth, whereas mortality is the declination through death in population during a specific period of time (usually one year) gives the natural increase in the population. An effort has been made to study the death rate and birth rate of the population in order to find out the fundamental determinants of growth and decline.

(vi) The socio-economic condition is another major area, which controls demographic structure of a population. Traditionally, Tangsas were shifting cultivators, but slowly they have switched over to wet paddy cultivation and also accepted different types of occupations. An effort has been made to observe the changes and its effect on population.

(vii) The opportunity of formal education has influenced the life style of the population. The literacy rate on the basis of sex has a strong determining factor of social demography. Effort has been made to find out the exact picture of literacy and to trace the discrimination of the basis of sex if any.

(viii) The health of a population depends on various factors. Food habits and nutritional aspects no doubt affect the demographic condition. Attempt has been made to observe nutritional status on the basis of dietary habit. The acceptance and rejection of modern health care facilities depends on the magico-religious beliefs and practices of the population. Their attitudes towards modern medicine, family planning are important dimensions of socio-demographic study. Efforts have been made to outline these spheres also.

(ix) At present, the government has been spending large amount for the welfare of the tribal communities. Attempt has been made to trace the developmental spheres and their attitude towards such measures. Finally, an effort has been made to project the changing scenarios.

Methodology

Standard anthropological methods and techniques have been used in the field either independently or in combination with other. Intensive fieldwork is a prerequisite in anthropological research.

The most important aspects of any scientific study is its methods, without which no investigation or experiment will be fruitful. Methodology encompasses the overall planning that includes a proper knowledge of the techniques and means of data collection, systematic and meaningful analysis and drawing of the relevant conclusion from the same. Methodology refers to the structure of procedures and transformational rules guiding data collection (Pelto, 1978).

In the present project, the general demographic data has been collected from each and every household through a household census schedule. In the course of intensive field investigation, the anthropologist heavily relies upon observation, aided by interrogation or questioning of the people. Both participant and non-participant observation has been used in the present study. Participant observation is a technique which opens up the prospects of gaining an 'emic' or insider view as against an 'etic' or outsider view of social and cultural realities.

Interview has been conducted with a number of informants to enquire about their origin, ethno-history, religion, economy, political system, kinship and other systems from both the historical and the contemporary perspectives. Unstructured interview is the most common technique in ethnographic research.

The case study represents a significant trend in ethnographic work.

To grasp a variety of empirical materials qualitatively as well as quantitatively, number of cases has been collected depending upon the type of problem.

Data on fertility and mortality has been collected through specially designed fertility schedule by interviewing methods. For the relevant information on fertility, the concerned women (who have at least one live birth and her husband alive has been considered) has been interviewed, but their husband and other members of the family has also been interviewed whenever necessary.

Socio-economic status has been traced by considering the general economic activities of the people. In the present project data on land holding, crop production, occupation, income, saving pattern, spending (which has been reflected through material possession) has been considered to assess the economic status. Moreover, the food habit, type of food consumed, daily intake, their awareness about nutrition, food items, prohibition and preference of certain food items during pregnancy has been considered to analyse the socio-economic status.

Data on menarcheal age has been collected on cross sectional reporting whether the girls had started menstruation or not at the time of interview and also retrospective information about the first occasion of menstruation for those who had reached menarche. Data has been collected from those girls of similar age groups who had not attained menarche. In assessing the dietary in-take of the families as well as individuals, questionnaire diet survey has been used.

In the present study genuine effort has been made to use methodological technique to collect systematic and precise information on the relevant variables so as to get a precise picture of socio-demographic situation of the Tangsas of Arunachal Pradesh.

2

The Setting

The Villages and Its People

In this chapter, an effort has been made to give a detailed description of the micro-field wherefrom the field data have been collected and incorporated. The present study has been confined among the two major sub-tribes of the Tangsas, i.e. Lungchangs and the Mukloms of Arunachal Pradesh. Data on Lungchang Tangsas has been collected from three villages, i.e. the New Changlang, the Old Changlang and the Rangkatu. In the same way, the data on Muklom Tangsas have been collected from three villages, i.e. the Laktong, the Simrang (New Thamlom) and the Yanman.

To exhibit a vivid scenario, data has been arranged systematically under two broad setting, viz. Section **A** and Section **B**. In Section **A** an effort has been made to give a detailed description of the micro-field, i.e. settlement pattern, location, general description, house type public utility services etc. Section **B** is entirely devoted to analyse the demographic characteristics of the selected villages.

SECTION A

New Changlang Village

The village New Changlang is situated in the south-eastern part of the Changlang district. The village is about 4 km away from the main Changlang town and is situated near the Deputy Commissioner's office. The village was established in the year 1984, when a few families from Old Changlang village shifted to this area (including the gaonbura) and started to settle in this village. They had shifted from Old Changlang village because of population pressure and some of the practical problems. As the Old Changlang village is situated at hill top, they were facing many problems in harvesting and bringing of agricultural products to home. Slowly more and more people have shifted to this village.

On the northern side of the village, most of the Government offices are situated, e.g. the Deputy Commissioner's office, District Court, S.P. office etc.

On the eastern side of the village, lies, wet paddy field along the river bank of Tirap. On the western side, the Town Middle School, Changlang is located. On the southern side also lies the wet paddy field.

The village is located at an altitude of about 2320 ft above the sea level. It is situated between 26°40'-27°40'N latitude and 95°11'-97°10'E longitude.

The People

The village is entirely inhabited by the Lungchangs, a sub-tribe of the Tangsas. They belong to the Tibeto-Burman Linguistic group and physically resemble with the Mongoloid population. At the time of survey, there are 39 households. Out of this, 32 households belong to the Lungchang sub-tribe. While remaining 7 households are from different communities.

The non-Lungchangs consist of tea labourers, Bengalis, Assamese, Nepalis etc. who are living together in the village.

Out of 32 Lungchang households, 2 households may not be considered as pure Lungchang, because the heads of these two households belong to the Assamese and Bengali community. These persons settled permanently in the village after marrying the Lungchang girls and started to follow the Lungchang custom and tradition. Such marriages are allowed in their community. So, in the present study, they are considered as Lungchang.

Settlement Pattern

The village New Changlang is situated slightly in a sloping area. A *pucca* road runs through the village which connects the D.C. office, Police Station, Fishery office etc. on the one end and the Town Middle School, Changlang on the other end. The houses are built systematically along with side of the road. Street light facility is there on the side of the road.

The soil of the village is blackish red, contains porous and very fertile.

At about ½ km away from the village, the only river of Changlang district, i.e. the river Tirap is flowing. Paddy fields of the villagers are seen just below the village and along the bank of the river Tirap. The village is covered with varieties of bushes and flora. There is a pond within the boundary of the village. Almost all the households have kitchen garden in which different types of vegetables (seasonal), arum, *masala* plants are grown.

The road condition, which connects the village with the main town, is good. The main village road is also good.

The villagers mainly depend upon Arunachal Pradesh State Transport Corporation (APSTC) and private vehicles, like Tata Sumo for communication to other places of Arunachal Pradesh and Assam. Besides, most of villagers have their own vehicles, like bike, scooter, car etc. It is also significant that the person having bi-cycle is almost absent. It may be due to the fact that the hilly areas are not convenient for using bi-cycle.

Most of the households have television and radio. Some of the villagers have their own telephone and mobile phone. But not a single family is found in the village, who subscribe daily newspaper regularly.

General Description

Educational Institutions

There is one Anganwadi School and one Primary School in the village. The name of the Primary School is "Bapuji Primary School" which was established in the year 1988. The students from nearby villages also come to this school. At the time of survey, there are 5 teaching staff and about 50-60 students. After completing primary education the students are to go to "Town Middle School" and "Government Higher Secondary School, Changlang", which is about 1½ km away from the village. For higher education, they have to go to "Rang-Frah Government College, Changlang". Some of the students go to Itanagar and Assam for higher studies.

Many students are getting education at VKV (Kharsang and Jairampur), R.K. Mission (Deomali), J.N.V. (Bordumsa) etc. The medium of school education is English.

Place of Worship

There is a *Rang-Frah* temple in the village. This is the first *Rang Frah* temple among the Tangsa, which was established in this village. The people used to go to the temple on every Sunday to offer their prayer to the almighty God Rang Frah. There is a priest, who was recruited by villagers very recently. Every year, on the full moon day of November, the villagers celebrate the Rang Frah Day in the community level.

Community Hall

There is one community hall in the village, where the villagers perform various cultural programmes like New Year, Rang Frah Day, Children's day etc. The village youth used to practice for different occasions in this community hall.

Play Ground

In the middle of the village there is a small playground. The children and the youth play volley ball, cricket etc. at the field.

Water Source

The villagers are facilitated with running water provided by the Public Health and Engineering Department. They use this water for drinking, bathing, washing and other household purposes. For agricultural purpose, they have to mainly depend on rain water, for wet rice cultivation. They also use water from stream, namely Jang kang wa, which is running by the side of their agricultural field. They make small canals from the stream and supply the water to the field. The river Tirap is the only river flowing through the district Changlang, where a number of streams meet. The villagers either individually or in group used to go for fishing in this river.

Electricity

The electricity facility is good in the village. Each and every house of the village has got the electricity connection. They have to pay according to the prescribe rate of State Electricity Department.

Market Place

There is no shop within the village. But at the entrance of the village, there are a few shops, which are run by other communities like Assamese, Bengali, Marwari, Manipuri etc. The villagers prefer to go to the Changlang town for purchasing their necessary goods and articles.

Cremation Ground

The villagers have a cremation ground in the eastern direction of the village. They cremate those dead bodies, who die on natural death. In case of accidental death, suicide and other unnatural death, they do not cremate dead bodies in this ground. There is no particular place for cremation of such death. In most cases, cremation is done in the deep jungle, far away from the village. Sometimes cremation is done on the spot of death itself. In case of still birth, the body of the baby is hanged on the branch of a tree, which bears fruits.

Old Changlang Village

The Old Changlang village is located on the northernmost part of the Changlang town, on the hill slopes of the Patkai range. Earlier it was known as the Changlang village. But in the year 1984, a few families shifted from this village and established a new settlement near Deputy Commissioner's office at Changlang. The new area is about 3 km away from the main village and located on the south eastern part of the main Changlang town. The village was named as New Changlang and the old one became known as the Old Changlang village.

The village is about 1.5 km away from the Changlang town if travelled by main road that lead to the village. There is also short cut route by foot which is only 200-400 metres away.

On the eastern side of the village, there is a road, which connects Changlang to Margherita. On the western and northern side, there is vast forest and the mountain tracts of the Patkai ranges. And the Changlang town is located just below the village.

It has already been mentioned that the village is on the hilly area and is divided into two parts by two small streams, i.e. the *Khamking-wa* and the *Khamsa-wa*, which originate in the mountain and flows through the village and enters the Changlang town. Finally, the streams fall at the river Tirap. The first part, i.e. the western side is called the *Khengjung*, which forms the original village (old one) and the other part, i.e. the eastern side is known as *Keng Nya* or *Ha Nya* (new area).

Settlement Pattern

The houses are located by the side of main village path. Some of the houses are situated on the other side of the hills. As the village is on the hill tops, houses are located in the plain area on the hill. At the time of field survey, there were 47 households on the *Khengjung* side and 28 households on the *Ha Nya* side. The village is exclusively inhabited by the Lungchang Tangsas.

The village is connected to the Changlang town by a road, the condition of which is not very good. It starts from the heart of the village and enters Changlang town after ups and down in the hill and running in a zigzag way.

Educational Institutions

There is one Anganwadi and one primary school in the village. The school is called the Government Primary School, Old Changlang village. At the time of survey, there were about 50-60 students with 5 teaching staff. The school building is made of concrete. There were also teacher's quarters near the school, but none of the staff stay there. Students after primary education go to the Town Middle school and the Government Higher Secondary School, Changlang for higher studies. Some students were also getting their education in some private school at Changlang town, while some are studying at VKV, Kharsang, J.N.V. Bordumsa (private school outside the Changlang town). After higher secondary, the students normally go to Rang Frah Government College, Changlang (Arts College) which is about 14 km away from the village. It was also found that some of the students were getting higher education at Itanagar and even some were moving outside the Arunachal Pradesh.

Place of Worship

There is one Rang Frah Mandir in the village which is built of bamboo and wood. Roofing is done with palm leaves. There is one priest which performs the rituals. The villagers come to the temple every Sunday and offer their prayer by singing song and lighting incense sticks.

Cultural Hall

There is a common hall in the village. It is built of concrete and various cultural functions are held here. The youth of the village fully utilize it for rehearsal/learning the art and dance.

Play Ground

There is a small play ground in the village. The field is entirely used for playing volleyball by the village youth.

Water Source

The villagers are getting the facility of drinking water provided by the Public Health Department. They also use water from the stream for irrigating their paddy field. Water is never a problem for the villagers.

Electricity

Each and every household is getting the electricity connection in their house. As reported they are getting the regular supply and there are not frequent power cut. The villagers are to pay according to the prescribed rate which is not very high.

Cremation Ground

The cremation ground of the Old Changlang village is situated on the eastern side of the village, which is about 1 km away from the village.

Market Place

The villagers normally prefer to go to the Changlang town for purchasing their essential items, which is just below the village. During field survey, it was found that there was a small shop in the village owned by villagers. It caters the emergent need of the villagers. The items which are available in the shop are salt, sugar, pencils, soap, and other minor stationary objects.

It is also revealed that a few villagers have private means of vehicles like scooter, bike and Maruti cars. The villagers mostly depend on Arunachal Pradesh State Transport Corporation and private vehicles like Tata Sumo for communication to other places of Arunachal Pradesh and Assam for which they have to come down to the Changlang town.

The villagers are enjoying the amenities of modern facility. More than 50 per cent of the villagers have their own television. Some families have Dish connection, while some have cable connection. Some have Mobile connection whereas others have Landline telephone. For postal service, the villagers are to go to the Changlang Post Office at Changlang town. Of course, for delivering the letters the postman comes to the village.

Rangkatu Village

Rangkatu village is one of the biggest and largely populated villages of the Lungchang Tangsas. The village is located in the eastern side of the district headquarters of Changlang. It is about 12 km away from the district head quarter or the Changlang town. The Rangkatu village is located in the left bank of the river Tirap and bounded by the Chokdok village (inhabited by the Lungchang Tangsas) in the east, Kengkhu village (Lungchang Tangsas) in the west and Rangkatu (Hills) in the north. The river Tirap is flowing in the southern side of the village. The village itself is on the hill slopes, surrounded by dense forest and thick jungles.

The village is mostly inhabited by the Lungchang Tangsas. The Lungchang people of this village had migrated with all other Lungchang group from Jangsung-Lungchang, which is believed to be the original abode of the Lungchang Tangsas. As per their verbal opinion it was somewhere in the Myanmar (Burma). They had to migrate to different areas, due to cold war that existed among the various tribal groups. Again the Lungchang people observed that in the Changlang-kan or Rangkatu-kan, the sun light falls comparatively earlier than other areas. So, they decided to shift to this area and finally, all the Changlang people came down to the present Changlang-kan or Rangkatu-kan by crossing the river Tirap by different crossing point or places. Rangkatu-kan is represented by the present Rangkatu and Old Rangkatu as well. The inhabitants of the present Rangkatu village are originally from the Old Rangkatu village, which is only a few km away on the northern side of the village. They have shifted to the present village around 1980s in search for more suitable land for cultivation.

Settlement Pattern

The Rangkatu village is situated on the hill slopes, covered with bushes and flora. A road runs through the village which connects the Changlang town with the Manmao circle. There are tea plantations in the mountain areas. *Jhum* fields are seen on the slopes of the hills. And wet rice fields are there just below the village along the river bank of the Tirap. The condition of the road is, however, is not good. It is not a pitch one. During rainy season, it becomes muddy. The road runs through dense forest and thick bushes, shrubs, crossing many streams and hills.

The houses are constructed in such as way that they arrange it more or less in a row on either side of a common narrow street which is facing each other. In other words, the settlement patterns are both cluster and lineal in nature.

At the time of survey, there are 65 households with a total population of 467. Out of the total 65 households, only a single family belongs to non-Lungchang community.

Educational Institutions

There is one Government Primary School in the village. At present there are 40-50 students with 4 teaching staff. Students after receiving the primary education, go to the Kengkhu Middle School of Kengkhu village, which is about 9 km away from the village. For higher education, they go to the Government Higher Secondary School, Changlang at Changlang town. Mostly they stay at hostels there. The study also reveals that many students are receiving education in other private school in and outside Changlang town. For college studies, they used to go to Rang Frah Government College, Changlang. Some also avail the opportunities in Itanagar or Assam.

An *Anganbadi* school is also run by an *Anganbadi* worker. However, there is no building, so, the worker had to run it at their own home. *Anganbadi* worker is a female who is paid Rs. 1870.99 per 2 months. There is also a helper who is paid Rs. 500.00 per 2 months. Students are provided biscuits, grams, cerelac, toys etc. Medicines are also provided to the villagers by the *Anganbadi* worker. Monthly reports are submitted at the B.D.O. at Changlang.

Place of Worship

The Lungchang Tangsas are the followers of the *Lord Rang Frah.* There is a Rang Frah Mandir in the village by the side of the road, which connects the Changlang town with Manmao circle. The Mandir is made of wood and bamboo and the roofing is done with palm leaves. Pictures of the Lord Rang Frah are kept inside the Mandir and villagers offer their prayer on every Sunday. They normally offer flowers and lighting incense sticks while worshipping the *God Rang Frah.* The villagers used to observe fasting on Sunday before coming to the Mandir. After returning from the temple they used to take water and eat food.

The villagers form a committee with Secretary and President to look after the management of the Mandir. They also select one of the villagers as a Priest of the Mandir to perform the ritual. According to the villagers, the priest is paid in every six months.

Water Source

The villagers are getting the facility of running water provided by the Public Health Department. They are getting sufficient water to meet all the household activities. The river Tirap is running just below the village and the young boys occasionally go to the river for bathing. They also use the stream water for irrigating their wet paddy field. However, they mostly depend on rain water for cultivation.

Electricity

Like other villages of Changlang, in Rangkatu village also each and every household has the electricity connection. The villagers are to pay the rent according to the prescribed rate.

Play Ground

Due to hiily area, there is no permanent playground. However, the children used to play wherever there is open space to play volleyball, cricket etc.

Cremation Ground

The Lungchangs cremate their dead bodies. But there is no cremation ground within the village. It is far away from the village on the eastern side of the village which is covered with shrubs and bushes.

Market Place

For purchasing necessary articles, the villagers used to go to the Changlang town, which is about 12-13 km away from the village. But there is one small shop in the village, which is owned by a villager. Only certain articles of the day-to-day use, e.g. soap, biscuits, matches, candle are available in the shop. The villagers used to sell domestic birds like fowl and ducks and vegetables to meet their immediate need. Sometimes, they sell other domestic animals like pig, goat at Changlang town. The villagers are expert in making bamboo baskets and handicraft. They sell such items in the market.

Compared to two other villages, the Rangkatu village is situated far away from the main township. There are only few families who have scooter and bikes for communication. The villagers are to walk on foot to come to the Changlang town. From there they get other means of communication to move out of Changlang town.

Television is possessed by only a few families. Only 2-3 persons have mobile phones.

The chapter also incorporated data on Muklom Tangsa which has been collected from 3 villages, i.e. Laktong, Simrang (New Thamlom) and Yanman villages of Arunachal Pradesh.

Laktong Village

The Laktong village is situated at a distance of about 2 km away from the Changlang town. The village is surrounded by the Assam Rifle camp on the eastern side. On the southern side or just below the village there are wet rice field. There is a Tutsa village on the northern side and the APST bus stand is also situated on the northern side of the village. The Laktong Middle School is situated on the western side.

According to the villagers, the inhabitants of the present village had shifted from different interior villages like Chingsa, Yankang and Wottom.

The word Laktong is derived from two words, i.e. the '*Lak*' means a kind of tree called *Hullong* or the Dipterocarpus macrocorpus and '*tong*' means available. It indicates that such kind of tree was easily available in those areas, so the village was named as Laktong. The village is populated by both the Muklom Tangsas and the Tutsa sub-tribe (another sub-tribe of the Tangsas). According to the villagers in the year around 1971-1972, only 1 or 2 families had settled on that area, who had shifted from a far away village called Yankang (Tutsa village). Later on a few families from both the communities, i.e. Muklom Tangsa and the Tutsa came to settle in the village. They have selected the site because it is near to the Changlang town and the wet rice cultivation is possible in the surrounding area.

Settlement Pattern

The village is situated on hill slops with rocky area. A road that runs just above the village connects the Changlang town passing through few villages. It then reaches the Tirap district passing through dense forest and hills.

The houses are situated on both sides of the main village road and the by-lanes. A stream runs by the side of the village in the western side. It originates in the hills and passes through the village and touches the wet paddy field.

Educational Institutions

There is one *Anganbadi* school in the village where the children are taught in the morning for about 2 hours.

The Laktong Middle School is situated just near the village so the students used to go there after completing their primary education in the Anganbadi School. After that, the students go to the Government Higher Secondary School for higher education. For college education, the students are admitted in the Rang Frah Government College, Changlang. Some students also take the opportunity of higher education, outside the Changlang, i.e. Itanagar. In certain cases, it was found that the students were taking the advantage of private schools in Changlang town, i.e. Rang Frah Vidya Niketan, Green Lawn etc.

Water Source

The villagers are getting the same facilities of water as in other villages. The Public Health Department is taking the steps, so, that every village in Arunachal Pradesh is getting the proper drinking water. The tap water is used for their daily household activities. For wet agricultural purposes, they have a good opportunity of using water from the stream. However, the villagers are to depend on rain water for *jhum* cultivation.

Electricity

The villagers are getting the electricity connection from State Electricity Board. The villagers were in opinion that they are not getting the regular power supply.

Cremation Ground

The cremation ground is situated on the western side of the village, near the wet rice field. The cremation ground is called as *Mangrot tong* in Muklom dialect.

Play Ground

As the village is situated on the hilly rocky area, there is no playground in the village. It was found that due to hill and forest there was no opportunity of developing a big play ground.

Market Place

There are small shops just above their village. The shops are owned by the villagers themselves. But they are to go to the Changlang town for purchasing the daily necessities. Some of the villagers sell domestic products like vegetables and birds like fowls and ducks in the Changlang town. This also helps them economically.

Simrang (New Thamlam) Village

Simrang or New Thamlam village is exclusively inhabited by the Muklom Tangsas. The village is located on the eastern side of the district head-quarters of Changlang. It is about 5 km away from the Changlang town. The road which connects the Changlang town with Manmao circle passes through the village. The village is situated on hill slops like most of the villages of Changlang.

The river Tirap flows just below the village, i.e. from the southern side to the eastern side near the PWD (Public Works Department) camp. The north and the western side of the village are covered with hills and forest and the area is known as *Laktham*. The area was fully covered with *Lak* (Hallong tree or *Dipterocorpus macro carpus*) tree. Such trees were easily available in the area that is why the area is referred as *Lakthams*.

Settlement Pattern

According to the villagers, they had migrated to this area from the Old Thamlam village (another village populated by the Muklam Tangsas), which is about 49-50 km away from the Khimyang circle. They had started to migrate from that village around 1971 in search of suitable cultivable land. The village is also known as the New Thamlam as they had shifted from Thamlam village, and settled in a new area. The area below is known as the *Simrang Sung*. So, the villagers were of opinion that the Lungchang Tangsas have named their village as the Simrang village.

The village is situated on the hill slopes covered with flora, bushes and shrubs all around. A road from Changlang town runs through the village, connecting a few Lungchang villages and ultimately reaches the Manmao circle on the eastern most side. The houses are located on one side of this road. Several by-lanes are formed from this road and houses are located on both sides of the by-lanes.

Educational Institutions

The "New Thamlam Primary School" is situated in the village. At the time of survey, there were 30-35 students with two teaching staffs. Students after receiving primary education have to go to the Government Higher Secondary School, Changlang town for higher studies. Many of them have taken the opportunity of private schools in Changlang and other areas. For college education, they normally go to "Rang Frah Government College, Changlang".

Place of Worship

The Muklom Tangsas are the believer of *Lord Rang Frah*. The Rang Frah Mandir or the Rangsom-Hom is situated just near the school. It is on the hill top and is constructed with wood and bamboo. Roofing is done by the palm leaves. Pictures of the Lord Rang Frah are kept inside the temple. Here the villagers used to offer their prayer three days in a week, i.e. on Wednesday, Saturday and Sunday. It was reported that the villagers observe fasting on Sunday. After offering prayer in the temple by 12 noon, they used to drink water or eat food. However, the children are exempted from such fasting. There are selected Secretary and President to look after the affairs of the Mandir. Moreover, the villagers are also involved in the affairs of the Mandir.

Playground

The youth and the children play games like cricket, volleyball etc. in the school playground which is situated within the school compound. Due to the hilly areas, the condition of the village is not good. However, they manage to play on the playground.

Cremation Ground

The Mukloms cremate their dead bodies. The village cremation ground is there just below the village, covered with shrubs and bushes.

Water Source

Like every village of Arunachal Pradesh, the villagers are getting regular water supply provided by Public Health Department. The water is used by the villagers for their daily necessities. The river Tirap is flowing just below the village, but the villagers are not in a position to use water from the river. Occasional fishing is done in the river. The villagers depend on rain water for agricultural purposes.

Electricity

During survey, it was found that most of the houses are connected with electricity facility. However, there are some families who cannot afford to pay the rent thereby deprived from the facility of electricity.

Market Place

There is no shop in the village. The villagers have to go to Changlang town for purchasing their daily necessities, which is about 5-6 km away. The villagers occasionally sell fowls, ducks, pigs etc. at the Changlang market. Sometime, they sell vegetables also. Their economic condition compels them to sell their product.

The villagers normally walk on foot to the Changlang town. The road, passing through the village is not a pitch one. The condition becomes muddy and bad during the rainy season. The road passes through dense forest, shrubs and bushes. It is also found that only a few families possess bike and scooter. As bi-cycle is not suitable in the hilly areas, not a single family possesses bi-cycle.

Only a few families have television set in their house. There is no landline or mobile connection in the village. It may be said that in comparison to other Lungchang villages, this village is not getting all the means.

Yanman Village

The village Yanman is situated 16 km away from the Changlang town.

The communication is very difficult as it is located at a hill top. The major facilities like electricity, water are available like other villages. The Rang Frah temple is there for religious purposes. In comparison to other villages the typical tribal set-up is reflected in this village.

A brief description of the villages inhabited by the Lungchang and the Muklom Tangsas considering the location, boundaries, settlement pattern and public utility services reveal that there are slight variation on the basis of village level and as sub-tribe level. All the villages are situated within the range of 2-16 km away from the district headquarters of Changlang. Most of the villages, which are situated near the township, were established later on. The interior villages are their original settlement. These newly established villages are getting all the modern facilities due to their location.

With regard to educational facilities except one all the villages have primary school within the village. Moreover, the Anganbadi School provides the primary level education. There is Government Higher Secondary school in the Changlang town. Besides many private educational institutions are there and some of the villagers are able to grab all the facilities of modern education. For higher education, some of the students move to Itanagar and Assam.

Both the Lungchangs and the Mukloms are the believer of *Lord Rang Frah*. In each village there is Rang Frah temple. The villagers normally refer it as *Mandir*. In most of villages it is constructed with wood and bamboo. Roofing is done by palm leaves. Besides regular prayer, every Sunday the villagers pray to God Rang Frah, offering flowers and lighting incense sticks. They observe fast on that day and after their prayer by 12 noon, they drink and eat.

Regarding the public utility service, it has been revealed that all the villages have received the water and electricity facility. Except a few families, all the families have electricity connection. The families which do not have connection are because of poor economic condition. There are provisions of playground in all the villages except two. It is because those villages are situated on the hill top and the plain surface required for playground is not available. Only 2 villages have shop within the village, which cater the minimum need of the villagers. But for purchasing essential items, they go to the Changlang town. Most of villagers go to the Changlang town on foot. Only a few villagers have bikes and scooters.

Dwelling

It has been found that the houses among the Tangsas do not show much variation as regards the designs and the materials used for construction of houses. But each sub-tribe has their own word used for referring the house. The traditional house type among the Tangsas are pile type, with some variation in layout. The houses are built on stilts, rectangular in shape with double shaped roof of palm leaf. Each house has independent stairs made of wood and it is placed on the right corner of the verandah. The dwelling houses of the villagers are constructed on a co-operative basis. It is the responsibility of the owner to collect the materials. They have a traditional custom where the co-villagers are informed about the date of starting construction. And the villagers irrespective of age and sex come together and extend their helping hand in construction of the houses and complete the entire process within one or two days. But at present such co-operative spirit are lacking among the Tangsas. They prefer to engage paid labourers. There are some individuals in the village who also work on wage basis.

The house is divided mainly into three parts. The front room has wall on sides, except the front which remain open. In front of this room, there is open verandah (*Pongran*) made of bamboo splits having sufficient gap. They use this part of the house for different purposes like to dry the paddy, cloth or to keep flowering pot or orchid. In the front room, one fireplace or hearth (*tap)* is placed slightly towards left side of the room. The walls of this front room are decorated by hanging skulls of buffaloes, deer, hornbill etc. which are killed in various occasions.

The middle portion is a hall like and divided longitudinally into two parts. The right side of the room is used as long corridor running through the room and the other part is divided into small compartment called *jumong* or *himong*. The length of the house depend on the number of members are there in the family. Each compartment has fireplace in each room. Sometimes one of the compartment is used as common kitchen. In case of joint family, sometimes each family use separate hearth, just near to their compartment, but they live under the same roof. The back part where generally a paddy pounder is installed known as *jumcheng* or *himkha*. Guests belonging to other sub-tribes are not allowed to go beyond this part.

The hearth in each household plays a significant role in the life of the members. Besides cooking, it has contributed in preservation and drying. Just above the hearth, there is a small square shaped ceiling (*khareng sa*) made of bamboo, which is used to keep or preserve some daily used materials. Above *khareng sa*, another big platform (*khareng-jung*) is built to keep some items like drum (*Nong*), cane strings, leather or skin of different animals, wooden and bamboo materials.

From the general outlook of the house type it appears that the house type of Lungchangs is slightly better than the houses of Muklom Tangsas. Most of the houses of Muklongs are in deplorable conditions, the front platform is small and narrow and the roof comes down very low.

Selection of Site

The Tangsas have a traditional belief regarding the selection of house site. It is a common practice that they never select their site near *nalah*. It is believed that harmful spirits normally come through the *nalah*. While selecting the site they normally put a bamboo into fire and split it horizontally. If the bamboo is split into equal proportion then the site is considered suitable for construction. The main post of the house is always considered sacred. Normally, the head of the family keep his bed near the main post keeping the head towards the post.

On the day of the entrance to the new house they observe a ceremony where the near relatives and villagers are invited. A fowl is sacrificed and a knowledgeable person read the omen from the sacrificed fowl.

A slight variation is also noticed among the Tangsas in recent years. Many of them have started to construct Assam type house with C.I. sheets. Regarding the type of house it is revealed that among the Lungchangs, out of 179 families as many as 129 are entirely platform type, the percentage being 72.07. The remaining cases both the Assam type and pile dwellings are found. Among the Mukloms out of 153 households as many as 118 families are living on platform type houses and the percentage is 77.0. And the rest of the families have both type of houses.

Dress and Ornaments

The Tangsa men and women have quite elaborate style of dress pattern. The costume of the man is made up of homemade *chequered lungi* of green and black colour, lined with red, yellow and white yarn, a shirt and a white turban. The traditional dress of women (about 39 inches in length and 12 inches in breadth) consisted of a *khasa* or *khatsa*, a single piece of cloth wrapped round the body from the breast down to the ankles, a blouse and in some cases turban. Some changes have been observed in recent years. The ladies, now wear a black skirt (*khailung*) reaching below the knee and sometimes coming down to the ankles, a blouse (*champhung*) a piece of white cloth (*pungmeng*) thrown over the body and a *khupak,* i.e. a piece of cloth wrapped round the head as turban-like.

The Tangsa women are good weaver. They weave most of their clothes at home. In general, they have a preference for geometric pattern, such as zigzag band with internal repetition, rectangular cross-thatching etc. Regarding the colour Dutta remarks, "Tangsas are particularly sensitive to scarlet-red, black and dark-green colours." The design of *mekhela* itself signifies the sub-tribes of Tangsas. Among the Lungchangs the women use colourful checks. Among the Mukloms broad horizontal colourful stripes are used. On the other hand the Tutsa women use colourful mountain like motifs.

The Tangsa men and women wear various ornaments for personal adornment. Men wear a few coloured beads string on a copper wire and a legging of fine can string dyed black with the juice of a kind of jungle fruit in the earlobe.

Women wear in their ears a transparent crystal bead known as *Jangphai* in Assamese. They also wear necklace made of coins. They use a pair of bangles made of metals and leggings made of bead.

In recent years, the younger generation started to use western costumes. As most of them are taking education in school, colleges, a visible change has emerged in the dress pattern. But still they prefer to use their traditional dress while at home, particularly the womenfolk. They have a respect for their tradition and want to maintain their identity.

Food and Drink

Rice is their staple food along with maize and millet. Fish, vegetables, meat etc. are included in their diet. They observe various festival and ceremonies round the year and these have given them the opportunity to eat beef and pork, because, animals are sacrificed invariably in their religious ceremonies. Rice beer, locally known as *chal, jaw, khem, ji* or *sai* (Singh, 2003) by the different sub-tribe is their favourite drink. Black tea (*phalapkha*) is preferred by most of them and they take it frequently. They take rice thrice daily, i.e. in the morning, noon and at evening. A few families take rice twice in a day, i.e. in the morning and night and take snacks at noon. As a whole the Tangsas prefer non-vegetarian food, but only a few families have preference for vegetarian diet.

SECTION B
Demographic Characteristics

Age and Sex Structure

An analysis of age and sex structure provides a clear understanding of demographic characteristics a community/tribe. Sex structure of a community reflects various dimension social system. Similarly, a study of age structure throws light on the future trend in the population.

Table 2.1: Distribution of Population by Age and Sex in the Village New Changlang

Sl. No.	Age group	Male		Female		Total	
		No.	Percentage	No.	Percentage	No.	Percentage
1.	0 – 4	7	3.55	2	1.01	9	4.56
2.	5 – 9	10	5.08	11	5.58	21	10.66
3.	10 – 14	8	4.06	11	5.58	19	9.64
4.	15 – 19	11	5.58	8	4.06	19	9.64
5.	20 – 24	8	4.06	15	7.61	23	11.67
6.	25 – 29	10	5.08	8	4.06	18	9.15
7.	30 – 34	10	5.08	11	5.58	21	10.66
8.	35 – 39	8	4.06	5	2.54	13	6.60
9.	40 – 44	8	4.06	8	4.06	16	10.13
10.	45 – 49	6	3.05	2	1.01	8	4.06
11.	50 – 54	2	1.01	1	0.51	3	1.52
12.	55 – 59	2	1.01	6	3.05	8	4.06
13.	60 – 64	3	1.52	3	1.52	6	3.05
14.	65 – 69	3	1.52	3	1.52	6	3.05
15.	70 – 74	2	1.01	–	–	2	1.01
16.	75 – 79	1	0.51	–	–	1	0.51
17.	80 – 84	1	0.51	–	–	1	0.51
18.	85 – 89	–	–	1	0.51	1	0.51
19.	90 – 94	–	–	1	0.51	1	0.51
20.	95 – 99	–	–	1	0.51	1	0.51
	Total	**100**	**50.76**	**97**	**49.24**	**197**	**100.00**

The population covered by the investigation according to age and sex in the three villages, inhabited by the Lungchang Tangsas has been presented in the Tables 2.1, 2.2 and 2.3.

The analyses of population in New Changlang village shows that the total population of the village is 197, among which 100 (50.76%) are male members and 97 (49.24%) are female members. Thus, in the village as a whole showed deficit of female in a slight proportion. The analysis also

Table 2.2: Distribution of Population by Age and Sex in the Village Old Changlang

Sl. No.	*Age group*	*Male*		*Female*		*Total*	
		No.	*%*	*No.*	*%*	*No.*	*%*
1.	0 – 4	18	4.26	17	4.02	35	8.27
2.	5 – 9	17	4.02	13	3.07	30	7.09
3.	10 – 14	25	5.91	26	6.15	51	12.05
4.	15 – 19	29	6.86	23	4.44	52	12.29
5.	20 – 24	16	3.78	11	2.60	27	6.38
6.	25 – 29	14	3.31	20	4.72	34	8.04
7.	30 – 34	13	3.07	12	2.84	25	5.91
8.	35 – 39	23	4.44	19	4.49	42	9.93
9.	40 – 44	18	4.26	13	3.07	31	7.31
10.	45 – 49	13	3.07	12	2.84	25	5.91
11.	50 – 54	7	1.65	5	1.18	12	2.84
12.	55 – 59	5	1.18	7	1.65	12	2.84
13.	60 – 64	6	1.41	10	2.36	16	3.78
14.	65 – 69	7	1.65	6	1.41	13	3.07
15.	70 – 74	9	2.12	3	0.71	12	2.84
16.	75 – 79	2	0.47	1	0.24	3	0.71
17.	80 – 84	1	0.24	1	0.24	2	0.47
18.	85 – 89	1	0.24	–	–	1	0.24
	Total	**224**	**52.96**	**199**	**47.04**	**423**	**100**

reveals that the highest frequency of male falls within the age group of 15–9 yrs, i.e. 11 (5.58%) in number and lowest frequency of male falls within the age group of 75–79 and 80–84 yrs. where there is single individual in each group. While the highest number of female is found within the age group of 20–24 yrs., i.e. there are 15 (7.61%) females and the lowest frequency of female fall within the age group of 85–89, 90–94 and 95–99 yrs., where single person is found in each age group. While considering the population of the village as a whole, the highest frequency is found in the age group of 20–24 yrs, i.e. there are 23 (11.67%) persons are found.

The analysis of age and sex structure in the village Old Changlang (Table 2.2) indicates that there are altogether 423 individuals in the village. Out of the total individuals 224 (52.69%) are male and 199 (47.04%) are female. Here a clear indication of female deficiency is revealed. The table also reveals that the highest frequency of male falls within the age group of 15–19 yrs, i.e. 29 (6.86%) individuals are found in that age group and the lowest frequency of male fall within the age group of 80–84 and 85–90 yrs. where there is one person in each category.

On the other hand the highest number of female is found within the age group of 10–14 yrs. where 26 (6.15%) females are located. The lowest number of females is found within the age group of 75–79 and 80–84 yrs. i.e. one female is found in each category, respectively. This also gives an idea that along with the female deficiency the number of females in the higher age group is not significant.

The distribution of population by age and sex in the Rangkatu village has been presented in Table 2.3. The analysis shows that it is the highest populated village under study. There are 467 individuals in the village out of which 241 (51.61%) are male and 226 (43.39%) are female. This again reflects female deficiency in the village. The total number of age group is divided into 20 categories with an interval of 4 yrs. From the table it is clear that the highest frequency of males fall within the age group of 15–19 yrs., where there are 38 (8.14%) individuals and the lowest frequency of males fall within the age groups of 90–94 and 95–99 yrs., where there is single individual in each category. It is also revealed that there is not a single individual in the age group of 85–89 yrs.

Table 2.3: Distribution of Population by Age and Sex in the Village Rangkatu

Sl. No.	*Age group*	*Male*		*Female*		*Total*	
		No.	*%*	*No.*	*%*	*No.*	*%*
1.	0 – 4	18	3.85	22	4.71	40	8.56
2.	5 – 9	33	7.07	35	7.49	68	14.56
3.	10 – 14	25	5.35	30	6.42	55	11.78
4.	15 – 19	38	8.14	19	4.67	57	12.21
5.	20 – 24	14	3.00	14	3.00	28	5.99
6.	25 – 29	16	3.34	22	4.71	39	8.35
7.	30 – 34	15	3.21	13	2.78	28	5.99
8.	35 – 39	16	3.34	17	3.64	33	7.07
9.	40 – 44	19	4.07	17	3.64	36	7.71
10.	45 – 49	13	2.78	13	2.78	26	5.56
11.	50 – 54	10	2.14	3	0.64	13	2.78
12.	55 – 59	4	0.86	4	0.86	8	1.71
13.	60 – 64	6	1.28	5	1.07	11	2.36
14.	65 – 69	4	0.86	1	0.21	5	1.07
15.	70 – 74	2	0.43	3	0.64	5	1.07
16.	70 – 79	2	0.43	3	0.64	5	1.07
17.	80 – 84	4	0.86	4	0.86	8	1.71
18.	85 – 89	–	–	1	0.21	1	0.21
19.	90 – 94	1	0.21	–	–	1	0.21
20.	95 – 99	1	0.21	–	–	1	0.21
	Total	**241**	**51.61**	**226**	**48.39**	**468**	**100**

On the other hand, the highest number of females is found in the age group of 5–9 yrs., where there are 35 (7.49%) individuals. The lowest number of females is counted in the age group of 65–69 and 85–89 yrs. where single female is recorded.

An analysis of age and sex structure among the Lungchang Tangsas in three villages clearly indicates the female deficiency. However, in the village New Changlang female deficiency is not so distinct. But in Old Changlang and Rangkatu villages the trend is distinct. From the analysis of tables, we may say that overall life span of Lungchang Tangsas is high and even in 95–96 yrs. age group individuals are recorded. Another significant trend is that in the Rangkatu village there are no female member in the age group of 90–94 and 95–99 yrs., whereas in the Old Changlang village both males and females are not noticeable in the age group of 90–94 and 95–99 yrs. There is only one male member is recorded in the age group of 85–89 yrs. It is significant to note that in the New Changlang village, there are females in the age group of 85–89, 90–94 and 95–99 yrs. where single female member is recorded whereas in these categories no male member is recorded in this village.

The overall deficiency of female among the Lungchang Tangsas may be interpreted that as they are patriarchal tribe, the sons get preference in the family. Moreover, the females as a whole are a doing hard work in most of the tribal societies and the Tangsas are not an exception. But at this stage, it is very difficult to come to definite conclusion about the trend of population.

In the present study the data for Muklom Tangsas have been collected from three villages. The Mukloms constitute one of the major sub-tribes of the Tangsas. The age and sex structure of the Mukloms have been presented in Tables 2.4, 2.5 and 2.6.

The analysis of distribution of population by age and sex in the Laktong village shows that there are altogether 190 individuals in the village, out of which 96 (50.53%) are male and 94 (49.47%) are female. This indicates a slight female deficiency. The highest frequency of male falls within the age group of 0–4, 10–14 and 15–19 yrs. where 13 (6.84%) individuals in each age group are. The lowest frequency of male falls in the age group of 55–59 and 80–84 yrs. where single person is noticed in each age group. No male member is recorded in the age group of 70–74 and 75–79 yrs.

While the highest frequency of females is recorded in the age group of 0–4 yrs. with 16 (8.42%) individuals and the lowest frequency is found in the age group of 60–64 and 75–79 yrs. There is only one female member

Table 2.4: Distribution of Population by Age and Sex in the Village Laktong

Sl. No.	Age group	Male		Female		Total	
		No.	%	No.	%	No.	%
1.	0–4	13	6.84	16	8.42	29	15.26
2.	5–9	11	5.79	12	6.32	23	12.11
3.	10–14	13	6.84	5	2.63	18	9.47
4.	15–19	13	6.84	10	5.26	23	12.11
5.	20–24	6	3.16	7	3.68	13	6.84
6.	25–29	5	2.63	5	2.63	10	5.26
7.	30–34	4	2.11	13	6.84	17	8.95
8.	35–39	11	5.79	7	3.68	18	9.47
9.	40–44	6	3.16	6	3.16	12	6.32
10.	45–49	6	3.16	3	1.58	9	4.74
11.	50–54	2	1.05	2	1.05	4	2.11
12.	55–59	1	0.53	–	–	1	0.53
13.	60–64	2	1.05	1	0.53	3	1.58
14.	65–69	2	1.05	3	1.58	5	2.63
15.	70–74	–	–	3	1.58	3	1.58
16.	75–79	–	–	1	0.53	1	0.53
17.	80–84	1	0.53	–	–	1	0.53
	Total	**96**	**50.53**	**94**	**49.47**	**190**	**100**

(0.53%) is found in each group. No female is recorded in the age group of 55–59 and 80–84 yrs.

The distribution of population by age and sex in the village Simrang (New Thamlom) has been presented in Table 2.5. The table shows that there are 209 individuals, out of which 104 (49.76%) are males and 105 (50.24%) are females. A slight deficiency of male is revealed in this village.

It is also found that highest frequency of males fall in the age group of 10–14 yrs., where 20 (9.57%) males are found and the lowest frequency of males fall within the age group of 60–64 and 85–89 yrs, i.e. 1 individual is found in each category, respectively.

On the other hand, the highest number of females is found in the age group of 15–19 yrs. with 22 (10.53%) members and the lowest number is recorded in the age group of 25–29, 50–54, 55–59 and 70–74 yrs., where single individual (0.48%) in each group is recorded. Another significant trend in this village is that there is not a single individual (both male and female) in the age group of 80–84, 90–94 and 95–99 yrs. There is only one male in the age group of 85–89 yrs. of age group. The general life span of the population may be considered as high, but the absence of individual above 80 yrs. is also noticeable.

Table 2.5: Distribution of Population by Age and Sex in the Village Simrang

Sl. No.	Age group	Male		Female		Total	
		No.	%	No.	%	No.	%
1.	0–4	10	4.78	8	3.83	18	8.61
2.	5 – 9	14	6.70	12	5.74	26	12.44
3.	10–14	20	9.57	14	6.70	34	16.27
4.	15–19	8	3.83	22	10.53	30	14.35
5.	20–24	8	3.83	10	4.78	18	8.61
6.	25–29	4	1.91	1	0.48	5	2.39
7.	30–34	2	0.96	6	2.87	8	3.83
8.	35–39	8	3.83	12	5.74	20	9.57
9.	40–44	10	4.78	6	2.87	16	7.66
10.	45–49	7	3.35	4	1.91	11	5.26
11.	50–54	4	1.91	1	0.48	5	2.39
12.	55–59	3	1.44	1	0.48	4	1.91
13.	60–64	1	0.48	2	0.96	3	1.44
14.	65–69	2	0.96	3	1.44	5	2.39
15.	70–74	2	0.96	1	0.48	3	1.44
16.	75–79	–	–	2	0.96	2	0.96
17.	80–84	–	–	–	–	–	–
18.	85–89	1	0.48	–	–	1	0.48
19.	90–99	–	–	–	–	–	–
	Total	104	49.76	105	50.24	209	100.00

The distribution of population by age and sex of the Yanman village has been presented in Table 2.6. There are altogether 517 individuals in the village, out of which 257 (49.7%) are males and 260 (50.29%) are females. The highest frequency of males fall in the age group of 5–9 yrs., where 37 (7.16%) individuals are found and the lowest frequency of male falls within the age group of 85–89 and 90–94 yrs., where single individual is noticed in each category.

On the other hand, the highest number of females is found in the age group of 5–9 and 10–14 yrs., where 41 (7.93%) females are recorded in each category. The lowest frequency falls within the age group of 55–59 and 100–104 yrs., respectively, where single individual is recorded in each category. No females are recorded in the age group of 85–89, 90–94 and 95–99 yrs.

Two important trends are noticed in this village. First, there is slight male deficiency though it is not significantly noticeable. Secondly, there is a female member in the age group 100–104 yrs., while there is no male member beyond 95 yrs. The overall life span of Muklom Tangsas may be considered as high.

Table 2.6: Distribution of Population by Age and Sex in the Village Yanman

Sl. No.	Age Group	Male		Female		Total	
		No.	Percentage	No.	Percentage	No.	Percentage
1.	0–4	31	6.00	34	6.58	65	12.57
2.	5–9	37	7.16	41	7.93	78	15.09
3.	10–14	31	6.00	41	7.93	72	13.93
4.	15–19	28	5.41	28	5.41	56	10.83
5.	20–24	22	4.26	14	2.71	36	6.96
6.	25–29	21	4.06	13	2.51	34	6.58
7.	30–34	8	1.55	19	3.68	27	5.22
8.	35–39	15	2.90	19	3.68	34	6.58
9.	40–44	23	4.45	9	1.74	32	6.19
10.	45–49	10	1.93	16	3.09	26	5.03
11.	50–54	7	1.35	4	0.77	11	2.13
12.	55–59	9	1.74	1	0.19	10	1.93
13.	60–64	2	0.39	9	1.74	11	2.13
14.	65–69	4	0.77	4	0.77	8	1.55
15.	70–74	5	0.97	3	0.50	8	1.55
16.	75–79	–	–	2	0.39	2	0.39
17.	80–84	2	0.39	2	0.39	4	0.77
18.	85–89	1	0.19	–	–	1	0.19
19.	90–94	1	0.19	–	–	1	0.19
20.	95–99	–	–	–	–	–	–
21.	100–104	–	–	1	0.19	1	0.19
	Total	**257**	**49.71**	**260**	**50.29**	**517**	**100.00**

The overall analysis of Muklom Tangsas reveals that in the Simrang (New Thamlom) and Yanman villages has slight male deficiency, whereas in the Loktong village a slight female deficiency is recorded. But, it is a fact that though deficiency in all the villages may not be considered as significant, yet such a trend is noticed in all the Muklom villages.

When a comparison is made on the basis of age and sex between the Lungchangs and Mukloms (Table 2.7) revealed that population among the Lungchangs is higher than the Mukloms. Among the Lungchangs there are 3 males and 5 females above 85 yrs. of age, whereas among the Mukloms there are 3 males above 85 yrs. of age. It is significant to note that among the Mukloms there is a female above 100 yrs. of age. The higher numbers of population in the lower age group may be interpreted due to the lower rate of child mortality.

Literacy

The infrastructural facilities with regard to education is visible among

Table 2.7: Distribution of Population by Age and Sex among the Lungchangs and the Mukloms

Sl. No.	Age Group	Male		Female	
		Lungchang	Muklom	Lungchang	Muklom
1.	0–4	43	54	41	58
2.	5–9	60	62	59	65
3.	10–14	58	64	67	60
4.	15–19	78	49	50	60
5.	20–24	38	36	40	31
6.	25–29	40	30	50	19
7.	30–34	38	14	36	38
8.	35–39	47	34	41	38
9.	40–44	45	39	38	21
10.	45–49	32	23	27	23
11.	50–54	19	13	9	7
12.	55–59	11	13	17	2
13.	60–64	15	5	18	12
14.	65–69	14	8	10	10
15.	70–74	13	7	6	7
16.	75–79	5	Nil	4	5
17.	80–84	6	3	5	2
18.	85–89	1	2	3	Nil
19.	90–94	1	1	1	Nil
20.	95–99	1	Nil	1	Nil
21.	100–104	Nil	Nil	Nil	1
	Total	**565**	**457**	**523**	**459**

the Tangsas. It has already been revealed that there is at least one primary school in each studied village. Besides, the children are getting the opportunity of higher education in Changlang town.

The distribution of population by age, sex, and educational states among the lungchanges has been presented in the following Tables 2.8, 2.9 and 2.10.

Sex and educational status of New Changlang have been presented in Table 2.8. The individuals above 3 yrs. of age are considered. Out of 185 individuals, 27 (14.59%) females are found in the category of illiterate. On the other hand only 5 (2.70%) males fall in the category of illiterate. While males and females are considered together, the highest frequency, i.e. 41 (22.16%) individuals are found in the category of High School (VIII-X) standard.

In case of male, there is one Doctor and 2 Engineers. It indicates that they are getting the opportunity of higher education. With regard to female, a female is working as nurse, while there is one Veterinary Doctor and one has passed B. Pharma.

Table 2.8: Distribution of Population by Sex and Education in the Village New Changlang

Sl. No.	Literacy	Male		Female		Total	
		No.	%	No.	%	No.	%
1.	Illiterate	5	2.70	27	14.59	32	17.30
2.	Primary (Up to IV)	22	11.89	13	7.03	35	18.92
3.	ME (V–VII)	15	8.11	16	8.65	31	16.76
4.	VIII–X	24	12.97	17	9.19	41	22.16
5.	HS (XI–XII)	16	8.65	11	5.95	27	14.60
6.	Graduate	6	3.24	3	1.62	9	4.86
7.	P.G.	2	1.08	1	0.54	3	1.62
8.	Doctor	1	0.54	–	–	1	0.54
9.	Engineer	2	1.08	–	–	2	1.08
10.	B. Pharm a.	–	–	1	0.54	1	0.54
12.	Nurse	–	–	2	1.08	2	1.08
13.	Veterinary doctor	–	–	1	0.54	1	0.54
	Total	**93**	**50.27**	**92**	**49.73**	**185**	**100.00**

Note: Children below 3 yrs. are not included.

Table 2.9: Distribution of Population by Sex and Education in the Village Old Changlang

Sl. No	Literacy	Male		Female		Total	
		No.	%	No.	%	No.	%
1.	Illiterate	28	7.33	54	14.14	82	21.47
2.	Primary (Up to IV)	47	12.31	39	10.20	86	22.51
3.	M.E. (V–VII)	36	9.43	24	6.28	60	15.71
4.	H.S (VIII–X)	63	16.49	43	11.26	106	27.75
5.	H.S.S (XI–XII)	18	4.71	15	3.93	33	8.64
6.	Graduate	5	1.31	4	1.05	9	2.36
7.	P.G	1	0.26	1	0.26	2	0.52
8.	Doctor	2	0.52	–	–	2	0.52
9.	ITI	1	0.26	–	–	1	0.26
10.	M. Phil	1	0.26	–	–	1	0.26
	Total	**202**		**180**		**382**	**100.00**

Note: Children below 3 yrs. are not included.

The distribution of population by sex and education in the Old Changlang village has been presented in Table 2.9. The table shows that there are total of 82 illiterate individuals in the village. Out of it 28 (07.32%) are male and 54 (14.14%) are female. The maximum number of literate population are found in the category of High School level (VIII–X), where there are 63 (16.49%) are male and 43 (11.26%) are female.

The next maximum number of population, i.e. 86 (22.51%) is found in the category of Primary level (up to IV). Here, literate male are 47 (12.30%) and literate female is 39 (10.20%). It is followed by total literate persons, i.e. 60 (15.71%) in the category of Higher Secondary level. Here 18 (4.71%) are male and 15 (3.93%) are female. This is followed by 9 (2.36%) individuals in the Graduate level with 5 (1.30%) males and 4 (1.05%) females. In the P.G. level, there is 1 male and 1 female. However, in the category of Doctor, ITI and M. Phil. category, no female member is found whereas 2 (0.52%) males are recorded in the category of Doctor and 1 male in the each category of ITI and M. Phil. Table 2.9 revealed that the villagers achieved success in the field of education, which is a positive sign.

The distribution of population by sex and education in the Rangkatu village has been recorded in Table 2.10. From Table it is revealed that there are 141 (32.49%) individuals who are categorized as illiterate, out of which 50 (11.52%) are male and 91 (20.97%) are female. The maximum number of literate population has been found in the category of primary level (i.e. up to standard IV) where 60 (13.82%) male and 50 (11.52%) female are recorded. It is followed by a total literate population of 82 (18.89%) in the category of class VIII–X standard. Here literate male is 55 (12.67%) and females 27 (6.22%). In the category of M.E. (V–VII) there are equal number of male and female i.e. 36 (8.29%) in each category. In the Higher Secondary level (XI–XII) there are 18 (4.14%) males and 6 (1.38%) female. In the category of Graduate and Post Graduate level no female member is recorded, whereas there are 3 (0.69%) and 1 (0.23%) male are found in each standard, respectively.

Table 2.10: Distribution of Population by Sex and Education in the Village Rangkatu

Sl. No.	*Literacy*	*Male*		*Female*		*Total*	
		No.	%	No.	%	No.	%
1.	Illiterate	50	11.52	91	20.97	141	32.49
2.	Primary (up to 4)	60	13.82	50	11.52	110	25.35
3.	ME (V–VII)	36	8.29	36	8.29	72	16.59
4.	VIII–X	55	12.67	27	6.22	82	18.89
5.	H.S. (XI–XII)	18	4.14	6	1.38	24	5.53
6.	Graduate	3	0.69	–	–	3	0.69
7.	P.G.	1	0.23	–	–	1	0.23
8.	Doctor, Engineer	–	–	–	–	–	–
9.	D. Pharma	1	0.23	–	–	1	0.23
10.	Nurse and Others	–	–	–	–	–	–
	Total	**224**	**51.61**	**210**	**48.39**	**434**	**100**

Note: Below 3 yrs. 18 males and 16 females are not included.

In this village the illiterate persons are comparatively high, but the record reveals that the illiterate persons are mostly from illiterate category while the new generation is interested in the getting education.

It has already been mentioned that the data on Muklom Tangsas have been collected from three villages. The distribution of population by sex and education in these three villages has been presented in Tables 2.11, 2.12. and 2.13.

The distribution of population by sex and education in the village Loktong has been presented in Table 2.11. It is clear from table that the number of illiterate people is highest, i.e. 48 (28.57%) in number which normally includes the aged persons and small children. The maximum number of literate individuals is found in the category of Primary (up to IV) and M.E. (V–VII) level, where there are 36 (21.43%) persons in each category. Out of 36 (21.43%) people in the primary level, 25 are male and 11 are female. Again, out of 36 (21.43%) people in the M.E. level, 22 (13.10%) are male and 14 (8.33%) are female.

Table 2.11: Distribution of Population by Sex and Education in the Village Laktong

Sl. No	*Literacy*	*Male*		*Female*		*Total*	
		No.	%	No.	%	No.	%
1.	Illiterate	13	7.74	35	20.83	48	28.57
2.	Primary (Up to IV)	25	14.88	11	6.55	36	21.43
3.	Middle (V–VII)	22	13.10	14	8.33	36	21.43
4.	H.S. (VIII–X)	17	10.12	8	4.76	25	14.88
5.	H.S.S. (XI–XII)	6	3.57	10	5.95	16	9.52
6.	Graduate	2	1.19	2	1.19	4	2.38
7.	Post Graduate	1	0.60	1	0.60	2	1.19
8.	Engineer/B.E.	1	0.60	–	–	1	0.60
	Total	**87**	**51.79**	**81**	**48.21**	**168**	**100.00**

Note: Children below 3 yrs. are not included in the table as they are too young. And their number is 22.

Thus, it can be said that comparatively the number of males have attained higher education than the female. It is followed by a total literate population of 25 (14.88%) in the H.S. level (VIII–X), out of which 17 (10.12%) are male and 8 (4.76%) are female. In the Higher Secondary level (XI–XII) 16 (9.52%) are recorded. Here, the number of female is 10 (5.95%) which is slightly higher than the literate male, i.e. 6 (3.57%) individuals. In Graduate category 4 (2.38%) members are there, where both the male and female are found in equal number, i.e. 2 (1.19%) persons are in each category. There is only 1 male who have completed the Engineering course. Some significant trend may be noticed in the analysis. In the lower level of educational category the percentage of male is slightly higher whereas from the Higher Secondary level, the percentage of female is either increasing or equal in number. It indicates that the villagers are giving equal opportunity of education to male and female.

Table 2.12: Distribution of Population by Sex and Education in the Village Simrang

Sl. No.	*Literacy*	*Male*		*Female*		*Total*	
		No.	*%*	*No.*	*%*	*No.*	*%*
1.	Illiterate	21	10.82	36	18.56	57	29.38
2.	Primary (Up to IV)	33	17.01	28	14.43	61	31.44
3.	M.E (V–VII)	17	8.76	14	7.22	31	15.98
4.	H.S (VIII–X)	17	8.76	16	8.25	33	17.01
5.	H.S.S (XI–XII)	6	3.09	4	2.06	10	5.15
6.	Graduate	2	1.03	–	–	2	1.03
	Total	**96**	**49.48**	**98**	**50.52**	**194**	**100.00**

The distribution of population by sex and education in the village Simrang (New Thamlom) has been presented in Table 2.12. From the table it is clear that there are altogether 57 (29.38%) illiterate individuals, out of which 21 (10.82%) are male and 36 (18.56%) are female.

The maximum number of literate persons are found in the category of Primary level (up to IV) where 61 (31.44%) are found, out of which 33 (17.01%) are male and 28 (14.43%) are female. It is followed by High School level (VIII–X) where 33 (17.01%) individuals are recorded, out of which 17 (8.76%) are male and 16 (8.25%) are female. In the category of Middle School level (V–VII) level, 31 individuals are found, where 17 (8.76%) are male and 14 (7.22%) are female. 10 individuals (5.15%) have achieved Higher Secondary level (XI–XII) with 6 (3.09%) male and 4 (2.06%) female. 2 (1.03%) male members are recorded in Graduate level. There are no individuals in with technical education. An analysis of educational level indicates the trend of equal educational opportunity for both male and female. But unfortunately, in higher level of education the number is not that significant.

The distribution of population by sex and education of the village

Table 2.13: Distribution of Population by Sex and Education in the Village Yanman

Sl. No.	Literacy	Male		Female		Total	
		No.	%	No.	%	No.	%
1.	Illiterate	57	12.15	120	25.59	177	37.74
2.	Primary (up to IV)	71	15.14	51	10.87	122	26.01
3.	Middle (V–VII)	46	9.81	29	6.18	75	15.99
4.	H.S. (VIII–X)	44	9.38	27	5.76	71	15.14
5.	H.S.S. (XI–XII)	13	2.77	7	1.49	20	4.26
6.	Graduate	3	0.64	–	–	3	0.64
7.	ITI	1	0.21	–	–	1	0.21
	Total	**235**	**50.11**	**234**	**49.89**	**469**	**100.00**

Yanman has been presented in Table 2.13. It is revealed that there are 177 (37.74%) illiterate persons in the village with 57 (12.15%) male and 120 (25.59%) female. The children below 3 yrs. of age are not included as they are too young to go to school. Excluding these young children, the total population in this village is 469.

It is clear from Table 2.13 that the maximum number of literate persons fall in the primary section (up to IV) where there are 122 (26.01%) individuals, of which 71 (15.14%) are males and 51 (10.87%) are female. It is followed by Middle School level (V–VII) where there 46 (9.81%) male and 29 (6.18%) are females. In the next level, i.e. at the High School level, there are 71 (15.14%) individuals, out of which 44 (9.38%) are male and 27 (5.76%) are female. Twenty (4.26%) individuals had their education up to Higher Secondary level (XI–XII) of which 13 (2.77%) are male and 7 (1.4%) are female. There are 3 persons (0.64%) who had attained education up to Graduate level. Only 1 person is found who had his education from ITI. From the table it is revealed that in all the level of education, the number of males is higher than the female. In the same way, there are no individuals who have attained medical or technical education.

The analysis of population by sex and education among the Lungchang and the Muklom Tangsas reveal that both male and female are getting equal opportunity of education (Table 2.14). The educational level signifies that females are not deprived of education as a whole. Except in one village, i.e. the Laktong inhabited by the Muklom Tangsas, in all other village the percentage of educated male are higher than the female. In the village Laktong, in the lower level of education, the percentage of male are slightly higher whereas from Higher Secondary level, the percentage of female is either higher or equal in number.

Table 2.14: Distribution of Population by Sex and Education among the Lungchangs and Mukloms

Sl. No.	*Literacy*	*Male*		*Female*	
		Lungchang	*Muklom*	*Lungchang*	*Muklom*
1.	Illiterate	129	91	172	191
2.	Primary (up to IV)	129	129	102	90
3.	Middle (V–VII)	87	85	76	57
4.	H.S. (VIII–X)	142	78	87	51
5.	H.S.S. (XI–XII)	52	25	42	21
6.	Graduate	14	7	10	2
7.	Post Graduate	3	1	2	1
8.	Doctor	3	Nil	Nil	Nil
9.	Engineer/ITI	3	2	Nil	Nil
10.	B. Pharma.	1	Nil	1	Nil
11.	Nurse	Nil	Nil	2	Nil
12.	Veterinary Doctor	Nil	Nil	1	Nil
13.	M. Phil.	1	Nil	Nil	Nil

When the educational level is compared in the sub-tribe level, it is found that the percentages of highly educated persons are slightly higher among the Lungchang Tangsas. There are 3 males and 2 female graduates are there among the Lungchangs. It is also encouraging picture that 3 Doctors and 3 Engineers are recorded among the Lungchangs. There are 2 persons in B. Pharm. course out of which one is male and the other is female. Similarly, 2 Nurses and 1 Veterinary Doctor are recorded among the Lungchangs.

Among the Mukloms, the number of graduates is significant. There are 7 male and 2 female graduates. In the Post Graduate level there is 1 male and 1 female. There is only 1 Engineer and 1, ITI belonging to male category. The overall Sex and Education pattern are better in case Lungchangs. It may also be interpreted that villages situated near the township provide better opportunities for education. As most of the Lungchang villages are situated near the township they are in a better position of getting educational facilities. Another significant trend is that those villages which are situated slightly in interior areas, the number of highly educated persons are less, be it Lungchang or Mukloms. The study also indicates that though the Tangsas have a preference for male children, yet the girls are not deprived of the educational facilities.

3

Socio-Economic Life

Economy is an important constituent of the community life and plays a deciding role in the formation of the cultural and social structure of society. In the study of economy, one has to give emphasis on non-economic factors like social and cultural relation. In the words of Firth (1951:123), "economic organization is a type of social action. It involves the combination of various kinds of human sciences with one another and with non-human goods in such a way that they serve given ends."

Every community has its own way to meet its basic needs for the existence of its members failing which they are threatened with extinction. Nature provides the raw materials, but the customs and traditions of a cultural group determine how raw materials are utilized for economic end. Economy is a result of the interaction of those portions of the environment that are utilized by the culture in the form of resources and those aspects of the culture that are techniques for utilizing the resources. The way in which resources, technology and work are combined to satisfy the material requirements of the human beings and of social groups may be called as economic organization. In the words of Firth (1951:138) economic anthropology deals primarily with the economic aspects of social relation. Various Anthropologists has defined economic activities from different angles. Economic activity is connected with all such activities of men are designed to secure him physical survival (Majumder and Madan, 1970:191). It is agreed by all social scientists that economic life deals with material wants of the people. The association with the fulfilment of material wants also constitutes part of economic life. Paddington opines (1952:18) "economic system is designed to satisfy material wants of the people, to organize production, to control distribution and to determine the rights and claims of ownership within the community". Thus, a study of economic life of a community helps us to understand an important feature of their culture.

The study of economic system may be looked at with two perspectives. One looks at the economic system from the point of view of production, consumption and distribution. The second perspective is actual application of these three aspects in relation to a particular community. The mode of production implies technique and organization of economic activities relating to production. This leads to the understanding the role and status that exist in a society. Maurice Godlier developed economic anthropology from Marxian perspective and emphasized on social relation which emerge out of modes of production. The structure of society itself emerges from the modes of production. For understanding of economic life, special analytical concepts are necessary because social organization and culture-kinship, political organization, religion-effect economic organization and performance so directly and sensitively related that only a socio-economic approach may reveal various dimensions. Such type of study was carried by Good fellow among the Bantus and Firth (1939) of Tikopean economics. Firth himself admitted that he analysed economic structure, because many social relationships were made most manifest in their economic content. Indeed, the social structure in particular and other aspects of political structure was clearly dependent on specific economic relationships arising out of the system of control of resources. While these relationships in turn, were linked with the religious activities and institutions of the society.

Modern economy, thus, studies all the activities related to production, distribution, exchange and consumption. Till today, there is no simple and precise definition of the tribal economy.

The most important characteristics of the tribal economy are the close relationship between their economic life and the natural environment. They have a very simple technology which is well suited in their environment. The tribal totally dependent on the gift of nature and that is why they rarely experience famine or starvation. Because of it their economy may be termed as subsistence type. In simple way, tribe is always considered as economically independent group of people having their own specific economy and thus having a living pattern of labour, division of labour and specialization. Gift and ceremonial exchange, trade and barter consumption norms, values, attitudes, capital formation all are unique according to their cultural pattern.

In the present chapter, the economy of the Tangsas under study has been presented. The Tangsas as a whole are dependent on agriculture.

They practice both *jhum*/shifting and wet/settled cultivation. There are instances where they go for terrace cultivation. Thus, agriculture is their main occupation and livelihood. However, due to the impact of modern education, there is a tendency to go for different salaried jobs.

From early stage, the Tangsas were fascinated by hill-tops, mountain ranges, thick forests, riversr, etc. The Tangsa villages were situated within the midst of thick forest and mountain ranges. There was no necessity to make a demarcation line between forest end and area under habitation. They lived happily in the forest and there was no dearth of forest land for *jhum* cultivation. A plot once cleared by a farmer yielded harvest for 3-4 yrs. and was abandoned for some time to become a part of the forest. Moreover, the Tangsas were in the habit of frequent movement from one area to another, either for due to exhausting resources and due to increase of population size. Though now-a-days also, they have forest land in their surrounding areas, yet these are not sufficient for their livelihood. The individual property with well demarcation boundary in their households is the characteristics of the Tangsas.

It has already been mentioned that the present data were collected from 6 villages, covering two major sub-tribes, i.e. the Lungchangs and the Mukloms sub-tribe of the Tangsas. The mode of operation by and large is same in both the sub-tribes. The land is operated either by the owner themselves or in the share basis.

Land Holding Pattern

Land is the most precious possession of the Tangsas. Here an effort has been made to present the landholding pattern of the Lungchangs and the Mukloms, the two major sub-tribes of the Tangsas. Though both the sub-tribes follow more or less same pattern of agriculture, yet minor difference are noticed both on the sub-tribe level as well as village level. They are practicing mainly two types of agriculture, viz. *jhum* cultivation and wet cultivation.

Tables 3.1, 3.2, and 3.3 represent the land holding pattern of Lungchang Tangsas of Arunachal Pradesh.

Though there are families who possess more than 13 *bighas* of land yet the average holding per family is not significant. In the village New Changlang out of 39 families, 23 families have homestead land ranging from 1–3 *bighas*. It is followed by 4 families who have 7–9 *bighas* of land. There are 3 families who have homestead land ranging from 4–6 *bighas* of land.

Table 3.1: Landholding Pattern of the Village New Changlang

Sl. No.	*Land possession (in bighas)*	*Home stead (No. of families)*	*Cultivable (No. of families)*	*Others (No. of families)*
1.	Nil	9	15	24
2.	1–3	23	7	4
3.	4–6	3	6	3
4.	7–9	4	5	2
5.	10–12	–	1	–
6.	13 +	–	–	6
	Total	**39**	**34**	**39**

There are 3 families who have homestead land ranging from 4-6 *bighas* of land. Table 3.1 also indicates that there are 9 families who do not have homestead land of their own. With regards to cultivable land, there are 7 families who have land ranging from 1–3 *bighas* of land. It is followed by 6 families who possessed land within the range of 4–6 *bighas* and 5 families have cultivable land within the range of 7–9 *bighas.* There is only one family who has cultivable land above 10 *bighas* of land. Those who do not have homestead land of their own normally stays in others land, earn their livelihood either by *jhum* cultivation or other means. It is also revealed that who utilize other type of land possesses above 13 *bighas* of land. Besides homestead and cultivable land, the villagers utilize other type of land either for cultivating seasonal vegetables or tea cultivation. In many cases, they do not utilize the land at present and wait for utilizing it in later stage.

The picture of land holding pattern in the village Old Changlang has been presented in Table 3.2. Table shows that out of 75 families, 71 have homestead land ranging between 1–3 *bighas.* Only 4 families have homestead land within the range of 4–6 *bighas.*

Table 3.2: Landholding Pattern of the Village Old Changlang

Sl No.	*Land Possession (bighas)*	*Home stead (No. of families)*	*Cultivable (No. of families)*	*Others (No. of families)*
1.	Nil	–	15	52
2.	1–3	71	2	–
3.	4–6	4	6	1
4.	7–9	–	15	2
5.	10–12	–	26	3
6.	13 +	–	11	17
	Total	**75**	**75**	**75**

In the category of cultivable land, there are 26 families who have more than 10 *bighas* of land. It is followed by 15 families having 7–9 *bighas* of land. There are 11 families who have 13 *bighas* of cultivable land, 6 families have 4–6 *bighas* of land and only 2 families possessed land within the range of 1–3 *bighas*. It is also revealed from the table that 15 families do not have cultivable land.

There are 17 families who have above 13 *bighas* of other type of land which is followed by 3 families having 10–12 *bighas* of land, whereas, 52 families do not have other type of land.

The analysis of landholding pattern of Rangkatu village has been presented in Table 3.3. It indicates that out of 65 families, 64 families have homestead land ranging from 1–3 *bighas*. There is only 1 family who possesses homestead land within the range of 4–6 *bighas*.

In the category of cultivable land there are 22 families having land ranging from 4–6 *bighas* of land. It is followed by 19 families who have land within the range of 7–9 *bighas*. There are 14 families having land within 1–3 *bighas*. It is also revealed that 8 families have more than 10 *bighas* of cultivable land. Only two families have above 13 *bighas* of cultivable land.

Table 3.3: Landholding Pattern of the Village Rangkatu

Sl. No.	*Land possession (in bighas)*	*Homestead (No. of families)*	*Cultivable (No. of families)*	*Others (No. of families)*
1.	Nil	–	–	18
2.	1–3	64	14	2
3.	4–6	1	22	20
4.	7–9	–	19	11
5.	10–12	–	8	7
6.	13 +	–	2	7
	Total	**65**	**65**	**65**

It has also been revealed that there are 20 families, who have other type of land ranging from 4–6 *bighas*. 11 families have such type of land ranging from 7–9 *bighas*. There are 7 families who have land above 10 *bighas*. There are another 7 families who have above 13 *bighas* of land.

An analysis of landholding pattern among the Lungchang Tangsas of 3 villages revealed that in New Changlang village there are 9 families who do not have homestead land, whereas in Old Changlang and Rangkatu all the families have homestead land. With regards to cultivable land, the position is much better in Old Changlang village, where 26 families have more than 10 *bighas* of land. And there are 11 families who have above 13 *bighas* of land. The picture of Rangkatu village may also be considered better where 8 families have above 8 *bighas* of land and 2 families have above 13 *bighas* of land.

It is a common trend in all the villages where there are families who have other type of land. Such lands are utilized either for cultivating seasonal vegetables or tea cultivation. Sometimes they give these lands on lease basis.

The present project also covers the Muklom Tangsas of Arunachal Pradesh. The data have been collected from the village Laktong, Simrang and Yanman. Landholding pattern of these three villages have been presented in Tables 3.4, 3.5 and 3.6.

Table 3.4: Landholding Pattern of the Village Laktong

Sl. No.	*Land possession (bighas)*	*Homestead (No. of families)*	*Cultivable (No. of families)*	*Others (No. of families)*
1.	Nil	–	15	32
2.	1 – 3	33	–	–
3.	4 – 6	2	10	1
4.	7 – 9	–	9	1
5.	10 – 12	–	1	1
6.	13 +	–	–	–
	Total	**35**	**35**	**35**

The landholding pattern in the village Laktong has been presented in Table 3.4. It is revealed from the table that out of 35 families, 33 families have homestead land between 1–3 *bighas*. Only 2 families possessed 4–6 *bighas* of homestead land.

In the category of cultivable land there are 10 families who have land within the range of 4–6 *bighas*. It is followed by 9 families having 7–9 *bighas* of cultivable land. There is only 1 family who has above 10 *bighas* of cultivable land. It is also revealed that there are 15 families who do not have cultivable land, i.e. wet land.

In this village there are no significant numbers of families who have other type of land. Only 1 families have other type of land within the range of 4–6 *bighas*. There are another two families who have 7–9 *bighas* of land and 10 *bighas* of land respectively above 10 *bighas* of land.

The landholding pattern in the Simrang village reveals that all the 32 families have homestead land within 1–3 *bighas*. In the category of cultivable land, there are 18 families who have land within the range of 4–6 *bighas* of land. It is followed by 9 families having (1–3) *bighas* of land. There are 4 families who possess 7–9 *bighas* of cultivable land. There is only 1 family who does not have any cultivable land.

Table 3.5: Landholding Pattern of the Village Simrang

Sl. No.	*Land possession (in bighas)*	*Homestead (No. of families)*	*Cultivable (No. of families)*	*Others (No. of families)*
1.	Nil	–	1	6
2.	1 – 3	32	9	–
3.	4 – 6	–	18	14
4.	7 – 9	–	4	10
5.	10 – 12	–	–	2
6.	13 +	–	–	–
	Total	**32**	**32**	**32**

There are 14 families who have other type of land within the range of 4–6 *bighas*. It is followed by 10 families who possess such type of land within the range of 7–9 *bighas*. Only 2 families have above 10 *bighas* of such type of land.

The landholding pattern of the village Yanman has been presented in Table 3.6. It is revealed that out of 86 families 85 have homestead land between 1–3 *bighas*. There is only 1 family who does not possess any homestead land.

Table 3.6: Landholding Pattern of the Village Yanman

Sl. No.	*Land Possession (Bighas)*	*Homestead (No. of Families)*	*Cultivable (No. of Families)*	*Others (No. of Families)*
1.	Nil	1	1	36
2.	1–3	85	24	5
3.	4–6	–	47	25
4.	7–9	–	10	16
5.	10–12	–	4	2
6.	13 +	–	–	2
	Total	**86**	**86**	**86**

In the category of cultivable land, there are 47 families who have land within the range of 4–6 *bighas*. It is followed by 24 families having

1–3 *bighas* of land. There are 10 families having 7–9 *bighas* of land, whereas 4 families have more than 10 *bighas* of cultivable land. There is only 1 family who does not have any cultivable land. It seems that 1 does not have any land.

There are 25 families who have other type of land within the range of 4–6 *bighas*. It is followed by 16 families who have utilized other type of land within the range of 7–9 *bighas*. Out of 86 families, 36 do not have any such type of land. But there are 2 families each have more than 10 *bighas* and 13 *bighas* of land, respectively.

The analysis of landholding pattern among the Muklom Tangsas revealed that most of the families have homestead land except 1 family in the village Yanman. With regards to cultivable land there are 4 families who have above 10 *bighas* of land. There is not a single family with more than 13 *bighas* of land.

When a comparison is made between the Lungchangs and the Mukloms with regard to the land holding pattern it is revealed that most of the families possess 1–3 *bighas* of homestead land. There are 158 families among the Lungchangs and 150 among the Mukloms who possess the land within that range. With regards to the cultivable land maximum number of families have 4–6 *bighas* of land, while the position of the Lungchangs may be considered as better as 39 families possess 7-9 *bighas* of land and 35 families have more than 10 *bighas* of land, while 13 families among the Lungchangs have more than 13 *bighas* of cultivable land. In case of Mukloms there are only a few families who possess above 10 *bighas* of land. It may be due to the fact that as most of the Muklom villages are located in the hill top they do not have enough cultivable land in the river valley.

Table 3.7: Landholding Pattern among the Lungchangs and Mukloms

Sl. No.	*Land Possession (Bighas)*	*Homestead (No. of Families)*		*Cultivable (No. of Families)*		*Others (No. of Families)*	
		Lungchang	*Muklom*	*Lungchang*	*Muklom*	*Lungchang*	*Muklom*
1.	Nil	9	1	30	17	94	74
2.	1–3	158	150	27	33	6	5
3.	4–6	8	2	35	75	24	40
4.	7–9	4	Nil	39	23	15	27
5.	10–12	Nil	Nil	35	5	10	5
6.	13 +	Nil	Nil	13	Nil	30	2
	Total	**179**	**153**	**179**	**153**	**179**	**153**

Patterns of Land Ownership

The pattern of land ownership varies from tribe to tribe and region to region according to socio-economic and traditional customs of the particular tribe or group. Among the Tangsas, the patterns of land ownerships are as follow:

(a) Individual Ownership of Land

The individual ownership of land among the Tangsas include cultivated areas, e.g. wet cultivation field, any kind of garden including horticulture, bamboo and palm grooves etc.

(b) Village Ownership of Land

All the areas, where *jhum* cultivation is done are the property of the village. Moreover, the areas where public institutions are there, e.g. school, community halls, and health centre are the property of the village community. Therefore, except an individual ownership of land, the rest of the areas are considered as village land.

The intensive study in six villages revealed that there are few families who entirely depend on *jhum* cultivation. There are families ranging from 3 to 3.07 per cent in all the villages who entirely depend on *jhum* cultivation. There are mainly two types of cultivation i.e. *jhum* cultivation and settled cultivation. There are few families who follow terrace cultivation.

Inheritance of Land

The Tangsas are generally patrilineal in nature, where descent is traced through the male line. The composition of family differs both within a village and between the villages. That does not affect the inheritance process and it always revolves around male members only. Inheritance systems of landed properties are neither primogeniture nor ultimogeniture in nature. The parents normally prefer to hand over their properties to a son whom they consider efficient, are in a position to look after them in their old age. But in general, property is handed to the eldest son. And it is his duty to distribute the properties among the brothers. There are cases also, where father during his life time divided his landed properties and other among his sons.

In case of absence of male child in a family, his younger or elder brother's son will inherit the landed properties of that particular person. Sometimes one may adopt a male child and in that situation he will inherit the properties accordingly. Female members usually inherit movable properties like ornaments, weaving implements etc. at the time of marriage. The daughters are permitted to construct the houses within the homestead of her parental land if it is available. With slight variations according to familywise, this is the normal practices followed by the Tangsas. In no case the villagers are allowed to sale their land to outsiders.

Procedures of Jhum Cultivation

As *jhum* or shifting cultivation is widely practiced by the Tangsas, an effort has been made in this study to project a brief picture of the procedure of *jhum* cultivation. As Tangsas are hill people, *jhum* cultivation is their traditional means of cultivation. The system of *jhum* cultivation among the Tangsas has socio-economic and religious and cultural significance for the community. The *jhum*/shifting cultivation is as old as human civilization and this type of cultivation is prevalent widely in whole of Asia and Pacific region. The Neolithic culture continued to survive up to the present days in hill tracts of north-east India. Among the Lungchangs, the *jhum* cultivation is referred as "Kharangpok-som" or "Khangpok-som", where 'Kharang/kang' means dry/hilly; '*Pok*' means field and '*som*' means cultivate, respectively. Among the Mukloms it is referred as *Chajungsam*. The *jhum* cultivation consists of various stages and procedures.

The first stage of *jhum* cultivation is the selection of the site. All the villagers interested in *jhum* cultivation assemble together in a particular place as decided by them. In the meeting, the villagers unanimously fixed the date of selection including the other necessary spheres which are related to the cultivation.

In the next stage, as fixed by them all the male members of the village go to the site and choose the plot of land, keeping in mind the soil fertility and his interest. In the selection of plot, they take the decision by observing omen, i.e. whether that plot is suitable for them or not. In this process, after surveying the plot of land, they decide to clean any small portion of land in one corner of the plot. Then the person erects a *kann-knah*, the ownership prohibited symbol, which is usually used by the Lungchangs. It is normally a bamboo or wooden stick with sharp pointed head, inculcate with few portion of bushes or shrubs on it.

The male member sitting in front of this symbol observes an omen to know the suitability of the plot. If it indicates any bad sign, he leaves the plot and selects another. It may happen that the same plot may be suitable for another person. Thus, the omen indicator varies from person to person. After the selection of site, they are to work hard, because they have to make it dried very soon. They clear the weed and the big trees as well. The cutting is systematically done from top to bottom, i.e. high slop to down slop in a systematic linear manner or column-wise.

The date of setting the fire is jointly decided by the villagers. When they think that the soil is dry enough to set fire they hold a meeting for setting fire on the field. It is referred as *Pakchak* (setting fire on the field) by the Lunchangs and *Sal-rukh* by the Mukloms. They avoid odd days of the week and consider Monday, Wednesday, Friday or Sunday for this purpose. In the very next day of fire, millet seeds may be sown or broadcast.

In case of paddy, seeds are sown after the cleaning and arranging of half burnt wood and debris. Paddy seeds are sown by two ways, i.e. either broadcast by hand and later on mixed with the help of scraper. In other method, seeds are sown by digging soil using sticks. In the last stage of seed sowing, they are to observe a taboo. On that day, the family-members are not allowed to husk rice or the person who broadcasted the seed usually does not take fish/meat on that day. Moreover, the family members are not allowed to go to the field.

In case of *jhum* cultivation, they erect fencing after broadcasting and sowing of seed. The height of fencing is approximately 1.5 to 2.0 metres from the ground and the breadth depends on coverage of the sowing area.

On the day of harvesting, they are to observe a small ritual. A bamboo stick is made and designed accordingly by stripping a bamboo. In the upper portion of the bamboo, a little amount of boiled water is carried. After reaching the field, the bamboo stick is erected in a sacred place, called *Maanroung*. After performing some ritualistic activities, he/she starts harvesting.

The ritualistic harvesting is normally done by woman, among the Lungchangs. But there is no hard and fast rule and a male member may perform it.

Climate and season are the fundamental determinants of the *jhum* cultivation, which are obviously observed by all the tribes of North East India. *Jhuming* being rain fed agriculture, all the cycles of cultivation exist accordingly climatic changes. A regular calendar based on natural sources may also be used, e.g. calendar like summer and winter, appearance of monsoon, flowering of different trees and shedding of leaves, changing behaviour in animals, resting of birds etc. which tell them the different periods of cultivation throughout the year.

The cutting of trees, grass, bushes etc. used to be completed in February-March. In March-April, the Lungchang farmers used to go for sowing of *kochu,* chilli, oil seeds, vegetables, paddy, millet, maize and variety of other crops. The millet, maize, etc. used to be harvested in October-November every year. In July, paddy, millet and vegetables were grown for the second time in a year. These crops were also harvested in November-December. During recent years, among the Lungchangs the *jhum* cultivation is almost completely replaced by wet paddy cultivation. Of course, *jhum* crops such as vegetable, chilli, ginger, *kochu* etc. are still raised in *jhum* field.

Shifting cultivation also plays an important role in the life of Mukloms. The major crops raised by Mukloms include, maize, millet, paddy, bean, tapioca, oil seeds, vegetables etc. Sowing of these seeds is completed by the end of January. In July they perform a festival called *Chamtuk* to celebrate the success of cropping season. It marks the beginning of harvesting season for certain crops. Some crops are harvesting in July, while other are harvested in November-December, depending upon the maturity of crops. So, they are to perform *Chamtuk* ritual twice in a year. After harvesting certain crops in July, the Mukloms again start the next phase of *jhum* cultivation. These crops are harvested in December-January. Thus, it is found that cultivation of *jhum* crops is carried out in two phases and certain crops are raised twice in a year. The process is similar among the Lungchangs and the Mukloms.

Wet Cultivation

Each sub-tribe has their own agricultural cycle. And the sub-tribes living in close vicinity have much similarity in cycle and performing the rituals. The nomenclature of some of the agricultural festivals differs from one village to another. The Tangsas were originally shifting cultivators. The available literature (Dutta, Bhagawati, Rao) indicate about their dependence on *jhum* cultivation. But, gradually changes are apparent.

The Tangsa villages, situated at the top of hills frequently faced conflict situation from the other hill tribes like Singphos and Kacharis. Slowly many of the villages were shifted to the roadside and river banks. After shifting to new locations, these villages have got the opportunity of frequent contact with the various Governmental agencies. They came to know about the advantages of settled wet cultivation. With the initiative of village level workers they have shown interest to this effective mode of production strategy. During the last four decades, these become a part of their tradition itself. This transition may be considered as one of the significant step as it came from within rather than imposing from outside source. They themselves realize the benefit of settled cultivation, which ensure a better production and upgradation of their subsistence economy to a considerable extent. They have developed within last four decades a distinct cycle for settled cultivation like their *jhum* cycle which have seasonal implication. In the process, a large group of the Mukloms, the Mossangs, and the Lungchangs acquired land for wet cultivation. The Lungchangs of Changlang, Kengkhu, Rangkatu and other villages situated on the northern bank of Tirap River have secured control over a fertile tract on the bank of Tirap and its tributaries. The wet paddy cultivation is referred as *Panikheti* in Assamese and *Nah-Pok* in Lungchang dialect. *Nah* means wet or mud and *Pak* means field, respectively whereas among the Mukloms it is known as *Nal-tong*.

The process of wet paddy cultivation starts in the month of May when seedlings are prepared in a small plot of land. The plot is prepared with the help of *Jang* (*dao*), *Khurpi* and *Khochak* (spade). This particular plot is called *Taka-soow*. Generally, it is selected in the outskirt or corner of the field, so, that it is easier to transplant in the actual plot.

The actual cultivation of wet field is started by cutting of grasses from the field. It is referred as *Nahsam*, by both the Lungchangs and the Mukloms. This is usually done in a group by the male members. Sometimes the owner arranged the labour force on the family and kinship level. In such cases *dung* (food), *jaw* (local beer) and *ngam* (meat) are provided to the working group. Sometimes it is done on return of cash.

Next step is burning/setting fire to the debris, which is referred as *Nahthing-chak* or *Na-amchok* by the Lungchangs and the Mukloms referred it as *Nal-ruk.* It is done within the plot of land with a belief that it will enhance the fertility of the soil. If there is continuous raining then the debris are thrown or dumped outside the field.

Before tiling, they are to repair or clean the canal (*nala*), which is known as *Nalatoli*. In this process, one person from each household is to take part in the irrigation system. The actual tiling is done with the help of oxen (*Manpong*) in all the Lungchang and the Muklom villages. Once first tilling is over, water is allowed to flow through canal in order to make soil wet. They rarely use modern technology like tractor etc. The main reasons behind it are due to uneven land and size of the cultivable land. Mostly the fields are small in size and subsistence in nature except few of them. Like the plain people, they plough the land three times in a single cultivation of a year.

After completing the tilling, seedlings are uprooted carefully. This is termed as *Takaphei*. The seedlings are known as *Taka* by the Lungchangs, while the Mukloms refer it as *Tika-tong*. Seedlings are up-rooted mostly by the female members. When the seedlings attained 20-25 cm of height then it is considered matured enough for transplantation. An approximate distance between the seedlings should be 15-20 cm but in reality it depends on fertility of land or soil. It means, in more fertile soil, the distance or gap between the seedlings are more and *vice versa*. Weeding is done by women folk, but in case of nuclear families, even men also extend their helping hand.

Before harvesting of the crops, a common ritual is performed in the name of god of crops (*Toungkoow-Chamkoov*). It is a very simple ritual, where all the concerned villagers assemble in a particular place near their wet cultivation. A pig is sacrificed in the name of god of crops. The villagers spend the day eating food, drink and meat and return back to home in the evening. In the very next day they are to observe a taboo, when the villagers are not allowed to visit the field. This ritual is referred as *Chamrjm* or *Nahrong* by the Lungchangs.

Harvesting starts only after the performance of *Chamrip* ritual. Reaping is done mostly by the female members, but males also help in it according to the demand of the situation. If a family is unable to complete reaping, then the co-villagers extend their helping hand. The community of fellow feeling which was an essential part of *jhum* cultivation may be traced in such situation.

The paddy is not immediately taken to the household. Handful of paddy consists of a bundle and is kept in the plot for drying. After four or five days, those bundles are packed and collected in the conical basket (*jing*) or cloth and kept in a selected place.

After storing the paddy, they wait for two or more than two weeks for thrashing, which is known as *Chamrag*. A day before it, the concerned family seeks the help and support from the co-villagers in matters of thrashing. A pig or hen is sacrificed by the owner in the name of paddy spirits and a feast is arranged with food, drink and meat for the participants. In the process, paddy is spread on the clean ground and let it crashed with the help of numbers of pairs of oxen. It is one of the oldest methods of thrashing paddy. It was reported by the villagers that in Rangkatu village even in 2004, the thrashing was done with the hands by beating in the ground itself, with the help of bamboo sticks. They also admit that the process change from time to time according to the convenience and mutual understanding of the villagers. These are the normal process of thrashing among the Lungchangs in general the villagers of Rangkatu in particular.

Grains are collected and stored in *Chamra-ab-the*, big cylindrical baskets made up of bamboo slits for temporary period. Finally grains are transported from the temporary storing place to the permanent granary at the homestead. Sometimes, this may be done entirely by the family members and sometime they are to engage marginal labour. But marginal labourers also belong to the village itself. They construct the granary usually a little bit away from the original house in order to prevent from fire. While constructing the granary, they use banana leaves in a unique way for the safety of the seeds. Wild banana leaves are tied in each post of the granary to prevent the rats from climbing.

Economic Unit

Among the Tangsas, the mode of production is styled 'familial' or 'domestic'. Family is considered as a unit of production. All members of the family together form the production unit. The pattern of labour is based on well-organized division of labour according to sex and age. The sex-wise division of labour is more prominent and women are considered physically weak. Both the male and female folk work according to the physical capacity and their skill. In some activities skill of women is counted.

Like any other societies, the Tangsas also consider that women are not in a position to do hard work, but are considered as expert in lighter works, like sowing and broadcasting of seeds, weeding, transplanting of seedling, reaping of crops etc. As the most of the Tangsas continue both *jhum* and settled cultivation, the male folk are considered more specialised in felling down of big trees, selection of *jhum* field, construction of farm hut etc. in *jhum* cultivation. In case of wet cultivation also, the division of labour is well represented. The Tangsas have now realized that they are getting more products in wet cultivation and the works are considered as lighter in comparison to *jhum* cultivation. It is roughly estimated by the Tangsas that per acre yield in respect of wet paddy cultivation ranges between 25–40 *mond* per acre (Rao, 2006:194). The women are engaged in works like cleaning and burning of debris, transplantation, weeding etc. While male are engaged in hard and tedious works like cutting of grasses, tilling, levelling, and repairing of plot contours and canals, construction of farm houses. Of course, there are various stages in both *jhum* and wet cultivation, where both the male and female jointly work as a unit. Children are also equally capable to work in certain stages of cultivation and in miscellaneous work relating to agricultural operations. There are not much variation in the division of labour in *jhum* and settled cultivation. But, it is a fact that the family work as a unit.

Land Operation

Among the Tangsas in general and Lungchang in particular, two unique modes of land operation are noticed, i.e. (a) lease-out of land, (b) lease-in of land, particularly with regards to wet/settled cultivation. The Lungchangs are to follow such type of land operation since the beginning of wet cultivation.

As the settled cultivation is more family oriented, the complete operation of cultivation may be possible with the joint efforts of the family members. In most of cases it is revealed that the families have no other alternative than to lease out the cultivation. Such situations are due to shift to the salaried job by the male members or the absence of male members who can help in cultivation.

In the same way, some families take land on lease in order to meet their family's need and improve livelihood. When a family needs money for marriage or for construction of houses they prefer to cultivate on lease basis.

The Tangsas follow different processes of lease operation, which varies from family to family: Two families enter into a lease system on mutual understanding. In most cases they agree on fixed share (cash/kind). But normally it depends on the productivity of crops.

If a particular family has more than enough land, then that family may lease out the land to support another family with whom they have strong kinship bond. In such cases no fixed rule is followed in lease system, and allowed to give certain amount which one can spare. Lease system is agreed on the basis of fixed period and usually for a period of one year.

There are some families, who are to make their living as wage earner. They do not have enough land for cultivation. A case is represented below:

> *R.K., 26 yrs. read up to class IX. He is a married person. After taking rice in the morning, he leaves the house in search of work. If he gets wage work he is to work up to 3 P.M. whatever*

> *the work he get, he accept it. During cultivation season, normally he becomes more busy. He gets Rs. 50.00 in a day. His original home was in Rangkatu village, where he has some family land. But as New Changlang village is near to the Changlang town, he shifted to this village. Moreover, his wife belongs to this village. Here, they are staying in other's land. But as reported, he manages to provide food to his family as a wage earner. His two daughters are studying in Government H.E. they are getting free books. He is to buy uniform, pencil etc. Though there is hardship, yet he is managing his family.*

Another case is reported by J.T. (female) 70 yrs.

> *She is a widow and is getting old age pension of Rs. 1800.00 annually from the government. She has a ration card and she gets rice worth Rs. 6.50 per kg. She has taken meal twice daily. She is staying alone. She cannot do hard work. Her son-in-law provides her food. But as he too is a wage-earner he cannot provide it regularly. She collects roots, fruits, stem, and leaves etc. from nearby forest. She takes meat or fish once in a month if her son-in-law provides her. She purchases her necessary cloth from her old age pension. To repair her kaccha and small hut, she gets help from daughter and son-in-law. Sometimes the villagers also help in repairing. For medical check-up, she goes to hospital, where she gets some free medicines. But some medicines she is to purchase, which she cannot afford. Sometimes she works in her small kitchen garden, where she grows colocacia, potatoes, etc. Somehow in a meagre way she is leading her life.*

The above cases reveal that they are to earn their livelihood by various means on different situation. The villagers who can engage labourers prefer to engage those needy people from the village itself. Some of the families also engage labourers on monthly wage basis ranging between Rs. 1000-1500 per month. The workers are mainly from tea-garden of West Bengal, Bihar and plains of Assam.

The intensive study in the villages reveal that the Tangsas are getting various forest products (food stuffs), e.g. vegetables, roots, shoots, fruits from the surrounding forest and consumed it in different ways like boiling, steaming etc.

The varieties of crops produced by the Tangsas varies in different seasons throughout the year, namely paddy (*chem*), maize (*haipung*), tapioca (*phateink*), big yam (*thah*), chili (*medi*), all types of gourd, lettuce, seasam etc. Paddy of different varieties are grown by them in both irrigated as well as in non-irrigated cultivation. Some of the high yielding varieties of paddy are also grown by them.

They also grow three varieties of Tapioca, e.g. red, black and yellow. They grow these extensively to feed the domestic animals and to prepare local wine as well as for home consumption. It was the staple food to the people earlier, but at present also it is popular for preparing local wine.

The Lungchangs also grow three varieties of maize, mainly on *jhum* field. Similarly Foxtail millet was their staple food when they entirely dependent on *jhum* cultivation. But now they rarely cultivate it due to their dependence on wet cultivation. But still it is considered best for preparation of local wine.

The Tangsas as a whole give proper care in selecting the seeds. Selection of crop seeds is done by systematic way. Before harvesting, matured and healthy crops are identified by the experienced persons and leave it for fully matured. And later it is harvested in a special way. They consider Sunday, Tuesday, Thursday and Saturday as auspicious day for reaping those paddies. They take particular attention in selecting matured and healthy seeds.

The Tangsas perform various rites and rituals in connection with cultivation of crops. The socio-economic and socio-religious life of the Tangsa villages revolves around cultivation. The nomenclature of some of these festivals differs from one village to another even among the same sub-group of the Tangsas. This was very common when they entirely dependent on *jhum* cultivation. When they have started settled cultivation, they have rescheduled some of their traditional festivals, ceremonies and rituals, which were linked to the cycle of *jhum* cultivation. Some of these have either been dropped or readjusted to the process of wet paddy cultivation.

During investigation it was reported that though the Lungchangs and the Mukloms have almost abandoned in cultivating paddy in the *jhum* field, but the Tutsa, Havis Tangsas still continue paddy cultivation in the *jhum* field.

Livestock

Livestock/domestication of animals play a significant role in tribal economy and the same is also reflected in Tangsa economy. Herds of cattle play a vital role in different agricultural pursuits, transportation, fertilization etc. From ancient times, the Tangsas kept a variety of domesticated animals such as pig, cows, buffaloes, fowls, birds etc. They keep pigs and fowls within the premises of their house. But, they take special precautions to confine the pigs within the compounds. Sometimes they make small enclosure for the pigs, but in most cases they tie the pigs with ropes across the belly and then tied to a post or a tree. They supply sufficient feeds to the pigs. The villagers are in opinion that there is a taboo in keeping the pigs free, and if they violate this taboo they are to pay fine for the act. Though the common villagers are not in a position to give a valid reason but a section of the villagers comment that as the pigs damage the vegetables and other products by digging the soil they put a taboo on it. However, the cows and buffaloes are let off in grazing or jungle and the owner keeps an eye on the movement and the whereabouts their herds. To recognize the cows and buffalos each family puts a mark by cutting the ears in different ways. The Tables 3.8, 3.9 and 3.10 reveal the particulars of livestock in each village.

Table 3.8: Particulars of Livestock in the Village New Changlang

Sl. No.	*Domestic animals and birds*	*Total*	*No. of families in possession*	*Average number per family*
1.	Cow	12	4	3.00
2.	Bullock	23	11	2.09
3.	Buffalo	4	2	2.00
4.	Goat	35	11	3.18
5.	Pig	26	14	1.86
6.	Fowl	63	16	3.94
7.	Duck	47	8	5.88
8.	Others (Dog)	34	15	2.27
	Total	**244**	–	–

The investigation reveals that they rear different animals for various reasons. The analysis of data in New Changlang village reveals that most common animal domesticated by the villagers is goat. Out of 39 families 11 have goats and the average number per family is 3.18. Pig is very commonly reared by the villagers, and there are 14 families who possess 26 numbers of pigs and the average number per family is 1.8. Then it is followed by bullocks and cows, respectively. As the Tangsas have recently opted for wet cultivation, the number of bullocks is not significant. There are 11 families who possess 23 numbers of bullocks and the average

Table 3.9: Particulars of Livestock in the Village Old Changlang

Sl. No.	*Domestic Animal*	*Total*	*No. of families in possession*	*Average No. per family*
1.	Cow	2	2	1.00
2.	Bullock	79	39	2.03
3.	Buffalo	14	3	4.67
4.	Goat	54	19	2.84
5.	Pig	74	42	1.76
6.	Fowl	334	56	5.96
7.	Duck	24	6	4.00
8.	Other (Dog)	14	12	1.17
	Total	**595**	–	–

number per family is 2.09. There are two families, who have domesticated buffalos; the numbers of buffalos are 4.

Besides these, 16 families possess 63 fowls and the average number per family is 3.94. Another commonly domesticated bird is Chinese duck, that are domesticated by 8 families and the average number per family is 5.88.

Besides animal, 16 families possessing 63 fowls and its average number of per family are 3.94. Another commonly domesticated bird is Chinese Duck by 8 families and the average number per family is 5.88.

The analysis of distribution of families according to possession of domestic animals in the Old Changlang is presented in Table 3.9. It is clear from Table that most common animal found is the bullock and out of 75 families 39 possessed bullocks the number being 79. The average number per family is 2.03. The data itself indicate that the number of families switching to wet cultivation is increasing day by day. The bullock is followed by pig reared by 74 families. The average number per family is 1.76. This is followed by goat and the number of families is 54. The average number per family is 2.84.

Table 3.9, also reveals that the most common domesticated bird is fowl, the total number being 334 possesses by 56 families. The average number per family is 5.96. There are 24 ducks, which are reared by 6 families. The average number per family is 4.

The distribution of families according to possession of domestic animals in the Rangkatu village is presented in Table 3.10. It is seen that the most common animals found in the village are bullocks, the total number being 80, which are possessed by 40 families. The average number per family is 2.00. The same trend of switching over to wet cultivation is reflected by increasing number of bullocks in the village. The goat is

Table 3.10: Particulars of Livestock the Village Rangkatu

Sl. No.	Domestic animal	Total	No. of families in possession	Average No. per family
1.	Cow	41	24	1.71
2.	Bullock	80	40	2.00
3.	Buffalo	3	2	1.50
4.	Goat	75	21	3.57
5.	Pig	32	22	1.45
6.	Fowl	500	58	8.62
7.	Duck	50	18	2.78
8.	Others (Dog)	70	26	2.69
	Total	**851**		

reared by the Tangsas in a large number. There are 75 goats, distributed in 21 families. The average number per family is 3.57. Pig is also reared by the villagers. The number of buffalos is not significant. There are 3 buffalos domesticated by 2 families.

Most of the families rear fowls and ducks in large quantity. There are 500 ducks, reared by 58 families. The average number per family is 8.62. A study of possession of domestic animals among the Lungchang Tangsas of 3 villages reveals more or less the same trend. The increased number of bullocks is entirely due to the introduction of wet paddy cultivation. It is also evident that as the Tangsas settle in New Changlang village in later stage, the number of bullocks is not significant. Pig is reared by almost all the families of Lungchang villages. There are only a few families who possess buffalo. Fowls and ducks are reared by majority of the families. The rearing of animals plays significant role both in the religious and economic life. In most of their religious rituals, animal sacrifice is a must. The people are to pay bride price on the occasion of marriage and they need pigs, buffaloes, cows and fowls etc. for it. Earlier animals kept by the Tangsas are used as a kind of buffer stock of food for survival. Because, while living in the hills, the Tangsas frequently faced famine and in such situation, domesticated animals substitute the food. As a whole domesticated animals are considered important and valuable asset of a family. The *mithuns* are semi-domesticated animal. Earlier *mithun* played an important role at the time of marriage either for the bride price or celebrating the feast. But now, only in rare cases some families go for rearing it.

The present project also covers Muklom Tangsas. The pattern of livestock among the Mukloms has been presented in Tables 3.11, 3.12 and 3.13.

Table 3.11: Particulars of Livestock in the Village Laktong

Sl. No.	*Domestic animals*	*Total*	*No. of families in possession*	*Average No. per family*
1.	Cow	2	1	2.00
2.	Bullock	21	10	2.10
3.	Buffalo	–	–	–
4.	Goat	1	1	1.00
5.	Pig	28	22	1.27
6.	Fowl	72	17	4.23
7.	Duck	7	2	3.50
8.	Others (Dog)	12	10	1.20
	Total	**143**		

Table 3.11 reveals that the maximum number of families rear pigs. Out of 63 families, 22 rear pigs. It is followed by bullocks and 10 possess 21 numbers of bullocks. Goat is reared by a single family and it is significant that not a single family have buffalo. Ducks and fowls are commonly reared by most of the families of Laktong village. As reported, except bullocks, most of the animals are reared for their domestic consumption and for selling.

Table 3.12: Particulars of Livestock of the Village Simrang

Sl. No.	*Domestic animals*	*Total*	*No. of families in possession*	*Average No. per family*
1.	Cow	3	2	1.50
2.	Bullock	39	19	2.05
3.	Buffalo	–	–	–
4.	Goat	11	5	2.20
5.	Pig	50	25	2.20
6.	Fowl	224	28	8.00
7.	Duck	–	–	–
8.	Others (Dog)	44	22	2.20
	Total	**371**		

The distribution of families according to the possession of live stock in the village Simrang revealed that out of 32 families as much as 25 rear pigs for various socio-religious purposes. There are 50 pigs possessed by 25 families. It is followed by bullocks where 19 families have 39 numbers of bullocks. There are only 5 families who rear goats. The fowls are reared by most of the families, whereas there is not a single family who has ducks.

Table 3.13: Particulars of Livestock in the Village Yanman

Sl. No.	*Domestic Animals/Birds*	*Total*	*No. of families in Possession*	*Average No. of family*
1.	Cow	59	23	2.57
2.	Bullock	52	30	1.73
3.	Buffalo	4	1	4.00
4.	Goat	22	7	3.14
5.	Pig	35	28	1.25
6.	Fowl	267	54	4.94
7.	Duck	3	1	3.00
8.	Others (Dog)	41	28	1.46
	Total	**483**		

It is revealed from the table that out of 86 families, the highest number, i.e. 30 families possess bullocks. It is followed by pigs as 28 families rear pigs. The number of cows is also significant. There are 23 families who possess 59 numbers of cows. Fowls are domesticated by majority of the families, whereas only 1 family possesses three ducks.

Table 3.14: Particulars of Livestock among Lungchangs and Mukloms

Sl. No.	*Domestic Animals/Birds*	*Lungchang*	*Muklom*
1.	Cow	30	26
2.	Bullock	90	59
3.	Buffalo	7	1
4.	Goat	51	13
5.	Pig	78	75
6.	Fowl	130	99
7.	Duck	32	3
8.	Others (Dog)	53	60

The analysis of possession of livestock among the Lungchangs and the Mukloms (Table 3.14) revealed that as they have shifted to wet-cultivation majority of families possess bullocks. Among the Lungchangs out of 179 families 90 and among the Mukloms out of 153 families 59 possess bullocks. It is followed by the pigs, which are reared both the sub-tribes. Among the 78 Lungchang families and 75 among the Mukloms rear pigs. It is also found that 51 families among the Lungchangs and 13 families among Mukloms rear goats. Cow is reared mostly by both the Lungchangs and the Mukloms. There are 30 families among Lungchangs and 26 among the Mukloms possess cows. Though buffalo and *mithuns* were common semi-domesticated animals in early stage, but there is not a single family who possesses *mithun*. And only 7 families among the Lungchang and 1 family among the Mukloms have buffalo.

Occupational Mobility

The main occupation of the Tangsa is cultivation. All the members in the family are engaged in various agricultural activities according to age and sex. Very young and aged persons are, however, exempted from the hard agricultural activities. In recent years, a trend towards non-agricultural activities is evident among the Tangsas. Along with the inroad of education and urban influences, more and more people have started to take up non-traditional occupation.

Occupation determines the mode of living, thinking and behaviour, etc. An idea about the distribution of population according to age, sex and occupation has been presented here.

Table 3.15: Distribution of Population according to Sex and Occupation in the Village New Changlang

Sl. No.	*Nature of occupation*		*Male*		*Female*		*Total*	
	Primary	*Secondary*	*No.*	*%*	*No.*	*%*	*No.*	*%*
1.	Agriculture	–	10	5.08	–	–	10	5.08
2.	Service	–	19	9.64	7	3.56	26	13.20
3.	Service	Agriculture	6	3.05	–	–	6	3.05
4.	Agriculture	Other activities	4	2.03	–	–	4	2.03
5.	Service	Housewife	–	–	4	2.03	4	2.03
6.	Business	Agriculture	6	3.05	–	–	6	3.05
7.	Housewife	Agriculture	–	–	14	7.11	14	7.11
8.	Housewife	Agriculture and petty business	–	–	14	7.11	14	7.11
9.	Wage earner	–	6	3.05	–	–	–	–
10.	Housewife	–	–	–	11	5.58	11	5.58
11.	Petty business	–	–	–	–	–	–	–
12.	Student	–	41	20.81	40	20.30	81	41.12
13.	Dependent	–	8	4.06	7	3.56	15	7.61
	Total		**100**	**50.76**	**97**	**49.24**	**197**	**100**

Table 3.15 shows the distribution of population of New Changlang village according to sex and occupation. Table 3.15 shows that out of the total 197 individuals, the higher number falls under the category of students, i.e. 81 (44.16%). The number of male students are 41 (20.8%) and female 40 (20.30%). There are 26 individuals, who are entirely

engaged in service and the number of males are 19 (9.64%) and female are 7 (3.56%) in number. There are 6 male members who are primarily involved in the service and secondarily in agriculture. In the same way, 6 male members are entirely dependent on business work and secondarily dependent on agriculture. There are 6 male members who are to earn their living as wage earners. There are 4 female members who primarily involved in service and secondarily serve the family as housewife. This indicates that Tangsa women are not lagging behind and the proper educational facilities help them to engage in service.

Table 3.16: Distribution of Population according to Sex and Occupation in the Village Old Changlang

Sl. No.	Nature of Occupation		Male		Female		Total	
	Primary	Secondary	No.	%	No.	%	No.	%
1.	Agriculture	–	35	8.28	–	–	35	8.28
2.	Service	–	28	6.62	5	1.18	33	7.80
3.	Service	Agriculture	13	3.07	–	–	13	3.07
4.	Agriculture	Other activities	14	3.31	1	0.24	15	3.55
5.	Service	Housewife	–	–	14	3.31	14	3.31
6.	Business	Agriculture	13	3.07	–	–	13	3.07
7.	Housewife	Agriculture	–	–	46	10.87	46	10.87
8.	Housewife	Agriculture and petty business	–	–	8	1.89	8	1.89
9.	Wage Earner	–	–	–	–	–	–	–
10.	Housewife	–	–	–	17	4.02	17	4.02
11.	Patty business	–	11	2.60	–	–	11	2.60
12.	Student	–	75	17.73	69	16.31	144	34.04
13.	Dependent	–	35	8.28	39	9.22	74	17.50
		Total	**224**	**52.96**	**199**	**47.04**	**423**	**100.00**

Note: Below 3 yrs. and pension holders are considered as dependent.

Table 3.16 shows the distribution of population by pattern of occupation and sex in the Old Changlang village.

Table 3.16 reflects that there are 35 (8.25%) male members who are exclusively engaged in agriculture. Whereas 28 males (6.62%) and 5 females (1.18%) are entirely involved in various services. It is also evident from the table that 14 females (3.31%) members are engaged primarily in service and only secondarily act as housewife.

There are 13 (3.07%) number of males who primarily involved in various types of business and secondarily engaged in agriculture. It is also to be noted that there is not a single family, who have to earn their living as wage earner.

The distribution of population by pattern of occupation and sex among the Lungchangs of Rangkatu village has been presented in Table 3.17.

Table 3.17: Distribution of Population according to Sex and Occupation in Rangkatu

Sl. No.	Nature of occupation		Male		Female		Total	
	Primary	Secondary	No.	%	No.	%	No.	%
1.	Agriculture	–	39	8.35	78	16.70	117	25.05
2.	Agriculture	Other activities	44	9.42	29	6.21	73	15.63
3.	Service	–	9	1.93	1	0.21	10	2.14
4.	Service	Agriculture	19	4.07	1	0.21	20	4.28
5.	Business	Agriculture	3	0.64	1	0.21	4	0.86
6.	Housewife	–	–	–	4	0.86	4	0.86
7.	Student	–	87	18.63	64	13.70	156	33.40
8.	Dependent	–	40	8.67	43	9.21	83	17.77
	Total		**241**	**51.61**	**226**	**48.39**	**467**	**100.00**

It is revealed that a significant number of individuals, i.e. 39 (8.35%) male and 78 (16.70%) females are entirely involved in agricultural pursuits. This indicates that agriculture is the main occupation of villagers, who practice wet rice cultivation. *Jhum* cultivation is also pursuing by some of the villagers. The individuals who are primarily dependent on agriculture and secondarily in other activities (petty business) are noticeable. There are 73 (15.63%) persons, male 44 (9.42%) and female 29 (6.21%) fall in this category. On the other hand the individuals entirely dependent on service are not significant. There are only 9 (1.93%) male and 1 (0.21%) who are solely engaged in different types of service. It may be presumed that as the village Rangkatu is situated far away from the Changlang town, the individuals are not getting suitable opportunity to engage themselves in various services.

The analysis also reveals that in recent years, due to availability of modern education, the literacy rate is increasing as a whole and both male and female are getting opportunity to engage them in different salaried job. The following case may reveal the advantage of modern education.

> *Ms. M.T. (25 yrs.) reported how she got help and co-operation from the family members in attaining higher education. She has completed her P.G. in Education from ARGO University, Arunachal Pradesh. She did her degree course from Pragjyotish*

College under Guwahati University and schooling from Changlang Government School. Her elder brother, who has completed B.E. and now working as Civil Engineer in Changlang helped her financially during her educational carrier. Her father who was an Assistant Clerk in D.C. office took various measures to help her. Her mother, though illiterate was very supportive in pursuing her education. In spite of financial constraints and opposition from the co-villagers her mother supported her 7 children in pursuing higher education. Her eldest sister after completing her Polytechnique course was engaged in job.

There are also instances, where members are working as teacher and all these are possible due to easy accessibility of modern education.

Mr. K.J. (55 yrs.) is working as teacher in Government Secondary School, Khonsa. He did his schooling from Changlang Government Higher Secondary School. Then he completed his degree course from J.N. College, Pasighat and M.A. from NEHU and B.Ed. from Arunachal University. For the attainment of higher education, his brother-in-law helped him financially. His father, who is a farmer, encourages him morally and financially. After completing his M.A. he got a job as teacher in Government Secondary School, Khosa. Then he did his B.Ed. on deputation and working as teacher. Now, he is helping his brother-in-law financially, whenever needed.

Though the Tangsas are engaged in various services, their journey to achieve is not quite smooth.

Mr. W.T. (47 yrs.) informed that at present he is as teacher in Government Primary School, Simray (New Themlom). He completed his school from Government school and graduated from Pasighat College. His father was a cultivator and died when he was too young. When he was studying in school, he used to stay in school hostel. From class III, on wards he did various works to earn money. During vacation also, he stayed in hostel and tried to earn money by doing different types of works. When in college, he used to get stipend of Rs. 120 p.m. and from that stipend, he used to save money. He paid his admission fee from that money and now working as teacher in Primary School, Simray (New Themlom).

The study was also conducted among the Muklom Tangsas. The distribution of population by patterns of occupation and sex among the Mukloms have presented in the following tables.

Table 3.18: Distribution of Population according to Sex and Occupation in Laktong

Sl. No.	*Nature of occupation*		*Male*		*Female*		*Total*	
	Primary	*Secondary*	*No.*	*%*	*No.*	*%*	*No.*	*%*
1.	Agriculture	–	12	6.32	12	6.32	24	12.63
2.	Agriculture	Other activities	5	2.63	–	–	5	2.63
3.	Service	–	10	5.26	6	3.16	16	8.42
4.	Service	Agriculture	1	0.53	–	–	1	0.53
5.	Business	–	12	6.32	2	1.05	14	7.37
6.	Business	Agriculture	3	1.58	–	–	3	1.58
7.	Wageworker	–	–	–	–	–	–	–
8.	Housewife	–	–	–	19	10.00	19	10.00
9.	Student	–	38	20.00	25	13.16	63	33.16
10.	Dependent	–	15	7.89	30	15.79	45	23.68
		Total	**96**	**50.53**	**94**	**49.47**	**190**	**100**

Table 3.18 shows the distribution of population by patterns of sex and occupation among the Mukloms of Laktong village. It is revealed that a significant number of individuals, i.e. 24 (12.63%) are entirely involved in agricultural pursuits. The males and females are equal, i.e. 12 in number.

The number of individual who are entirely dependent on business is also significant. There are 14 (7.37%) individuals who are entirely dependent on business. It is significant that a good number of individuals are engaged entirely on service. There are 16 (8.42%) such individuals. There is not a single individual who is to earn his living on wage basis. The number of students and dependents are significant.

Table 3.19 shows the distribution of population by sex and occupation in the village Simrang. The number of individuals who are exclusively engaged in agriculture is significant. There are 66 (31.58%) individuals who are entirely dependent on agriculture, out of which 30 (14.35%) are males and 36 (17.22%) are females. The number of individuals entirely involved in service is 7 (3.35%). There are 12 individuals (5.74%) who follow service as primary and agriculture as secondary. There are two

Table 3.19: Distribution of Population according to Sex and Occupation in Simrang

Sl. No.	Nature of occupation		Male		Female		Total	
	Primary	Secondary	No.	%	No.	%	No.	%
1.	Agriculture	–	30	14.35	36	17.22	66	31.58
2.	Agriculture	Other activities	–	–	–	–	–	–
3.	Service	–	5	2.39	2	0.96	7	3.35
4.	Service	Agriculture	12	5.74	–	–	12	5.74
5.	Business	Agriculture	–	–	–	–	–	–
6.	Wageworker	–	1	0.48	1	0.48	2	0.96
7.	Housewife	–	–	–	4	1.91	4	1.91
8.	Student	–	39	18.66	37	17.70	76	36.36
9.	Dependent	–	17	8.13	25	11.96	42	20.10
		Total	104	49.76	105	50.24	209	100.00

individuals who are to earn their livelyhood by wage work. In this category there is 1 male and 1 female. The number of students and dependents are high.

The village Yanman is a big village having 86 families. The distribution of population by patterns of occupation and sex of Yanman village has been presented in Table 3.20. Table reveals that there are 146 (28.24%) individuals who are exclusively engaged on agriculture. The number of males are 59 (11.41%) and females 87 (16.83%). There are 52 individuals who take agriculture as their primary means and other activities as secondary. Here the number of males is 45 and females are7. There

Table 3.20: Distribution of Population according to Sex and Occupation in Yanman

Sl. No.	Nature of Occupation		Male		Female		Total	
	Primary	Secondary	No.	%	No.	%	No.	%
1.	Agriculture	–	59	11.41	87	16.83	146	28.24
2.	Agriculture	Other Activities	45	8.70	7	1.35	52	10.00
3.	Service	–	7	1.35	2	0.39	9	1.74
4.	Service	Agriculture	5	0.97	1	0.19	6	1.16
5.	Business	–	1	0.19	1	0.19	2	0.39
6.	Business	Agriculture	4	0.77	3	0.58	7	1.35
7.	Wage worker	–	–	–	–	–	–	–
8.	Housewife	–	–	–	5	0.97	5	0.97
9.	Student	–	83	16.05	76	14.70	159	3.25
10.	Dependent	–	53	10.25	78	15.09	131	25.34
		Total	**257**	**49.71**	**260**	**50.29**	**517**	**100.00**

are 9 (1.74%) individuals who take service as their service as sole occupation. The number of males is 7 and that of females are 2. It is revealed that 7 individuals (1.35%) pursue business as primary means of lively hood and agriculture as secondary. There is not a single individual who are to work on wage basis. As usual the number of students and dependents are significant.

Possession of Material Items

The study of possession of material items reflects the impact of urbanization on the one hand and the status image on the other.

The Lungchang Tangsas as a whole are influenced by modernization and the picture of possession of material items is more or less same in all the villages. The possession of material items among the Lungchangs has been presented in Tables 3.21, 3.22 and 3.23.

The analysis of possession of material items in the New Changlang village has revealed that in comparison to by-cycle, the number of families having two-wheelers is significant. Out of 39 families there are 14 (1.77%) who possess two-wheelers and 3 families have bi-cycles. There are 4 families (1.25%) who have car/jeep.

In case of other means of communication, the common media used by the villagers is T.V. There are 18 (1.00%) families who have T.V. connection in their household. Another commonly used media is Radio. There are 9 families who have refrigerators. There are 10 families who have landline telephone and 12 families have the facility of mobile phones. A few families also contributed for daily newspapers.

Table 3.21: Possession of Material Items in the Village New Changlang

Sl No.	*Material items*	*Total*	*No. of families*	*Average No. per family*
1.	By-cycle	3	3	1.00
2.	Two-wheeler	14	12	1.17
3.	Four-wheeler	5	4	1.25
4.	Radio	14	13	1.08
5.	Television	18	18	1.00
6.	Refrigerator	9	9	1.00
7.	Telephone (L)	10	10	1.00
8.	Telephone (M)	12	12	1.00
9.	Any other	16	16	1.00

The analysis in the Old Changlang village reveals that with regards to the means of communication, the picture is slightly better than the New Changlang village. Out of 75 families, there are 51 who have T.V. with Dish connection. There are 25 families who possess Radio.

For the purpose of interacting with the outside world, the 15 families have landline telephone connection and there are 12 mobile phones. Two families possess refrigerators. There is not a single family who possesses bi-cycle, may be because of hilly and rough road condition. There are 13 families who have two-wheelers and 6 families have cars.

Table 3.22: Possession of Material Items in the Village Old Changlang

Sl. No.	*Material items*	*Total*	*No. of families*	*Average No. per family*
1.	By-cycle	–	–	–
2.	Two-wheeler	13	13	1
3.	Four-wheeler	6	6	1
4.	Radio	25	25	1
5.	Television	51	51	1
6.	Refrigerator	2	2	1
7.	Telephone (L)	15	15	1
8.	Telephone (M)	12	11	1.09
9.	Any other	21	21	1

The village Rangkatu is situated far away from the Changlang town. The analysis of material possession is presented in Table 3.23. It is revealed that their condition is not encouraging and out of 65 families only 17 have televisions and 22 families possess radios. There are only 2 families who have landline telephone connections and 4 numbers of mobile phones in the village.

Table 3.23: Possession of Material Items in the Village Rangkatu

Sl. No.	*Material items*	*Total*	*No. of families*	*Average No. per family*
1.	By-cycle	–	–	–
2.	Two-wheeler	13	11	1.18
3.	Four-wheeler	1	1	1.00
4.	Radio	22	22	1.00
5.	Television	17	17	1.00
6.	Refrigerator	–	–	–
7.	Telephone (L)	2	2	1.00
8.	Telephone (M)	4	4	1.00
9.	Any other	17	17	1.00

The means of communication reveal that there are 11 families who have 13 numbers of two-wheelers. This means that 2 families'each posses more than one two-wheelers. There is only one family who has a car, and, the absence of bi-cycle indicates the inconvenience of using bi-cycle in the hilly areas.

The possession of material items among the Mukloms have been presented in Tables 3.24, 3.25 and 3.26. There are slight variations between the Lungchangs and the Mukloms with regards to the possession of material items.

Table 3.24: Possession of Material Items in the Village Laktong

Sl. No.	*Material items*	*Total*	*No. of families*	*Average No. per family*
1.	Bi-cycle	–	–	–
2.	Two-wheeler	7	7	1.00
3.	Four-wheeler	–	–	–
4.	Radio	11	11	1.00
5.	Television	15	15	1.00
6.	Refrigerator	–	–	–
7.	Telephone (L)	2	2	1.00
8.	Telephone (M)	1	1	1.00
	Total	**36**	**36**	**1.00**

The possession of material items in the village Laktong has been presented in Table 3.24. It is revealed that out of 36 families 7 possess two-wheelers, there are 15 families who have TV and 11 have radio. It is also revealed that there are two families who have land line connection and one has mobile phone. There is not a single family who possesses car or bi-cycle. Thus, it may be said that with regards to material possession the position of Laktong village may not be considered as good.

Table 3.25 shows the distribution of families according to the possession of material items in the village Simrang. It is revealed that out of 32 families 12 have TV and among these families 5 have Dish connection. There are 6 families who have radio. It is found that there is only 1 family who possesses a two-wheeler. With regards to telephone connections 1 family has land line connection and 1 has mobile phone.

The above data indicates that, in connection to the means of communication the condition of the Simrang village is not good.

Table 3.26 presents the possession of material items in the village Yanman.

Table 3.25: Possession of Material Items in the Village Simrang

Sl. No.	*Means of communication*	*Total*	*No. of families in possession*	*Average No. per family*
1.	Bi-cycle	–	–	–
2.	Two-wheeler	1	1	1.00
3.	Four-wheeler	–	–	–
4.	Radio	6	6	1.00
5.	Television	13	12	1.08
6.	Refrigerator	–	–	–
7.	Telephone (L)	1	1	1.00
8.	Telephone (M)	1	1	1.00
	Total	**21**	**20**	**1.05**

Table 3.26: Distribution of Families according to Possession of Material Items in Yanman

Sl. No.	*Means of Communication*	*Total*	*No. of Families in Possession*	*Average No. of family*
1.	Bicycle	–	–	–
2.	Two-wheeler	4	4	1
3.	Four-wheeler	–	–	–
4.	Radio	11	11	1
5.	Television	12	12	1
6.	Refrigerator	–	–	–
7.	Telephone (L)	–	–	–
8.	Telephone (M)	–	–	–
	Total	**27**	**27**	**1**

Table 3.27 indicates that out of 86 families only 4 have two-wheelers. There is not a single family who has car or bi-cycle. There are 12 families who have TV and 11 have radio. There is not a single family who has land line or mobile phone connection. The overall picture of possession of material item is not good. This may be due to their location and situation in remote areas. The village is situated about 16 km away from Changlang town and located in a hilly area (Table 3.27).

When a comparison is made between the Lungchangs and the Mukloms with regards to the possession of material items it is revealed that the position of the Lungchangs is much better than the Mukloms. Out of 179 families among the Lungchang Tangsas maximum number of families possesses TV, the number being 86. Among the Mukloms out of 150 families 39 have TVs. Next common item is radio and among the

Table 3.27: Distribution of Families according to Possession of Material Items among the Lungchangs and Mukloms

Sl. No.	*Means of Communication*	*Lungchangs*	*Mukloms*
1.	Bicycle	3	Nil
2.	Two-wheeler	36	12
3.	Four-wheeler	11	Nil
4.	Radio	60	28
5.	Television	86	39
6.	Refrigerator	11	Nil
7.	Telephone (L)	27	3
8.	Telephone (M)	27	2

Lungchangs 60 families possess radio and among the Mukloms 28 families have radio. There are 36 families among the Lungchangs and 12 among the Mukloms who possess two-wheelers. There are 11 families among the Lungchangs who possess four-wheeler and among the Mukloms not a single family who possesses four wheelers. There are as many as 27 families have land line connections among the Lungchangs and 3 among the Mukloms have land line telephones. While there are 27 families among the Lungchangs and 2 families among the Mukloms have mobile phones. It is significant to note that 11 families have refrigerators among the Lungchang. And all these 11 families are from New and Old Changlang villages. Among the Mukloms not a single family possesses refrigerator.

Saving by Different Means

It is encouraging to find that there is a tendency of savings among the Tangsas (Tables 3.28, 3.29 and 3.30). A study of 3 Lungchang villages reveals that the percentage of families who go for different means of saving is encouraging.

Table 3.28: Distribution of Families according to Savings in the Village New Changlang

Sl. No.	*Deposits*	*Number of Families*	*Percentage*
1.	Saving Banks	25	64.10
2.	Post office	–	–
3.	Both (SB/PO)	4	10.26
4.	Nil	10	25.64
	Total	**39**	**100.00**

The analysis of data in the New Changlang village reveals that out of 39 families, 25 families have deposit in the bank. There are 4 families who have account both in the bank and post office. There is not a single family who deposit their money in the post office. 10 families do not have any means of saving. Though re-investment in agriculture is not clearly evident, yet the means of saving reflect an encouraging picture.

The analysis of data in the Old Changlang village has been presented in Table 3.29. It is revealed that out of 75 families, 57 (76.00%) have their account in the bank. There are two families who have account both in the bank and post office. There is only 1 family who has account in post office. There are 15 numbers of families who have neither any account in the bank or in the post office.

Table 3.29: Distribution of Families according to Saving by Different Means in the Village Old Changlang

Sl. No.	*Deposits*	*No. of Families*	*Percentage*
1.	Saving Banks	57	76.00
2.	Post Office	1	1.33
3.	Both (SB\PO)	2	2.67
4.	Nil	15	20.00
	Total	**75**	**100.00**

The different means of saving in Rankatu village has been presented in Table 3.30. While analysing the trend of saving, it is revealed that the number of families who do not have any means of saving is noticeable. Out of 65 families, there are 33 (50.77%) who do not have any means of savings. There are 27 (41.54%) families who have their account in the bank. Similarly, 5 families have saving account both in the bank and post office.

Table 3.30: Distribution of Families according to Savings in the Village Rangkatu

Sl. No.	*Deposits*	*No. of Families*	*Percentage*
1.	Saving Banks	27	41.54
2.	Post Office	–	–
3.	Both (SB/PO)	5	7.69
4.	Nil	33	50.77
	Total	**65**	**100**

1. Display Board Showing the Distance

2. Township

3. Tirap River

4. Jhum Field

5. Gaonburah's House

6. Main Post of the House

7. Gaonburah

8. Main Post of the House

9. House Type

10. House Type

11. Kitchen

12. Village Children

13. Priest

14. Priest

15. Old Woman

16. Student

17. Village Panorama

18. Authors and Field Worker in front of God Rang Frah

19. Priest of the Temple

20. Children in Front of Temple

21. Temple

22. Women Return from Market

23. Anganbadi Centre

24. Village Panorama

It may be said that as the village Rangkatu is situated far away from the Changlang town, they are not in a position to utilize the facilities of bank and post office easily. Moreover, the means of communication is not good enough to communicate with the town.

Table 3.31: Distribution of Families according to Saving in the Village Laktong

Sl. No.	*Deposits*	*No. of Families*	*Percentage*
1.	Saving Banks	29	82.86
2.	Post Office	–	–
3.	Both (SB/PO)	–	–
4.	Nil	6	17.14
	Total	**35**	**100.00**

Note: Village near the SBI.

A study of saving patterns among the Mukloms shows a slight variation from the Lungchangs. The different means of saving among the Mukloms have been presented in Tables 3.31, 3.32 and 3.33.

The analysis of the data in the village Laktong indicates that out of 35 families 29 (82.86%) have bank accounts in SBI State Bank of India. There is not a single family who has account neither in the Post Office nor in the Bank. While there are 6 families (17.14%) who do not have any means of savings.

Table 3.32: Distribution of Families according to Saving in the Village Simrang

Sl. No.	*Deposits*	*No. of Families*	*Percentage*
1.	Saving Banks	14	43.75
2.	Post Office	–	–
3.	Both (SB/PO)	4	12.00
4.	Nil	14	43.75
	Total	**32**	**100.00**

The analysis of data in the village Simrang shows that out of 32 families 14 (43.75%) have bank accounts in SBI whereas there are 4 families who have their accounts either in the bank and the post office. There are 14 (43.75%) families who have neither any account in the bank or post office.

Analysis of data in Table 3.33 reflects that out of 86 families, more than half of the families, i.e. 60 (69.77%) do not have any account either in the Bank or Post Office. There are 25 families (29.07%) who have accounts in the SBI. There is not a single family who has account in the

Table 3.33: Distribution of Families according to Savings in the Village Yanman

Sl. No.	*Deposits*	*No. of Families*	*Percentage*
1.	Saving Banks	25	29.07
2.	Post Office	–	–
3.	Both (SB/PO)	1	1.16
4.	Nil	60	69.77
	Total	**86**	**100.00**

Post Office, whereas there is only 1 family who has account both in the Bank and the Post Office. As the village is situated far away from the main Changlang town, all the families are not in a position to utilize the facilities of saving by different means.

Table 3.34: Distribution of Families according to Savings by Different Means among the Lungchangs and Mukloms

Sl. No.	*Deposits*	*Lungchangs*	*Mukloms*
1.	Saving Banks	109	68
2.	Post Office	1	–
3.	Both (SB/PO)	11	5
4.	Nil	58	80
	Total	**179**	**153**

Both the Lungchangs and the Mulkoms have utilized the various means of saving. But the position of Lungchangs is much better than the Mukloms. Among the Lungchangs, 109 families have saving accounts in the SBI; while there are only 68 families among the Mukloms who have Saving Bank accounts. It is also found that there are 11 families among the Lungchangs who have utilized the facilities of both the Bank and the Post Office.

Studies of economic life reveal that overall economic scenario of the Tangsas may not be considered encouraging. Though few have certain knowledge about modern means of improving economic condition yet due to their general economic conditions all of them are not in a position to avail the facilities and their economy may still be considered as subsistence economy.

4
Family System

The unique characteristic of human being is that he lives in society which implies that he is a social animal. Social life is an essence of human life. In course of the development human being is to develop various types of institutions and organizations for their survival. This no doubt implies that social life is essential both for the necessity and survival of human being. Two most important and basic institutions are family and marriage. In this chapter an emphasis has been made to describe family and marriage system of the Tangsas.

Family

Family is an important and primary unit of any social organization. Beside biological role, family performs an important social role. It is the most permanent and most pervasive of all social institutions. The family is often called the basic social institution, because of its important functions of procreation and socialization. To an individual, family means his first school and next best security after his mother's womb. Worldwide it is the family tie that may be considered the most important and significant tie. As emphasized by Radcliffe Brown, the main condition that determines the family "the necessary conditions of existence of the social organism."

Though family is a universal social institution and is regarded fundamental, both for the individual and society as a whole, yet different scholars defined family from various perspectives. Murdock (1961:1) defines family as "a social group characterized by common residence, economic co-operation and reproduction. It includes adult of both sexes, at least two to whom maintain a socially approved sexual relationship, one or more children, own or adopted of the sexually cohabiting adults."

Thus, the family lives together, pool its resources and works together and produce offspring. In other words, according to Murdock, the family has three essentials: (i) common residence, (ii) economic co-operation, and (iii) reproduction.

According to Lewis "Family, the key institution in society, consists of one or more women living with one or more men and their children. It has socially approved sex relationship. The family is characterized by various rights and obligations." According to Lowie, "a family is a group based on marital relations, rights and duties of parenthood, common habitation, reciprocal relations between parents and children."

The form and size of familial grouping has varied from time to time, and different types and size of family has been observed in different societies in times and space perspective. Thus, family can be considered as a dynamic institution which is forever changing.

Family has different forms in different societies. It is, therefore, not possible to come out with a universal definition of family, but various social thinkers has attempted to define it as a social institution.

Majumdar has defined family in the following words. "Family is a group of persons who live under the same roof and are connected by nuclear and kinship ties and owns a consciousness of kind on the basis of locality, interest and mutuality of obligation." Beals and Hoijer have defined the family as "The family may briefly be defined as social groupings; the members of which are united by bond of kinship."

In the present chapter, an emphasis has been made to focus the family system among the Tangsas. It has already been mentioned that Tangsa has been divided into various sub-tribe, which are further divided into various exogamous clans. They maintain the tribal endogamy, but clan exogamy. Here the family has been analysed from various spheres, e.g. size, type, pattern, relationship, economic function, religious function, emotional function etc. Though the family among the Tangsas has some uniform features, yet slight variation has been noticed in sub-tribe level. The study has been confined among the Lungchangs and the Mukloms.

A Tangsa family is patrilocal in residence and patrilineal in heritance. A Tangsa family is a residential unit, fulfilling diverse activities.

The family among the Tangsas is the primary unit of the individual's life. It is the normal rule that sons stay with their parents till they attain maturity and are married. Normally, after marriage, they started to live in separate households. This is the normal practice followed by the Tangsas as a whole. It was reported that among the Ao Nagas, the newly married couple have to live separately in a new house constructed by the husband. As Tangsas have identified themselves with Nagas, same type of system may be noticed among both the tribes. But there is no hard and fast rule of living separately after marriage. Sometimes they live in a separate household, but the hearth is jointly shared by all. In certain cases, they live under the same roof but maintain separate hearth. Thus, the nature of residence after marriage varies from family to family. The daughters after marriage or after a year of marriage go to their husband's home and become the members of their family.

Though the Tangsas have a preference for joint living, yet the analysis of data both among the Lungchangs and the Mukloms have revealed that the number of nuclear family is higher in all the villages.

Family Size

The family size is variable, as this depends to some extent on the biological attributes of the couple. The size decreases when children grow up and break away from their parents to establish their own conjugal unit.

Table 4.1: Distribution of Family Size in Village New Changlang

Sl. No.	*Family size*	*Number*	*Percentage*
1.	Single (1)	2	5.13
2.	Small Family (2 – 3)	4	10.26
3.	Medium Family (4 – 6)	24	61.54
4.	Large Family (7 – 9)	7	17.95
5.	Very Large Family (10+)	2	5.13
	Total	**39**	**100.00**

Table 4.2: Distribution of Family Size in Village Old Changlang

Sl. No.	*Family size*	*Number*	*Percentage*
1.	Single (1)	3	4.00
2.	Small Family (2 – 3)	8	10.66
3.	Medium Family (4 – 6)	39	52.00
4.	Large Family (7 – 9)	20	26.67
5.	Very Large Family (10+)	5	6.67
	Total	**75**	**100**

For understanding the size of the family under investigation, it has conveniently been divided into 5 categories. Distribution of families according to size among the Lungchangs inhabited in three villages, i.e. New Changlang, Old Changlang and Rangkatu has been presented in Table 4.1, 4.2 and 4.3.

The distribution of family size in the New Changlang village reveals that out of 39 households, 24 (61.54%) fall in the category of medium size, i.e. 4–6 member group. Next is the category of large, i.e. 7–9 members group, consisting of 7 (17.95%) families. There are only two families (5.13%) in the village, which fall under the category of very large family, consisting more than 10 members.

The analysis of data in the Old Changlang village shows that out of 75 families, 39 (52%) families fall in the category of medium size, where number of individuals range from 4–6 members. It is followed by the large family size, where 20 (26.67%) families are found having 7–9 members. Very large family where more than 10 members reside together is not uncommon among the Tangsas. There are 5 (06.67%) such families are found in the Old Changlang village.

Table 4.3: Distribution of Family Size in Village Rangkatu

Sl. No.	*Family size*	*Number*	*Percentage*
1.	Single (1)	–	–
2.	Small Family (2 – 3)	7	10.77
3.	Medium Family (4 – 6)	30	46.15
4.	Large Family (7 – 9)	15	23.08
5.	Very Large Family (10+)	13	20.00
	Total	**65**	**100.00**

The family size in the Rangkatu village reveals more or less same trend. The medium size family consisting of 4–6 members is highest in the village. There are 30 (46.15%) families belonging to medium size. It is followed by large family and there are 15 (23.08%) families where the number of members ranges from 7–9. Very large family consisting of more than 10 members is significant in this village. There are 13 (20.00%) such families in this village.

The analysis of family size among the Lungchang Tangsas in 3 villages of Arunachal Pradesh reveal more or less same picture. The medium sizes, i.e. 4–6 member families are common in all the villages. The highest number of families is found in this category. It is followed by large family. But with regard to very large family consisting more than 10 members it is found that there are significant differences in three villages. In the Rangkatu village, which is situated far away from the Changlang town, there are 13 (20.00%) such families, whereas, in the Old Changlang village, there are 5 (6.67%) such families. In the New Changlang village there are only 2 such families.

In the present project data has been collected from the Mukloms. The study has covered 3 villages. Distribution of families according to size has been projected in Tables 4.4, 4.5 and 4.6.

Table 4.4: Distribution of Family Size in Village Laktong

Sl. No.	*Family Size*	*No. of Families*	*Percentage*
1.	Single Person (1)	2	5.71
2.	Small (2 – 3)	3	8.57
3.	Medium (4–6)	23	65.72
4.	Large (7–9)	6	17.14
5.	Very Large (10 +)	1	2.86
	Total	**35**	**100.00**

Table 4.5: Distribution of Family Size in Village Simrang

Sl. No.	*Family size*	*Number of Families*	*Percentage*
1.	Single Person (1)	–	–
2.	Small (2–3)	5	15.62
3.	Medium (4–6)	13	40.63
4.	Large (7–9)	9	28.13
5.	Very Large (10 +)	5	15.62
	Total	**32**	**100.00**

The analysis of family size in the Laktong village shows that out of 35 families, 23 falls in the category of medium size where number of members range from 4–6 numbers. The percentage of medium size family is 65.72. It is followed by the large family size with 6 (17.14%) families, where number of individuals range from 7–9 members. There are 3 (8.57%) families, which belong to small size and the number ranges from 2–3 members. There are 2 families (5.71%) which are inhabited by single individual. There is only 1 (2.86%) family where more than 10 members reside (Table 4.5).

The family size in Simrang (New Thamlom) reveals more of less same trend. Out of 32 households, there are 13 (40.63%) families which fall in the category of medium size, where number of individual's ranges from 4–6 members. It is followed by large family where there are 9 (28.13%) families, whose number of members range from 7–9 individuals. There are 5 families (15.62%) belonging to small size. The numbers of very large family where more than 10 members reside are significantly higher in this village, i.e. there are 5 (15.62%) such families.

Table 4.6: Distribution of Family Size in Village Yanman

Sl. No.	*Family Size*	*Number*	*Percentage*
1.	Single (1)	–	–
2.	Small family (2–3)	14	16.28
3.	Medium family (4–6)	29	33.72
4.	Large family (7–9)	37	42.02
5.	Very large family (10+)	6	6.98
	Total	**86**	**100.00**

The distribution of families according to size in the Yanman village reveals that there are 86 families in the village. Out of these 37 families fall in the category of large family, where number of members range from 7–9. The percentage of such family is 42.02 in the village Yanman. It is followed by medium family size where 29 (33.72%) such families are found, whose number range from 4–6 individual. In the village, 14 (16.28%) small size family and 6 (6.98%) very large size family are found.

The analysis of family size among the Muklom Tangsas in 3 villages projects more or less same trend. The medium size, i.e. 4–6 member families is highest in number in two villages. Whereas in the Yanman village, large size family, i.e. 7–9 members are dominant and the medium size family are also significant. With regard to the number of very large family consisting more than 10 members a significant trend is observed. The number of such families is found in the highest number in Yanman village and it is followed by Simrang (New Thamlom). But such family is almost insignificant in the village Laktong, where there is only one such family is found.

An attempt has been made to compare the family size of the Lungchangs and the Mukloms. Table 4.7 does not project much variation. In both the sub-tribes maximum number of families are found in medium

Table 4.7: Distribution of Family Size among Lungchangs and Mukloms

Sl. No.	*Family Size*	*Lunchang*	*Muklom*
1.	Single (1)	5	2
2.	Small family (2–3)	19	22
3.	Medium family (4–6)	93	65
4.	Large family (7–9)	42	52
5.	Very large family (10+)	20	12
	Total	**179**	**153**

size category, i.e. 4–6 members. Table 4.7 also indicates that vary large family, i.e. more than 10 members are higher among the Lungchangs.

The analysis of family types and composition in New Changlang village has been presented in Table 4.8. The study reveals that nuclear

Table 4.8: Distribution of Family Type and Composition in Village New Changlang

Family type	*Sl. No.*	*Family members*	*No. of household*	*%*
Nuclear	1.	Husband, wife, unmarried child.	18	46.15
	2.	Husband, wife	2	5.13
	3.	Husband, wife, unmarried child, husband's unmarried brother.	1	2.56
	4.	Husband, wife, unmarried child, husband's nephew	1	2.56
		Total	**22**	**56.41**
Joint/Extended	1.	Husband, wife, unmarried child, husband, widower/widow parent.	2	5.13
	2.	Husband, wife, husband's widow/ widow parent.	1	2.56
	3.	Husband, wife, married son, daughter-in-law, grandchild.	3	7.70
	4.	Husband, wife, unmarried child, husband's unmarried brother/sister, widow/widower parent	3	7.70
	5.	Husband, wife, married son, daughter-in-law, grandchild.	3	7.70
	6.	Husband, wife, unmarried child, husband's widow parent and widow aunt.	1	2.56
		Total	**13**	**33.33**
Broken	1.	Widower.	1	2.56
	2.	Widow, unmarried child	2	5.13
		Total	**3**	**7.70**
Miscellaneous	1.	Single man	1	2.56
		Total	**1**	2.56
		Grand Total	**39**	**100.00**

family is found in highest frequency. Out of 39 families, there are 18 families that fall in the category of nuclear family, the percentage being 46.15. This is followed by extended family with 13 (33.33%) families. The type and composition of family project diverse picture. The typical joint family, i.e. husband and wife with married sons, grandchild and unmarried daughters are not very significant. At the same time, they care for their parents. And even after the death of father/uncle the widow stay in the same family.

Type and Composition of Family

Different types of family are found among the Tangsas. The type and composition of family vary according to the customs and traditions of a community. In the present study, families are categorized into 4 different types according to the prevalent context of the Tangsas. Distribution of family type and composition of the Lungchang Tangsas of Arunachal Pradesh have been presented in Tables 4.8, 4.9 and 4.10.

The analysis of family type and composition in the Old Changlang village shows equal number of nuclear and joint/extended family, having 33 (44%) families in each category. It is followed by broken family where there are 7 (9.33%) such families.

The distribution of family type and composition in the Rangkatu village has been presented in Table 4.10. It is found that the percentage of joint or extended family is highest in this village. There are 35 (53.85%) such families. It is followed by nuclear family type, where 26 (40%) such families are found.

The analysis of types and composition of Lungchang Tangsas of Arunachal Pradesh projects a significant trend. The number of nuclear family is highest in the New Changlang village, which is situated near the Changlang town. Whereas, the Old Changlang village which is situated slightly far away from the township shows equal number of nuclear and joint/extended family. But the number of joint/extended family is found in highest number in the Rangkatu village which is situated far away from the Changlang town. Thus, it may be said that joint/extended family are normal and preferred type of family among the Lungchang Tangsas. But, the study indicates that nuclear family is still dominant among the Tangsas. In many cases, a single household is unable to accommodate too big family. Moreover, in recent years, there is a tendency to switch over to new salaried job and in such cases; they prefer to live in nuclear family.

Table 4.9: Distribution of Family Type and Composition in Village Old Changlang

Family type	*Sl. No.*	*Family members*	*No. of households*	*%*
Nuclear	1.	Husband wife, unmarried child.	27	
	2.	Husband wife, unmarried child, Wife's relative.	2	
	3.	Husband wife, unmarried child, married daughter's brother-in-law.	1	
	4.	Husband and wife.	3	
		Total	**33**	**44.00**
Joint/extended	1.	Husband wife, unmarried child, husband's widower parent.	2	
	2.	Husband wife, husband's widower parent.	1	
	3.	Husband wife, unmarried child, husband's widower/widow parent.	3	
	4.	Husband wife, husband's unmarried brother, widower parent.	1	
	5.	Husband wife, unmarried daughter, widow daughter-in-law, grandchild, married son, daughter-in-law, grandchild.	1	
	6.	Husband wife, married son, daughter-in-law, Grandson, unmarried child.	12	
	7.	Husband wife, unmarried child, widower brother and his child, married bro., sister-in-law and their unmarried child.	1	
	8.	Husband wife, unmarried child, married brother, sister-in-law, their child and widow/widower parent.	3	
	9.	Husband wife, unmarried child, Husband's unmarried brother/sister, widower/ widow parent.	5	
	10.	Husband wife, unmarried child, husband's unmarried sister.	1	
	11.	Husband wife, married son, daughter-in-law, grandchild.	1	
	12.	Husband wife, unmarried child, husband's unmarried uncle/aunty, wife's relative.	2	
		Total	**33**	**44.00**
Broken	1.	Widow, unmarried child	2	
	2.	Widower	1	
	3.	Widow	2	
	4.	Widower, widow mother, unmarried brother, widow sister and her child	1	
	5.	Widower, unmarried child	1	
		Total	**7**	**9.33**
Miscellaneous	1.	Head with relative.	1	
	2.	Head, unmarried brother/sister.	1	
		Total	**2**	**2.67**
		Grand Total	**75**	**100.00**

Table 4.10: Distribution of Family Type and Composition in Village Rangkatu

Family type	*Sl. No.*	*Family members*	*No. of household*	*%*
Nuclear	1.	Husband, wife, unmarried child	26	40.00
	2.	Husband, wife, unmarried child, husband unmarried cousin	1	1.54
		Total	**27**	**41.54**
Joint/extended	1.	Husband, wife, unmarried child, hus's widower/widow parent	5	7.69
	2.	Husband, wife, unmarried child, widow parent, unmarried uncle/aunty	1	1.54
	3.	Husband, wife, unmarried child, unmarried brother/sister, widower/widow parent	4	6.15
	4.	Husband, wife, unmarried child, widow daughter-in-law, unmarried grandchild.	1	1.54
	5.	Husband, wife, unmarried child, married brother with his wife and unmarried child and widow parent	4	6.15
	6.	Husband, wife, married son, daughter-in law, grandchild, unmarried child	7	
	7.	Husband, wife, unmarried child, unmarried brother/sister	4	6.15
	8.	Husband, wife, married son, daughter-in-law, grandchild unmarried brother/sister	1	1.54
	9.	Husband, wife, married brother with his wife, unmarried child, widow sister-in-law and her unmarried child, widow/widower parent	1	1.54
	10.	Husband, wife, married son with his wife and unmarried child, widow sister-in-law and her widow/widower parent	1	1.54
	11.	Husband, wife, married son daughter-in-law, unmarried child	1	1.54
	12.	Husband, wife, unmarried child, married brother, his wife and his unmarried child	3	4.62
	13.	Husband, wife, married son, daughter-in-law, widow/ widower parent	1	1.54
	14.	Husband, wife unmarried child, married brother, his wife, unmarried child	1	1.54
		Total	**35**	**53.85**
Broken	1.	Widow, unmarried child	2	3.08
		Total	**2**	**3.08**
Miscellaneous	1.	Head with unmarried grandson.	1	1.54
		Total	**1**	**1.53**
		Grand Total	**65**	**100.00**

In the present project, data has also been collected from the Muklom Tangsas and the study covered 3 villages.

Distribution of Family Type and Composition

Distribution of family type and composition of Muklom Tangsas have been presented in Tables 4.11, 4.12 and 4.13. The analysis of family type and composition in the Laktong village reveal that more than 50 per cent of families fall in the category of nuclear family type. Out of 35 families, 19 (54.29%) families are of nuclear type, whereas in 1 family only husband and wife reside, whereas 18 families consist of husband and wife with unmarried children.

The next highest position is occupied by joint/extended type, i.e. 12 (34.29%) such families are found in the village. Here different types of arrangements are noticed. It is significant to notice that there are 2 families (5.71%), in the villages which are put in the miscellaneous type. Here each family consists of single person, i.e. widow or widower.

Table 4.11: Distribution of Family Type and Composition in Village Laktong

Family Type	*Sl. No.*	*Family Members*	*No. of Households*	*%*
Nuclear	1.	Husband, wife	1	
	2.	Husband, wife, unmarried child	18	
		Total	**19**	**54.29**
Joint/ Extended	1.	Husband, wife, unmarried child, married son, daughter-in-law, unmarried grandchild	3	
	2.	Husband, wife, unmarried child, widow/widower parent	4	
	3.	Husband, wife, unmarried child, unmarried brother/sister, widow/widower parent	1	
	4.	Husband, wife, unmarried child, widower father-in-law	1	
	5.	Husband, wife, unmarried child, unmarried brother/sister	1	
	6.	Husband, wife, married son, daughter-in-law, unmarried grandchild	1	
	7.	Husband, wife, unmarried child, unmarried brother/sister, unmarried nice, widow/widower parent	1	
		Total	**12**	**34.29**
Broken	1.	Widower, unmarried child	1	
	2.	Widow, unmarried child	1	
		Total	**2**	
Miscell-neous	1.	Widower	1	
	2.	Widow	1	
		Total	**2**	**2.71**
		Grand Total	**35**	**100.00**

The analysis of family type and composition in Simrang (New Thamlom) village reflects the more or less same trend. Here almost 60 per cent of families are of nuclear type. Out of 32 families, 19 (59.37%) families belong to nuclear category. It is followed by joint/extended type of families, i.e. 11 (34.37%) in number. Here the arrangement is analysed on the context of that village.

Table 4.12: Distribution of Family Type and Composition in Village Simrang

Family Type	*Sl. No.*	*Family members*	*Number of households*	*Total*
Nuclear	1	Husband, wife	3	
	2	Husband, wife, unmarried child	16	
		Total	**19**	59.37
Joint/extended	1	Husband, wife, unmarried child, unmarried brother/ sister	1	
	2	Husband, wife, unmarried. Child, widow/widower parents	1	
	3	Husband, wife, unmarried child, married brother, sister-in-law and their unmarried child	2	
	4	Husband, wives, unmarried. Child, unmarried, nephew, widow/widower parent	1	
	5	Husband, wife, unmarried child, unmarried brother/sister, unmarried cousins, widow/widower parents	1	
	6	Husband, wife, unmarried child, married brother, sister-in-law and their unmarried child, widow/widower parent	1	
	7	Husband, wife, unmarried child married son, daughter-in–law, grandchild	1	
	8	Husband, wife, unmarried child, unmarried brother/sister, widow/widower parent	2	
	9	Husband, wife, unmarried child, unmarried uncle, widow/widower parent	1	
		Total	**11**	**34.37**
Broken	1	Widow, unmarried child	1	
	2	Widower, unmarried child, unmarried brother/sister.	1	
		Total	**2**	**6.26**
		Grand Total	**32**	**100.00**

The analysis of family type and composition of Yanman village has been presented in Table 4.13. The highest frequency of family type has been found in the category of nuclear family where more than 50 per cent of families fall. Out of 86 families, as much as 44 (51.16%) families are of nuclear type. It is followed by joint/extended family type with 29 (33.72%) families. The number of broken family is significant. There are 13 (15.12%) families are recorded as broken family.

Table 4.13: Distribution of Family Type and Composition in Village Yanman

Family Type	*Sl. No.*	*Family Members*	*No. of Households*	*%*
Nuclear	1.	Husband, wife, unmarried child	42	
	2.	Husband, wife	2	
		Total	**44**	**51.16**
Joint/extended	1.	Husband, wife, married son, daughter-in-law, unmarried grandchild, unmarried child	3	
	2.	Husband, wife, unmarried child, unmarried brother/Sister.	6	
	3.	Husband, wife, married son, daughter-in-law, unmarried-grandchild, unmarried child, widower/widow parent	8	
	4.	Husband, wife, unmarried child, married cousin, his wife, their unmarried child, parent	1	
	5.	Husband, wife, unmarried child, married cousin, his wife, their unmarried child	1	
	6.	Husband, wife, unmarried child, unmarried brother/sister, widower parent	4	
	7.	Husband, wife, married son, daughter-in-law, unmarried grand-child, unmarried child	3	
	8.	Husband, wife, married son, daughter -in-law, unmarried child	3	
		Total	**29**	**33.72**
Broken	1.	Widow, unmarried child	10	
	2.	Widower, unmarried child	3	
		Total	**13**	**15.12**
Miscellaneous	1.	–	–	–
		Grand Total	**86**	**100.00**

The analysis of family type and compositions of Muklom Tangsas show various significant trends. While interviewing the Muklom Tangsas, almost all of them were in opinion that they prefer joint/extended family. But, the analysis reveals that in each village more than 50 per cent of families fall in the category of nuclear type. The Mukoms are also considered as conservative Tangsas in comparison to the Lungchangs. So, such findings need more in depth study. Regarding the very large family where more than 10 members reside under the same roof is not significant. Here also distant counts. The Yanman village, which is situated in a very interior areas, there are 6 very large families. Whereas the number is slightly reduced in Simrang village, where there are 5 such families.

The number is insignificant in Laktong village where there is only one such family. It is also to be mentioned that in the Laktong village there is 1 family which is inhabited by a widow and in another case it is occupied by a widower.

Table 4.14: Types of Family among the Lungchangs and Mukloms

Sl. No.	*Type*	*Lungchang*	*Muklom*
1.	Nuclear family	82	82
2.	Joint family	81	52
3.	Broken	12	17
4.	Miscellaneous	4	2
	Total	**179**	**153**

A comparison of family type and composition among the Lungchangs and the Mukloms has been presented in Table 4.14. It is revealed from the table that equal number of nuclear families is found among the Lungchangs and the Mukloms. It is also noticed that among the Lungchangs the number of joint families are higher than the Mukloms. While among the Mukloms the number of nuclear family is distinctly visible. Though there are no cultural norms of establishing nuclear family among the Tangsas like the Ao Nagas yet the preference for nuclear family is clearly visible among the Tangsas. The type and composition of nuclear and joint family differ from village to village depending on the situation and context.

Overall among the Tangsas, the family tie is very strong. The sons always consider that it is their duty to look after their aged parents. So, while they started to separate from original home after marriage, one of the son either the eldest or the youngest stays with the parents. But when they do not have sons, the problem arises. In such situation, sometimes, they are to live alone. The married daughter and son-in-law never forget their responsibilities. But due to economic condition, they cannot take full responsibility.

While a brief comparison is made between the Lungchangs and the Mukloms a slight variation is noticed among these sub-tribes. There are differences in ideal and real picture also.

Family Pattern

Patrilineal and patrilocal types are the normal form of family organization among the Tangsas. They maintain tribal endogamy but clan exogamy.

Descent among the Tangsa is traced through father and residence is patrilocal. Father is considered as the head of the family. He is highly respected by everybody and his decisions and words are treated as final. All family members work with team spirit.

The sons need not separate from their parental house immediately after marriage, but may do so if situation demands. In a joint family, a common house is shared by the whole family consisting of parents, married sons and daughters. Even after the death of the father, family does not break up and the members continue to live in the same house. Each married couples occupy a separate cubicle in the houses. Earlier when they entirely dependent on *jhum* cultivation, joint family was considered as ideal type of family. But along with the urbanization, there is a tendency to prefer nuclear family. Of course, among the Tangsas, the role of clan members is very significant. In diverse situations, they are to depend on their clan members. Daughters after marriage generally leave her parental house after a year or may go to stay with her husband as soon as marriage ceremony is completed. Though polygamy is socially accepted among the Tangsas, yet it is rarely practiced. Such type of marriage is normally held when the first wife is barren and does not possess any issue of her own.

Family among the Tangsas is a productive unit. Every member of a family contributes its respective share in maintaining the economy of the family. In general, pattern of labour in the tribal family is based on a well organized division of labour according to sex and age. Both the males and females work according to their physical capacity. The boys and girls are allotted different types of works, suited to their age. The grown-ups allowed to do all important and strenuous works but women are usually given light work as compared to men. The women take care of infants and do the household work, as their primary job. Herskovits traces the history of division of labour as "it seems reasonable that prior to the domestication of animals or plants, the men hunted and carried on those other aspects of the food quest that took them from home. It seems equally reasonable that the women being closely confined to the place of family habitation if only for physical reasons, made their contribution to the economy of the group by searching out roots and herbs and gathering fruits and nuts. In this, it is further assumed, a tradition becomes fixed that associated men with animals and women with plants." The division of labour among the tribe still projects the same trend.

Tangsas, traditionally depend on shifting *jhum* cultivation. Men and women join together as unit of production. The *jhum* cultivation, technology is not so complicated, but the entire process is very tedious and production is not very encouraging. Division of labour is well managed. Whatever the plot of land every member collectively works. Family, being the primary unit of a village, they have a well defined set up. Each member of the family is equally responsible to one another. They enjoy equal status and rights in the context of social, economic, legal and religious observance. In the same way each member enjoys equal rights in case of ownership of property. After death of the father, the eldest son takes the responsibility of managing the family affairs.

Self sufficiency and autonomy of a Tangsa village was further strengthened by economic independence. In a village *jhum* crops were raised locally and the entire agricultural produce, i.e. food grains and vegetables were consumed locally. In their daily life women folk get up from bed earlier than the men folk. After their morning routine, they take black tea with biscuits. School going children remain busy with their studies. Women members get busy in the preparation of morning meal. There is not much variation in their menu. Rice is their staple food, which is locally referred as "*dung*". Their major meal consists of rice and vegetables. They take meals three times every day. Most of them produce the seasonal vegetables at their own kitchen garden. They like to take boil items using some curry plants. They also collect herbs and shrubs from the forest and *jhum* field and use these in their daily menu. All have medicinal value and act as preventive measures. They also relish fowl and pork. Meat of buffalo and wild animals are included in the menu occasionally, particularly when these are sacrificed for some religious ceremonies.

Tea is their favourable drink which is taken without adding milk and sugar. It is locally known as *phalapkha*. Rice-beer '*ju*' is locally prepared and is taken by all irrespective of age and sex.

Division of work among the Tangsa male and female has prevailed since the time immemorial. Men, being the bread winner, have to take important role of earning for the family and receive a status in the society. He also keeps control of family finance. Even when women participate in earning a living it is rated as subsidiary and subordinate to that of men.

Living Arrangement in the Family

The members of a family share a common roof. Sometimes married son may live in a separate house within the compound but share the same kitchen. Sometimes alternative arrangements are made where married sons share the same roof but maintain separate hearth.

The traditional dwellings of the Tangsas are pile house, which are about 3-4 feet above the ground. The houses are on some pillars which are generally made of wood. Their traditional pile dwellings are built on stilts, rectangular in shape with double shaped roof of palm. The house is divided into three parts. The first room is used as common room, having walls on three sides and the front side is open. The room has a hearth—(*tap*) placed slightly towards the left side of the room. Besides being used as a common room, it is also used as a guest room. The skull of buffaloes, pigs and other animals killed in various festive occasions are hung on the walls of this room. In front of this room, an open veranda is there which is made of bamboo splits having sufficient gap. This part of the house is used for different purposes like to dry paddy, cloth, to keep flowering pot or orchid, or to sit in the open air. The middle room is divided longitudinally into two parts, one of which is used as a long corridor running along the length of the room and the other part is divided into a small compartment with fire place in each. The size of the dwelling house varies according to the number of family members. The larger the number, the longer is the house. There are two verandas in each house, where one is on the front side and the other is on the back side of the house. They have the kitchen at the end of the house just adjacent to back veranda. In case of joint family sometimes each family use separate hearth just near to their compartment, but they live under the same roof. Just above the hearth, there is a small square shaped ceiling (*khang sa*) made of bamboo. They keep fish for drying, seeds of bitter gourd; seeds of different crops etc. are also preserved after drying. Hearth always plays an important role both in cooking as well for preservation. Above the *kharang sa*, another big platform (*kharang-jung*) is used to keep such materials like drums (*nong*), can strings, leather or skin of different animals, wooden and bamboo materials. It is a custom that food is served at first to the head of the family and other members. Women normally take their meal later on. Now-a-days, the Tangsas use both their traditional and modern utensils for cooking and serving.

Each family has its own granary. Granary is built at some distance from the main house. It is a small square house with sloping roofs on two sides built on fairly high stilts. The granary is not only serving for storage of paddy, but also utilized as a store house for other provisions.

The villagers also have their farm house which is used for keeping eyes on the birds and other wild animals. It is constructed in the same pattern as their dwelling house. These are also used as temporary residence during the cultivation season.

The houses are constructed on a co-operative basis. Reciprocal relationships are visible in such activities. The building materials for traditional houses are collected from the jungle by the owner of the house. The villagers are invited to help in the construction process. Rice-beer, rice and pork are served to the people who help in the construction of the house. They use palm leave for thatching and bamboo, wood, cane and wood are the materials that are used for constructions. But now-a-days, instead of seeking help from the villagers and kinsmen, many of the families prefer to engage paid labourers. Moreover in every villager, there are some persons who work on wage basis. In recent years, the people started to build modern *pucca* house. For construction of modern type of houses, they need brick, iron, tin etc. which are easily brought from the Changlang town or from Assam.

Inheritance of Property

The Tangsas call their property as *Tangsong*. Pattern of inheritance and ownership of property forms an important criterion to assess the position of an individual. The inheritance of property among the Tangsa is patriarchal. It regulates the transmission of property from one generation to the next through the male line. Generally, father is the guardian of all property. All the properties, movable or immovable are jointly shared by the family. The father, who is the head of the family, exercises the authority over the property. After the death of the father or when he becomes old, the property is divided equally among the sons. According to the customary rules, Tangsa women are not entitled to get any immovable property, but they can use it as long as the stay with the family. Usually, daughters inherit property like ornaments, handloom, valuable beads, necklaces, etc. If a person does not have any son or daughter or only a daughter, then the property goes to other male members of nearest kin.

However, during fieldwork, a case was reported where in the absence of son, the father divided his property among his daughters. As a patriarchal society, though they have preference for male child, yet now-a-days parent try to give education to the children irrespective of sexes. A case was reported where mother (though illiterate) extended her supporting hand to give proper education to her daughters. It is revealed from the field data that each village has at least a primary school. Prior to 1947, there was no educational institution in Arunachal Pradesh, the erstwhile NEFA. But, it is encouraging to note that even during 1947, there was one school in the village Rangkatu in the Changlang sub-division. Now, this village is situated in interior areas compared to others which are situated near the district headquarters. After the establishment of Changlang district, the Tangsa villages situated near the district headquarter are getting more facilities than these villages situated far away from it. In the present study, among the selected Lungchang Tangsa villages, the Rangkatu is considered as an interior village. It is no doubt a fact that there has been substantial increase in the rate of literacy since independence. But the progress of literacy still does not project a rosy picture. According to 1981 Census report, the percentage of literacy in respect of total population in the Changlang district is 23.42 as against 11.22 of the combined Tirap district in the 1971 Census.

There was a general trend of not giving proper opportunity to female child. Conservativeness and tradition were responsible for a general aversion of the people towards female literacy. The girls are considered as a helping hand in different household works. The socio-economic conditions also are determinant factor of not sending the girls to school. But, now-a-days, the people are giving up their earlier antipathy for school education and started to send their girls to school in increasing numbers. The field data reveal that educational level of both the male and female are almost same. But in case of attainment of higher education or status, it is still achieved by the male. Now, there are various opportunities available, e.g. Anganwadi, Adult Education, Food and Nutritional Programme and young girls are taking training in such institutions. Modern education has considerable impact on women and many of Tangsa women are employed in good jobs. The Adult Literacy Centre is taking steps not only to eradicate illiteracy, but to impart employment generation training and improve the skills in various fields of arts and crafts also. Adult Education Programme was introduced in Arunachal Pradesh during 1965-66. During the year 1986-87, there were only 77 Adult Education Centres in the Changlang districts. But the number of centres is increasing and it rose to 117 during 1996-97 and at present, the number of centres is increasing. The centres are attached to the primary schools and functioning in the evening.

Besides, these opportunities of formal education, family among the Tangsas plays a major role of socialization or enculturation from the birth of a child. Children learn various activities of their culture in the process of upbringing. And each member of the family contributes its respective share in fulfilling the economic needs according to age and sex. The

Tangsa women are good weaver. They weave all the necessary clothes in their loom. Weaving is also considered as one of the qualification of marriage. They have a preference for geometrical designs on their cloths. Dutta (1959) remarks "Tangsas are particularly sensitive to scarlet-red, black and dark-green colours." The girls learn the art of weaving in their family atmosphere.

Life Cycle Ritual of Lungchang Tangsas

The Tangsa religion is mainly based on animistic faith. They believe in all kinds of spirits: some are favourable towards mankind, while lots of others are responsible for the ills and suffering of human being. These spirits are to be propitiated by their customary rituals.

As a rule, both the Lungchang and Muklom Tangsas do not worship any idol in the form of God in the family. But all have a faith in the main post of the house and in the moment of any crisis, they bow before this pillar. In recent years they started to keep photos of *Lord Rang Frah* at their home and offer prayer family level.

Life cycle ritual or rite-de-passage is important events in the life of an individual. The role of various members is reflected in such occasions. But these rituals are confined not only among the family members, but these are the occasions where kin members get the opportunity of get together. In all such occasions, the kin members in various stages perform their ritualistic as well kin roles.

Here, an effort has been made to describe theses stages among the Tangsas. The birth of a baby is always considered as joyous occasion among the Tangsas. Lungchangs consider it as a gift of *God Rang Frah.* The entire family starts giving due attention to the pregnant lady. The health status of the lady is observed carelly. In general she gets usual treatment from her family in all respects with a slight variation and that is in the amount of care and social taboo. Most of the tribes do not observe any rites of pregnancy invariably, though there is some exception. But the Lungchang and the Muklom Tangsas observe certain ceremonies. Normally, if everything is favourable, no special ritual is performed to mark the pregnancy. In case of sickness or health related problems, they invariably perform specific ritual to please the spirit responsible for it. During field investation, it was reported that the family invariably perform a ritual known as *Poumthong* during the 7 or 8 month of pregnancy. This ritual is performed to appease the evil spirits, with a belief that no spirit would do any harm or create problems during delivery. This ritual is performed by the local priest. A female dog is killed by squeezing it neck. Then the dog is hanged on the *pipal* tree. One chick is also killed by squeezing the neck. This is done to know the sex of the baby and to find out whether the lady would face any problem during delivery. One cock and one hen are sacrificed to please the spirit. The meat of cock and hen are used for the feast which is arranged with rice and rice-beer. Mostly aged persons are invited for ritual. From the evening on the day of ritual till the next day meal time, the pregnant lady is to eat only *Khichiri* (prepared with rice and *dal*). They may add salt in it, but without turmeric. From the next evening she can have meal with her family members. There are also some restrictions for the other family members. From the day of performing this ritual, no one can eat meat or fish at home till the new moon appear on the sky. However, the pregnant lady is strictly prohibited to eat meat or fish till the appearance of new moon.

Sometime different version of the same ritual is also found. There is no difference of opinion in performing the *Poumthong* ritual. But, it was referred by (Rao, 2006: 237), "This ritual involves sacrifice of a pig and a fowl to please the spirits and protect the woman. The pig is sacrificed under a *pipal* tree. Before sacrificing the fowl, all ornaments, cloths, implements and baskets of the woman are placed under the tree and a fowl is sacrificed by holding it over these items. Prayers are offered to the spirits to release the soul of the pregnant lady from their clutches and allow her to live peacefully and work in the field."

Though there is variation of description of this ritual, yet all agree that it is performed for the safe delivery.

The Lungchang also perform *Naonasot* ritual after 3 or 4 days of the birth of a baby. *Nao* means child, *na* means ear and *sot* means piercing, thus, it indicate that this ritual is performed for piercing the ears of new born baby. They also keep the name for the newly born baby on the day itself. A cock is sacrificed by male head of the family to find out all omen of the baby by observing the claws of the cock. Then the piercing of ear is done and a black thread is tied in the pricked hole of the baby's ear. Before pricking the ear they apply a typical leaves of a plant dipped in water. The plant has medicinal value and known as *Theiram*. It is believed that this medicinal herb will prevent the prick of ear from septic. They also keep a name for the new born. After performing the religious part, a feast is organized with rice-beer, meat and rice. Only limited neighbours are invited for the feast.

The Lungchang and the Mukloms, the sub-tribe of Tangsas follows the fundamental rules that govern the marriage system in the Tangsa society.

Though the basic philosophy of marriage is same, yet slight variation is noticed in each sub-tribe (Detail in the Chapter heading Marriage System).

Death Ceremony Among the Lungchang Tangsas

The Tangsas consider birth, marriage and death as the three aspects of life process. The method of disposal of the dead body is different among the different sub-tribes. The Lungchangs and the Mukloms cremate their dead while the Yoglis bury their dead. Though Lungchangs and the Mukloms bury their dead, yet there are differences in the procedure of death ceremony. In the following pages, the death ceremony of the Lungchang Tangsas has been described.

The Lungchangs refer the ritual of death ceremony as *Mangpu.* When a person dies, they first inform all the members and kinsmen who are living in different areas. They sweep the house of the dead person. Then they wash the dead body with warm water. After ritual bath the dead body is kept in a bamboo mat inside the house. They cover the dead body with clean shawl. One mug of water is kept near the dead body so that person would not feel thirsty. A fowl is sacrificed on that day to prepare the special dish for the dead. Then they serve the meat with rice-beer and rice in front of the dead. The dead body is normally kept in the house till the arrival of close relatives to show their last respect to the dead. They keep the dead body for 1-3 days as per demands of the situation. In the cremation ground, they construct a small hut with bamboo and leaves. On the day of cremation, in the morning around 9 a.m. some villagers with head of the family go to the cremation ground. The villagers search firewood for the cremation and the headman put some fire in front of the small hut. Then a preparation is made in the deceased house to formally bid farewell to the departed soul. Either a pig/buffalo/cow is sacrificed. And a feast is arranged in the name of dead person, before moving to the cremation ground. Head, tail and leg portion of the sacrificed animal is prepared as a dish and ritually served to the dead person. The feast is arranged to take the last meal together before final departure. After the feast, by 1 p.m. they move to the cremation ground. The children are not allowed to go to the cremation ground. It is considered obligation to give some rice grains, chilli, colocacia, potato, maize, vegetables and seeds etc. along with the dead body. It is believed that the dead person requires these items for cultivation in the heaven. The belonging of the deceased such as utensils, like; bowl, plate, glass, dekchi, spoon, cloth, footwear, ornaments and his/her daily use items, e.g. *bidi*, cigarettes, beer etc. are offered to the dead person. Besides the material objects, even money amounting Rs. 10.00 to Rs. 100.00 are given in the name of dead person. All the items offered in the name of dead person are kept in the small hut in the cremation ground. When the party moves to the cremation ground along with the dead body, one of the family members is to carry water in a bamboo vessel so that the dead person would not feel thirsty. The fire is lighted by the eldest clan member first and then the process continued by the aged persons. When the body starts burning, female members slowly start leaving the cremation ground. But the male members return only after completing the whole funeral ceremony. After returning from the cremation ground, everybody take bath and change their cloth. During the return journey, one member from the last group brings a *dapung* (broom like plant) to the deceased's house. The next day after the cremation, the head (male/female) of the family is to perform a ritual with that *dapung* in front of the house. It is performed for the person, who carried water to the cremation ground. The ritual is performed by uttering some dialogues with a wish that the soul of the dead would not create any problem to the family members. It is hoped that the soul should go to heaven peacefully. On that day the family members and the paternal relatives of the dead only take *khichiri* (rice cooked in water and salt, but not fully boiled). A small quantity of it is placed in a *Nyapmi-jak* (*kaupat* or traditional leaf) and kept outside of the house in the name of dead person. From the cremation, up to 1 week, the family members are not allowed to go outside of the house. Others may go to their respective houses. They cannot eat green vegetables during this period. They can take pulse, potato, onion, garlic etc. which are grown under the earth. There is no bar in taking meat/fish. After 1 week, the aged persons of the village are invited to the dead man's house. The invitees are served with rice-beer. The villagers formally intimate that from that day, the relatives of the dead may go outside the house and will do their normal work.

Wulemrit Wulem Means Heaven and Rit Means Border

This ritual is performed by the Lungchangs to erase or reduce the border between the heaven and earth. This ritual is performed in the first *Mol* festival (annual festival of the Lungchangs) after the death of the person. This ritual is performed to bid farewell to the soul forever with a belief that the soul has no place on the earth and he/she has to go to the heaven forever. One pig is sacrificed on that day and a feast is arranged for the villagers/community members.

In case the family members are to wait for 1 yr for *Mol* festival, then this ritual may be performed during the appearance of new moon after the death of the person. They wish to complete this ritual as soon as possible to give relief to the soul as well as the family members. It is a custom that till the performance of this ritual; the family members have to serve food in the name of the soul whatever they eat. It is believed that if they forget to serve, the soul will remain hungry, and may cause harm to the family members. Thus, to give the eternal peace to the soul and for the safety of the family members, they try to complete this ritual as soon as possible.

Accidental Death

It is commonly believed that the accidental death as a bad omen. The soul of the dead would not get any place in the heaven and will go to hell (*san*). Therefore, instead of cremating the dead in the cremation ground, they burn the dead body anywhere in the forest or riverside. They keep thorny plant in front of the gate or below the step of the staircase. It is believed that this would prevent the soul to enter into the house. They do not perform any ritual for such death. Family members and the villagers do not go out of their house as a mark of respect to the soul. If anyone from the nearby villages gets the information of accidental death, they do not go outside the house and avoid doing their normal routine work.

Life Cycle Rituals of Muklom Tangsas

It has already been mentioned that each sub-tribe of the Tangsa has their own style of living, socio-cultural and religious faiths and beliefs. Yet some features are common to the Tangsas as a whole.

Birth of a baby is always considered as an auspicious event. Various measures have been followed by the Tangsas for the well being of both the mother and the child. The rituals and ceremonies, which have been observed by the Lungchangs have already been described. Among the Mukloms also birth of a child is considered as an important event in the family. The expecting mother is given special treatment since the beginning of pregnancy. If the mother suffers from illness, it is believed that the evil spirits are responsible for it. To ward off the evil spirits and the safe delivery a ritual is performed known as *Sowin*. This ritual is performed on the 8 month of the pregnancy. The priest (*Tingwa*) keeps, one *Wokhup* (chick) in the forest to die. It is believed that if it is done, the pregnant lady would not suffer from any complicacy during the delivery. There is some prohibition for both the wife and husband. They are not allowed to eat the meat of bear, wild pig, prawn, crab and monkey. They have a belief that all these things may create problems during delivery and it badly affects the new born. He may develop the anger or any bad habit. They are not supposed to kill snake. There is also a taboo to attend any death ritual, because it is believed that the spirits of the dead may cause harm to the mother and baby.

Nomanghun or Nao Chungrong

On the third day after the birth of the baby, a ceremony or sacrament known as *Nomanghun* or *Naochungrong* is performed. In this ritual a dish is kept on the floor and water is poured into it. Grandparents and parents select some names and names are written on chits. These chits are then put on the water one by one with two pieces of rice husks. If the two pieces of husks come together in the water, it is believed that the name written on that chit is suitable for the new born. When they do not use chit, then while putting rice-husks on the water, they recite some names. If the two pieces of husk come together, it is considered that the proposed name is suitable for the child. If the pieces of husks do not come together, then the same ritual is repeated by selecting other names. This is done until a favourable result is obtained and the name is decided after fulfilling the result. On that day the family members arranged feast which consist of meat, rice, rice-beer etc. for the relatives and the villagers.

More or less same belief and observance has been found among the Kumar tribe of Chhattisgarh. It is their general belief that some ancestors regain their life in the form of the child. "In certain cases, people may sit with a handful of paddy (*dhan*) and a *batki* (bowl) full of water. After naming some ancestors two grains will be slowly dropped from two opposite sides in the water contained in the *batki*. If two meet together within a short time, the child is named after that ancestor. Or else the process if repeated" (Khatua, 2008: 263). The similar beliefs that exist in two tribes situated far apart indicate that the primitive shifting tribes, who depend on nature, may develop the similar beliefs.

Up to one month from the birth of the baby, no member of family may eat fruits, vegetables which are grown in the creepers. It is believed that these things may cause wound or boil on the body of the baby. They are also not allowed to cut trees and creepers, because they believe that it would hamper the growth of the baby, i.e. the baby may not grow adequately.

Still-Birth

Birth of still born baby is considered a curse to the whole family. In case of still birth the baby is wrapped with cloths and then it is covered by flattened bamboo. This is then tied with cane rope. After that the dead body is buried under the *Changghar* of the bereaved family. The members of the family take frugal meal in a banana leaf. The whole village abstains from doing any work on that day. They do not go to the agricultural field. It is observed to seek the blessing from almighty *God Rang Frah.*

Birth of Twins

The birth of twin is considered to be a worst kind of curse among the Mukloms. They took various measures to kill the twins. The twins are used to be taken to the jungle where they were strangulated to death with a rope. Then it was kept in a bamboo basket and hung on a tree and the animals and insects consumed the dead bodies. The beliefs continued among the Mukloms until recently. A case of twin birth is presented below.

Mrs. L.N. 43 yrs. informed the death of her twin babies on 07.03.08. She reported that she gave birth to twin children. During that time, birth of twin children was considered as a curse and bad omen for the family. One of the twins was small in size and deformed. The small baby was kept in a bamboo basket and one bottle gourd in the name of the baby. The other baby was kept in another basket. Then the family members carried the baskets to the jungle and they were strangulated to death with a rope. They had to observe pollution period for 1 month from the disposal of the twin children. The members of the family used to remain inside the house and no one was allowed to enter their house except her own brothers and sisters. After one month, her brother arranged a small ritual where the priest and her brother performed customary worship and ritual to drive away the evil spirit. The priest prayed to *Lord Rang Frah* and sought his blessing for safety, security and well being of her family. A pig was sacrificed on that day and a feast was organized and the villagers and the visitors were entertained with rice, meat and rice-beer. After performing this ritual, their family was considered purified. Then they abandoned their old house and shifted to this new house. The villagers extended their helping hand in building the new house and their old house was destroyed.

At present, situation has changed and they started to understand that this is not the effect of spirit.

Disposal of the Dead

Both the Lungchangs and the Mukloms cremate their dead. The Lungchangs had their cremation ground from early stage, whereas, among the Mukloms, earlier dead body was cremated within their own compound. But, now-a-days, they cremate the dead bodies in an earmarked place at a short distance from their residential site known as *maangsattong* (cremation ground). Normally, cremation takes place after two days from the day of death. But in certain families dead bodies are kept for more than 3-4 days, so, that all the near relatives and friends can attend the funeral rite. Of course, the families who are economically well off keep the dead bodies for more than 3 days. Because as long the dead bodies are kept in the house, it is the responsibility of the family members to offer rice beer with rice and meat.

On the day of death, the dead body is washed and is covered with red clothes in case of women and white in case of male. The dead body is kept on *Khalbol* (mat made of bamboo) inside the house. On that day a chicken is also sacrificed and cooked. Then the meat, rice and water are offered near the dead body. This is done with a belief that in no case the soul should remain hungry. From this day, they start preparing rice-beer both for funeral ritual and entertaining the visitors who come to show their last respect to the departed soul. The same process, i.e. offering food to the dead body with rice and meat continued. The family members are to observe the same entertainment during the entire period.

On the day of cremation, one pig/cow/buffalo and a fowl are sacrificed and the heads of the animals are offered in the name of the deceased person. While sacrificing the animals the names of the dead ancestors are recited. It is believed that the ancestors would show the path of heaven (*ballam*) to the soul of the deceased. The villagers and the relatives who are present at the time take part in the feast which is arranged by the family members. After the feast is over, the dead body is carried in the bamboo mate by the *Phowa* (maternal uncle/brother) to the cremation ground. Funeral pyre is raised by keeping dry wooden logs on the top and green (wet) wooden material below, near the surface. At that time, a ritual called *Chitjunghol* is performed, where the two brothers of the deceased persons dig one hole near the funeral pyre. Both the brothers bring water in a bamboo vessel from the nearby river for three times, so, that the deceased could quench his/her thirst. It is a tradition among the Muklom Tangsas that the pyre is lit by *Sotwa,* the oldest person belonging to the deceased's clan or village. It is believed that soul would not be able to do any harm to the aged person. Young men are not allowed to light the funeral pyre. All the items, e.g. vegetables, utensils, cloths, ornaments, weapons, etc. are offered to the dead with a belief that the dead person could share these items with his/her ancestors in the heaven.

It has already been mentioned that there are variations in the performance of rituals among the sub-tribes of the Tangsas. But, it is also a fact that variation is noticed or recorded in different locality by different scholars. It was referred by Rao (2006: 244) that among the Mukloms, a memorial is erected (*samadhi*) on wooden poles by making used bamboo materials. It is a kind of small *tap* (house) in which image or replica of the body of dead person is installed, decorated with colourful dresses, ornaments etc. and regular prayers and offerings are made on all the festivals and other important social and religious events. For one year the family members are to observe mourning period and everyday a portion of meal is set aside and offered to the soul of departed person. The memorials are constructed on the entrance of the village as per the tradition among the Mukloms."

But intensive study among the Mukloms in three villages of Arunachal Pradesh revealed that along with the cremation, the clothes, boxes, things etc. of deceased person are also burnt. A *tap* is also made nearby the cremation where they keep all types of vegetable seeds like paddy, colocacia, maize etc. which the deceased may cultivate in the heaven.

After the cremation, everyone return to the deceased's house, where a feast is organized by the family. On that occasion meat of sacrificial animals are cooked and served with rice-beer to all the villagers, visitors and relatives. On that day the *sotwa* and close relatives of the dead lit a small stick near the cremation site so, that the soul need not stay in dark.

Next day, *Langban* ritual is performed where *Long* means kite and *Ban* means waiting. So, *Langban* means waiting for the kite. Normally, the aged and old person of the clan is to perform it. He waits outside the house with meat, rice-beer and water in a plate. When the kite is seen coming, he throws these after uttering "you kite have these things". Sometimes, kite may not come, even then they do it. It is believed that the soul of the deceased may visit the family in the form of kite.

Haltak

The Mukloms perform this ritual 3 days after the cremation. *Haltak* means dirty, black man due to burning. It is believed that God may not allow the dirty, striking soul to enter the heaven. So, to make the soul pure and fresh, they perform this ritual. On the occasion, the invitees are served with rice-beer. They believe that after performing this ritual, God may permit the soul to enter the heaven.

It was also reported that sometime one of the family member of the deceased cut the hair of the deceased and keep it inside a small bamboo tube. It is hanged on the neck. The person, who is carrying the hair, is to serve a portion of meal in front of that small bamboo hut. This is to be continued for one long year. After one year, on the same day, they make an image or replica of the deceased person. They are to perform every ritual which they actually did at the time of death.

Unnatural Death

Pre-mature death, death by accident, snake bite, attack of wild animals is considered as unnatural death. The Mukloms believe that *Sowin-Thaang* (spirits causing unnatural death) is responsible for unnatural death. These evil spirits are also believed to be the souls of those persons who die unnatural death. The souls of such persons are dwelling here and there in search of food, water, meat, homes and harboring evil spirits. So, to increase the number of evil spirits they cause the unnatural death.

In case of accidental death, only maternal uncle and brothers may attend the cremation. Maternal uncle pricks two thorns under the foot of the deceased, so, that the soul would not move here and there. In case of accidental death, they lit fire to the dead body (with clothes) on the accidental spot or sometimes somewhere away from the village. On that day, all the villagers remain within the house and never go outside. Anyone who hears the news remains within the house. No ritual is performed in such deaths.

5
Marriage System

Marriage is a socially recognized and the most wide spread institution in human society. Everywhere, it is a set of cultural pattern devised among other things, to guide the individual in the choice of his spouse. The function of marriage lies primarily in the social sanction; it supplies a stable background for care and rearing of children. As a social institution, Kapadia (1996:19) observes "marriage was desired not so much for sex or for progeny as for obtaining a partner for the fulfilment of one's religious duties." Fortes (1962:2) opines "marriage is a bridge between kinship side and the affinal side…"

Whatever may be the ritual related to marriage, it remains an alliance. This alliance can be for a life time or it may be short lived. Marriage is universal in human society, but no society considers marriage as a personal affair. It is a social alliance par excellence. All human societies have some in built mechanism for providing legitimacy to the couple. According to Beals and Hoijer (1965), "marriage is everywhere a set of cultural pattern to sanction parenthood and to provide a background for care and rearing of children. It is in fact, the major cultural mechanism to ensure the contribution of family and other grouping bonds of kinship." It has been defined by Kessing (1958), "marriage may be used as political or economic instrument as where alliances or property holding may be consolidated through marriage by leading families." Marriage is more or less permanent association of one or more males with one or more females, for the purpose of giving social sanction to pregnancy, satisfaction of biological and social needs. In this connection, Gough's opinion was "marriage is socially recognized and normally prescribed relationship between at least two persons that defined economy and sexual rights and other duties to each one and the other and provides the primary mechanism in a society by which offsprings are recognized as legitimate and accorded full birth status right common to normal members of (their) society or social stratum (Gough, 1909:32). Westermarck defines marriage "as a relation of one or more man to one or more women which is recognized by custom or law and involves certain rights and duties both in case of the parties entering the union and in the children born of it." Thus, it is very difficult to have a universal definition of marriage.

The nature of marital bond is basically same everywhere. It involves the social sanction generally in the form of a religious ceremony authorizing two persons of opposite sexes to engage in sexual and the correlated socio-economic relation with one another. The marriage ceremony consists of a series of ritual performances and every society or community has different custom and tradition of marriage ceremony.

Marriage Among the Tangsas

The Tangsas regard marriage as one of the most important event in the life of an individual. They are endogamous and confine their marriages within their own tribe. But they are organized into a number of patrilineal descent groups or clans. They are not allowed to marry within their own clan members. It is believed that violation of this rule adversely affect the entire community. Monogamy is ideal and general practice, and though polygamy is socially permitted, yet the percentage of polygamous marriage is negligible. Among the Tangsas, second marriage is allowed in case of death of the first wife or if the first wife is not able to bear a child.

Among the Tangsas various forms of marriage are performed. The variations with regard to the performance of actual marriage ceremony among the different sub-tribes are significant. However, certain rules and procedures of marriage are common among Tangsas as a whole.

The distribution of population by age, sex and marital alliances among the Lungchangs has been presented in Tables 5.1, 5.2 and 5.3.

Table (5.1) shows the distribution of the population of New Changlang village by age, sex and marital status. Out of the total population of 197, 53 males and 47 females are unmarried; the percentage being 26.90 per cent and 23.86 per cent, respectively.

On the other hand 43 males and 44 females are married and their percentage being 21.83 per cent and 22.34 per cent, respectively. The highest number of unmarried males fall within the age group of 15-19 yrs., i.e. 11 (5.58%) and unmarried females, i.e. 11 (5.58%) fall within the age group of 5–9 yrs. and 10–14 yrs. There are no married individual

Table 5.1: Distribution of Population by Age, Sex and Marital Status in New Changlang Village

Sl. No.	Age Group (yrs.)	Unmarried				Married				Widower		Widow		Total	
		Male		Female		Male		Female							
		No.	%	No.	%	No.	%	No.	%	No.	%	No.	%	No.	%
1.	0–19	36	**18.27**	32	16.23	–	–	–	–	–	–	–	–	68	34.49
2.	20–24	8	**4.06**	10	5.08	–	–	5	2.54	–	–	–	–	23	11.68
3.	25–29	6	**3.05**	3	1.52	4	2.30	5	2.54	–	–	–	–	18	9.14
4.	30–34	3	**1.52**	1	0.51	7	3.55	10	5.08	–	–	–	–	21	10.66
5.	35–39	–	–	1	–	8	4.06	4	2.03	1	0.51	–	–	14	7.11
6.	40–44	–	–	–	–	7	3.55	8	4.06	–	–	1	0.51	16	8.12
7.	45–49	–	–	–	–	6	3.05	1	0.51	–	–	–	–	7	3.55
8.	50–54	–	–	–	–	2	1.01	1	0.51	–	–	1	0.51	4	2.03
9.	55–59	–	–	–	–	2	1.01	5	2.54	–	–	1	0.51	8	4.06
10.	60–64	–	–	–	–	3	1.52	2	1.01	–	–	2	1.01	7	3.55
11.	65–69	–	–	–	–	3	1.52	1	0.51	–	–	–	–	4	2.03
12.	70–74	–	–	–	–	–	–	–	–	2	1.01	–	–	2	1.01
13.	75–79	–	–	–	–	1	0.51	–	–	–	–	–	–	1	0.51
14.	80–84	–	–	–	–	–	–	–	–	1	0.51	–	–	1	0.51
15.	85–89	–	–	–	–	–	–	1	0.51	–	–	–	–	1	0.51
16.	90–94	–	–	–	–	–	–	–	–	–	–	1	0.51	2	1.01
17.	95–99	–	–	–	–	–	–	1	0.51	–	–	–	–	1	0.51
	Total	**53**	**26.90**	**47**	**23.86**	**43**	**21.83**	**44**	**22.34**	**4**	**2.03**	**6**	**3.03**	**198**	**100.00**

Table 5.2: Distribution of Population by Age, Sex and Marital Status in the Village Old Changlang

Sl. No.	Age Group (yrs)	Unmarried				Married				Widower		Widow		Total	
		Male		Female		Male		Female							
		No.	%.	No.	%	No.	%	No.	%	No.	%	No.	%	No.	%
1.	0–4	17	4.02	18	4.26	–	–	–	–	–	–	–	–	35	8.27
2.	5–9	17	4.02	12	2.84	–	–	–	–	–	–	–	–	29	6.86
3.	10–14	26	4.02	28	6.62	–	–	–	–	–	–	–	–	54	12.77
4.	15–19	29	6.15	22	5.29	–	–	–	–	–	–	–	–	51	12.06
5.	20–24	15	6.86	6	1.42	1	0.24	4	0.95	–	–	1	0.24	27	6.38
6.	25–29	9	3.55	4	0.95	4	0.95	16	3.78	1	0.24	–	–	34	8.04
7.	30–34	6	2.13	2	0.47	6	1.42	9	2.13	1	0.24	–	–	24	5.67
8.	35–39	6	1.42	2	0.47	18	4.26	16	3.78	–	–	1	0.24	43	10.17
9.	40–44	2	1.42	1	0.24	15	3.55	11	2.60	1	0.24	2	0.47	32	7.57
10.	45–49	1	0.24	2	0.47	12	2.84	8	1.89	–	–	–	–	23	5.44
11.	50–54	–	–	–	–	7	1.65	5	1.18	–	–	1	0.24	13	3.07
12.	55–59	–	–	–	–	5	1.18	6	1.42	–	–	4	0.95	15	3.55
13.	60–64	1	0.24	–	–	5	1.42	6	1.42	–	–	2	0.47	14	3.31
14.	65–69	–	–	–	–	6	1.18	4	0.95	1	0.24	3	0.71	11	2.60
15.	70–74	1	0.24	–	–	5	1.42	–	–	3	0.71	2	0.47	11	2.60
16.	75–79	–	–	–	–	–	–	–	–	1	0.24	1	0.24	2	0.47
17.	80–84	–	–	–	–	1	0.24	–	–	–	–	–	–	1	0.24
18.	85–89	–	–	–	–	–	–	–	–	1	0.24	–	–	1	0.24
Total		**130**	**30.73**	**97**	**23.00**	**85**	**20.09**	**85**	**20.09**	**9**	**2.13**	**17**	**4.02**	**420**	**100.00**

Table 5.3: Distribution of the Population by Age Sex and Marital Status of the Population of Rangkatu Village

Sl. No.	Age Group (yrs)	Unmarried				Married				Widower		Widow		Total	
		Male		Female		Male		Female							
		No.	%	No.	%	No.	%	No.	%	No.	%	No.	%	No.	%
1.	0–4	18	3.85	22	4.71	–	–	–	–	–	–	–	–	40	8.56
2.	5–9	33	7.07	35	7.49	–	–	–	–	–	–	–	–	68	14.56
3.	10–14	25	5.35	30	6.42	–	–	–	–	–	–	–	–	55	11.78
4.	15–19	38	8.13	18	3.85	–	–	1	0.21	–	–	–	–	57	12.21
5.	20–24	11	2.35	5	1.07	3	0.64	9	1.93	–	–	–	–	28	5.99
6.	25–29	9	1.93	7	1.50	7	1.50	15	3.21	–	–	–	–	38	8.13
7.	30–34	–	–	1	0.21	15	3.21	12	2.57	–	–	–	–	28	5.99
8.	35–39	2	0.43	–	–	14	2.99	17	3.64	–	–	–	–	33	7.06
9.	40–44	–	–	–	–	19	4.07	16	3.42	–	–	1	0.21	36	7.70
10.	45–49	–	–	1	0.21	12	2.57	10	2.14	1	0.21	2	0.43	26	5.56
11.	50–54	1	0.21	–	–	9	1.93	3	0.64	–	–			13	2.78
12.	55–59		–	–	–	4	0.86	3	0.64	–	–	1	0.21	8	1.71
13.	60–64	1	0.21	–	–	4	0.86	3	0.64	1	0.21	2	0.43	11	2.35
14.	65–69	–	–	–	–	3	0.64	1	0.21	1	0.21	–	–	5	1.07
15.	70–74	–	–	–	–	2	0.43	2	0.43	–	–	1	0.21	5	1.07
16.	70–79	–	–	–	–	2	0.43	–	–	–	–	3	0.64	5	1.07
17.	80–84	–	–	–	–	–	–	–	–	4	0.86	4	0.86	8	1.71
18.	85–89	–	–	–	–	–	–	–	–	–	–	1	0.21	1	0.21
19.	90–94	–	–	–	–	–	–	–	–	1	0.21	–	–	1	0.21
20.	95–99	–	–	–	–	–	–	–	–	1	0.21	–	–	1	0.21
Total		**138**	**29.55**	**119**	**25.48**	**94**	**20.13**	**92**	**19.70**	**9**	**1.93**	**15**	**3.21**	**467**	**100**

within the age group of 10-14 yrs. This indicates that child marriage is not in practice in the village.

The table shows that 4 widowers and 6 widows are present in the village, whose percentages are 2.03 per cent and 3.05 per cent, respectively.

Table 5.2 shows the distribution of the population by age, sex and marital status of the population of Old Changlang Village. Out of the total population of 423, 130 male and 97 female are unmarried the percentage being 30.73 per cent and 22.93 per cent, respectively. On the other hand 85 male and 85 females are married the percentage being 20.09 per cent, respectively.

The maximum number of unmarried male falls in the age group of 15–19 yrs., i.e. 29 (6.25%) and unmarried females fall in the age group of 10–14 yrs., i.e. 28 (2.84%) and the maximum number of married male, i.e. 18 (4.26%) falls in the age group of 35–39 yrs. and married female, i.e. 16 (3.78%) each fall in the age groups of 25–29 yrs. and 35–39 yrs., respectively. There are no married individuals up to the age of 19 yrs. This indicates that child marriage in the village is not in practice. The table also shows that 9 widower and 17 widows are recorded in the village.

Table 5.3 shows the distribution of the population by Age, Sex and Marital status of the population of Rangkatu village. Out of the total population of 467, 138 males and 119 females are unmarried, the percentage being 29.55 per cent and 25.48 per cent, respectively.

On the other hand 94 males and 92 females are married and their percentage being 20.13 per cent and 19.70 per cent, respectively. The highest number of unmarried male is 38 (8.13%) which fall within the age group of 15–19 yrs. and unmarried females 35 (7.49%) which fall within the age group of 5–9 yrs. There are no married individual within the age groups of 10–14 yrs. This indicates that the child marriage is not practiced. The table also shows that 9 widowers and 15 widows are reported in the village, whose percentage are 1.93 per cent and 3.31 per cent, respectively.

Muklom Tangsas

The present study also includes Muklom Tangsas. The distribution of population by age, sex and marital alliances has been presented in the Tables 5.4, 5.5 and 5.6.

Table 5.4 shows the distribution of the population by age, sex and marital status of the population of Laktong village. Out of the total

Table 5.4: Distribution of Population by Age, Sex and Marital Status in the Village Laktong

Sl. No.	Age Group (yrs)	Unmarried				Married				Widower		Widow		Total	
		Male		Female		Male		Female							
		No.	%	No.	%	No.	%	No.	%	No.	%	No.	%	No.	%
1.	0–4	13	6.84	16	8.42	–	–	–	–	–	–	–	–	29	15.26
2.	5–9	11	5.79	12	6.32	–	–	–	–	–	–	–	–	23	12.11
3.	10–14	13	6.84	5	2.63	–	–	–	–	–	–	–	–	18	9.47
4.	15–19	13	6.84	10	5.26	–	–	–	–	–	–	–	–	23	12.11
5.	20–24	4	2.11	4	2.11	2	1.05	3	1.58	–	–	–	–	13	6.84
6.	25–29	4	2.11	2	1.05	1	0.53	3	1.58	–	–	–	–	10	5.26
7.	30–34	–	–	2	1.05	4	2.11	11	5.79	–	–	–	–	17	8.95
8.	35–39	–	–	–	–	10	5.26	6	3.16	1	0.53	1	0.53	18	9.47
9.	40–44	–	–	–	–	6	3.16	6	3.16	–	–	–	–	12	6.32
10.	45–49	–	–	–	–	6	3.16	2	1.05	–	–	1	0.53	9	4.74
11.	50–54	–	–	–	–	2	1.05	2	1.05	–	–	–	–	4	2.11
12.	55–59	–	–	–	–	1	0.53	–	–	–	–	–	–	1	0.53
13.	60–64	–	–	–	–	1	0.53	–	–	1	0.53	1	0.53	3	1.58
14.	65–69	–	–	–	–	1	0.53	1	0.53	1	0.53	2	1.05	5	1.05
15.	70–74	–	–	–	–	–	–	–	–	–	–	3	1.58	3	1.58
16.	75–79	–	–	–	–	–	–	1	0.53	–	–	–	–	1	0.53
17.	80–84	–	–	–	–	1	0.53	–	–	–	–	–	–	1	0.53
	Total	**58**	**30.53**	**51**	**26.84**	**35**	**18.42**	**35**	**18.42**	**3**	**1.58**	**8**	**4.21**	**190**	**100.00**

Table 5.5: Distribution of Population by Age, Sex and Marital Status in Village Simrang

Sl. No.	Age group (yrs.)	Unmarried				Married				Widower		Widow		Total	
		Male		Female		Male		Female							
		No.	%	No.	%	No.	%	No.	%	No	%	No.	%	No.	%
1.	0–4	10	4.78	8	3.83	–	–	–	–	–	–	–	–	18	8.61
2.	5–9	14	6.70	12	12.4	–	–	–	–	–	–	–	–	26	12.44
3.	10–14	20	9.57	14	6.70	–	–	–	–	–	–	–	–	34	16.27
4.	15–19	8	3.83	21	10.5	–	–	1	0.48	–	–	–	–	30	14.35
5.	20–24	4	1.91	6	2.87	4	1.91	4	1.91	–	–	–	–	18	8.61
6.	25–29	3.	1.43	–	–	1	0.48	1	0.48	–	–	–	–	5	2.39
7.	30–34	1	0.48	1	0.48	1	0.48	5	2.39	–	–	–	–	8	3.83
8.	35–39	2	0.96	1	0.48	6	2.87	11	5.26	–	–	–	–	20	9.57
9.	40–44	1	0.48	–	–	8	3.83	5	2.39	1	0.48	1	0.48	16	7.65
10.	45–49	–	–	–	–	7	3.35	4	1.91	–	–	–	–	11	5.26
11.	50–54	–	–	–	–	2	0.96	–	–	2	0.96	1	0.48	5	2.39
12.	55–59	1	0.48	–	–	2	0.96	1	0.48	–	–	–	–	4	1.91
13.	60–64	–	–	–	–	1	0.48	2	0.96	–	–	–	–	3	1.43
14.	65–69	1	0.48	–	–	1	0.48	1	0.48	–	–	2	0.96	5	2.39
15.	70–74	–	–	–	–	1	0.48	–	–	1	0.48	1	0.48	3	1.43
16.	75–79	–	–	–	–	–	–	1	0.48	–	–	1	0.48	2	0.96
17.	80–84	–	–	–	–	–	–	–	–	–	–	–	–	–	–
18.	85–89	–	–	–	–	1	0.48	–	–	–	–	–	–	1	0.48
19.	90–94	–	–	–	–	–	–	–	–	–	–	–	–	–	–
	Total	**65**	**31.1**	**63**	**30.14**	**35**	**16.75**	**36**	**17.22**	**4**	**1.91**	**6**	**2.87**	**209**	**100.00**

population of 190, 58 male and 51 females are unmarried and their percentages are 30.53 per cent and 26.84 per cent, respectively. On the other hand 35 (18.42%) males and 35 (18.42%) females are married. The highest number of unmarried male fall within the age groups of 0–4, 10–14 and 15–19 yrs., i.e. 13 (6.84%) in each group. And the highest number of unmarried females, i.e. 16 (8.42%) falls within the age group of 0–4 yrs. There are no married individuals from 0–14 yrs. which indicates that child marriage is not in practice. The table also shows that 3 widowers and 8 widows are present in the village, whose percentages are 1.58 and 4.21 per cent.

Table 5.5 shows the distribution of population by age, sex and marital status of the Mukloms of Simrang (New Thamlom) village. Out of the total 209 total individuals, 65 (31.10%) male and 63 (30.14%) females are unmarried. On the other hand 35 (16.75%) males and 36 (17.22%) females are married.

The maximum number of unmarried males falls in the age group of 10–14 yrs., i.e. 20 (9.57%) and unmarried females fall in the age group of 15–19 yrs., i.e. 21 (10.05%). And the maximum number of married males fall in the age group of 40–44 yrs., i.e. 8 (3.83%) and married females fall in the age group of 35–39 yrs., i.e. 11 (5.26%). There is no married individual up to the age of 14 yrs. This indicates that child marriage in the village is not in practice.

The table also shows that there are 4 widowers and 6 widows in the village.

Table 5.6 shows the distribution of population by age, sex and marital status of the Yanman village. The table reveals that out of the total 517 population, 169 (32.69%) males and 155 (29.98%) females are unmarried. On the other hand 82 (15.86%) males and 82 (15.86%) females are married.

The maximum number of the unmarried males fall in the age group of 5–9 yrs., i.e. 37 (7.16%) and females are 41 (7.93%) fall in each of the age group 5–9 and 10–14 yrs. And the maximum number of married males fall in the age group of 40–44 yrs., i.e. 21 (4.06%) and married females in the age group of 35–39 yrs., i.e. 18 (3.48%). There are no married individuals up to the age of 14 yrs.

This indicates that child marriage is not in practice in the village. The table also shows that there are 6 (1.16%) widowers and 23 (4.45%) widows in the village.

Table 5.6: Distribution of Population by Age, Sex and Marital Status in Village Yanman

Sl. No.	Age Group (Yrs.)	Unmarried				Married				Widower		Widow		Total	
		Male		Female		Male		Female							
		No.	%	No.	%	No.	%	No.	%	No.	%	No.	%	No.	%
1.	0–4	31	6.00	34	6.58	–	–	–	–	–	–	–	–	65	12.57
2.	5–9	37	7.16	41	7.93	–	–	–	–	–	–	–	–	78	15.09
3.	10–14	31	6.00	41	7.93	–	–	–	–	–	–	–	–	72	13.93
4.	15–19	28	5.41	25	4.83	–	–	3	0.58	–	–	–	–	56	10.83
5.	20- 24	18	3.48	11	2.13	4	0.77	3	0.58	–	–	–	–	36	6.96
6.	25–29	18	3.48	2	0.39	3	0.58	10	1.93	–	–	1	0.19	34	6.58
7.	30–34	1	0.19	1	0.19	7	1.35	16	3.09	–	–	2	0.39	27	5.22
8.	35–39	2	0.39	–	–	13	2.51	18	3.48	–	–	1	0.19	34	6.96
9.	40–44	2	0.39	–	–	21	4.00	6	1.16	–	–	3	0.58	32	6.19
10.	45–49	–	–	–	–	9	1.74	15	2.00	1	0.19	1	0.19	26	5.03
11.	50–54	–	–	–	–	7	1.35	4	0.77	–	–	–	–	11	2.13
12.	55–59	–	–	–	–	9	1.74	–	–	–	–	1	0.19	10	1.93
13.	60–64	–	–	–	–	1	0.19	3	0.58	1	0.19	6	1.16	11	2.13
14.	65–69	–	–	–	–	3	0.58	2	0.39	1	0.19	2	0.39	8	1.55
15.	70–74	1	0.19	–	–	3	0.58	1	0.19	1	0.19	2	0.39	8	1.55
16.	75–79	–	–	–	–	–	–	–	–	–	–	2	0.39	2	0.39
17.	80–84	–	–	–	–	1	0.19	1	0.19	1	0.19	1	0.19	4	0.77
18.	85–89	–	–	–	–	–	–	–	–	1	0.19	–	–	1	0.19
19.	90–94	–	–	–	–	1	0.19	–	–	–	–	–	–	1	0.19
20.	95–99	–	–	–	–	–	–	–	–	–	–	–	–	–	–
21.	100 +	–	–	–	–	–	–	–	–	–	–	1	0.19	1	0.19
	Total	**169**	**32.6**	**155**	**29.98**	**82**	**15.86**	**82**	**15.86**	**6**	**1.16**	**23**	**4.45**	**517**	**100.00**

Age at Marriage

The age at marriage cannot be answered in terms of universal application. It depends on many indigenous natural, social and economic conditions. The age at marriage in tribal society is considerably low. The analysis of age at marriage among the Tangsas revealed that child marriage is absent among them. The mean age at marriage of Lungchang female is 21.84 yrs. and the Muklom female is 21.94. On the other hand the range of age at marriage of Tangsa male is from 25–35 yrs. In the New Changlang village highest number of males is married at the age of 26 yrs. (6.25%) and it is followed by Rangkatu village where it is 25 yrs. (6.76%). In the Old Changlang village maximum number of males is married at the age of 28 yrs. (6.70%). Among the Mukloms in the Laktong village the maximum number of males married at the age of 30 yrs. (13.04%) and it is followed by 25 yrs. (6.85%) in Simrang village and 25 yrs. (8.06%) in the village Yanman.

Marriage Area

Regarding the marriage area it is found that normally they prefer to marry within their village. In certain cases they marry from outside the village, but the village exogamy is not the rule. Most of the marriages took place within a radius of 1 km, i.e. mostly within the village. The longest distance was found within the range of 40– 60 km.

Season of Marriage

It is a matter of convenience between the two families and it is decided upon by mutual agreement of both the families. The Tangsas usually prefer to marry at the time of their *Moh* festival. According to the villagers, the celebration of marriage during the *Moh* festival reduces the economic burden of the family as the same preparation fulfils the purpose of both the festival and marriage ceremony. They can marry at any time of the year depending upon the position of the moon. They consider the time between the new moon and full moon as auspicious for the celebration of marriage.

Preferential and Prohibition

In every human society some sort of prohibitions and preferences are attached concerning selection of mates for marriage. The most universal prohibition regarding marriage is the marriage between blood relationship. Among the Tangsas, parallel cousin marriage is allowed, but there are certain prohibitions that children of either brother are not allowed to marry as they belong to the same clan. The children of either sister may marry because a girl after marriage belongs to the other clan.

Preferential marriage, as is clear by the nomenclature, is the marriage custom in which some males and females are preferred for establishing matrimonial relationship. In such cases marriage is a means for uniting two families. The rules of preferential marriage are, however, customary and not written. Cross-cousin marriage is preferred among the Tangsas as the children belong to different clans.

In exceptional circumstances, widow marriage is allowed among the Tangsas. Polygamy is in general prohibited, but sometimes it occurs. As for example when a widow chooses her deceased husband's married brother the society permit such type of marriage. A widower after his wife's death can marry his deceased wife's sister (surrogate) with her consent.

Bride Price

Heavy bride price was prevalent among the Tangsas. But in recent years a change is noticed in amount of the items and materials.

Ways of Acquiring Mates

The ways in which mates can be acquired are indeed varied, particularly in the case of tribal communities. The tribal marriages are however, more on civil contract and not religious sacraments as among the advanced societies. The negotiated type of marriage is more prevalent among the Tangsas. The proposal for marriage is first put forwarded by the boy's family. The *Kamwa* (mediator) plays a significant role in arranging marriage ceremony.

There are differences of performing marriage on the sub-tribe level. Among the Lungchangs, the actual ceremony is held at the bride's family and the groom's party is to go the bride's house. Among the Mukloms the actual marriage ceremonies are preformed at groom's household. Following traditional procedure the bride is to come to the groom's household accompanied by the female members.

Earlier marriage by service was prevalent among the Tangsas. In this system the boy used to work for the girl's parents and stay at her residence to impress the girl and her parents. Marriage by service was common type of marriage among the tribal communities. Among the Tai Turungs also earlier marriage by service was practiced and heavy bride price was prevalent (Barua, 2001: 68). Though, it is not significant in recent years, but that custom is transformed into *bharutha* system, where all the expenses incurred in arranging and entertaining the guests in the bride's house on the day of marriage is borne by the groom's side (Barua, 2001: 68). As the Tangsas follow a patriarchal system a male child is preferred. But, the presence of bride price indicates the importance of females in their society.

Marriage Ceremony

The entire procedures of marriage pass through several stages. The *Kamwa*, the mediator or matchmaker plays an important role in the negotiation process. Marriage through negotiation is the common practice among the Tangsas. The *Kamwa* conducts negotiations with the guardians of the prospective groom and bride. This may happened in two ways– when a boy selects a girl, he talks to his parents about the girl. If his guardians found her suitable as bride, then they will send *Kamwa* to conduct the negotiation with the girl's family. Sometimes prospective bride is selected by the guardian itself. In such cases also they are to approach the mediator for negotiation.

The *Kamwa* goes to the girl's house with *Khaam* (rice-beer). If the girl's parents found the proposal suitable, they would accept the rice-beer, which was sent from the boy's family. Once the negotiation is finalized, the other procedures relating to marriage started.

Marriage by elopement is also found among the Tangsas. In such cases, both the families took measures to formalize their relations by performing marriage ritual.

Another type of marriage known commonly as advance marriage is practiced by the Tangsas. This type of marriage was common in earlier days. When the girl is the only child of their parents and still studying, then this type of marriage is preferred. In this type of marriage, bride is to stay with her parents for another one or two year even after her marriage. Sometimes bride is selected and some formalities are made by bride-groom's parents before one or two years of actual marriage.

Though various forms of marriages were prevalent among the Tangsas, in the past, but most popular and recognized form of marriage among the Tangsas was and still the marriage through negotiation, in which the society as a whole participated. Marriage is considered as an important sacrament and hence performs ritual, ceremonies and celebrates the occasion with the kin and community members. Marriage in the Tangsa society is a sacred bond of life-long partnership.

The celebration of marriage ceremony is a long process. Though the overall processes and values are similar, yet some differences are noticed in performing actual ritual, in different sub-groups of the Tangsas.

Role of *Kamwa* is significant among the Tangsas as a whole. The *Kamwa* acts as a mediator in negotiating the marriage. When the groom's family accepts the proposal, they fix a date with the *Kamwa* to visit the bride's family. Accordingly, the prospective groom and his parents along with the *Kamwa* go to the girl's family to fix the date of marriage and finalize the marriage proposal, so, that girl is reserved for him. They also discussed about the bride-price. As a token of acceptance, the *Kamwa* places before them a sum of Rs. 70.00 (Rupees seventy), which may be considered as an initial amount of bride-price.

Lungchang

The present study reveals that among the *Lungchangs*, the first ritual in connection with marriage is *Jungho*. This is normally performed about 2 months prior to actual marriage. It is the responsibility of the groom's parents to send certain materials to the bride's house to show their respect. The groom's parents collect some fishes and make 99 pieces out of it. Out of these, 55 fresh pieces of fish with 5 kg of rice and a bottle of pure rice-beer (*ruhi*) is ceremoniously sent to the bride's family. The mediator or *Kamwa* carries all these things to the bride's house on an auspicious day. This gift is particularly sent to honour the maternal uncles who along with his near kin members and relative arrange a feast to enjoy it. When the *Kamwa* carries all these things to the bride's house, due respect is shown to the *Kamwa*, by the bride's family after offering a bottle of rice-beer. The remaining 44 pieces of fish are dried in the groom's house, which are to be sent to the bride's house on the day of marriage. After the completion of ritual till the day of marriage, the prospective bride and groom are to follow certain restrictions. They are not allowed to talk freely with other boys and girls. There are some prohibitions in their movement also.

All the procedures reveal that the girl's family gets some importance in the marriage ceremony. Day before the day of marriage, the same

Kamwa is to perform his responsibility of visiting the bride's house. He is to carry a packet, which contains 39 pieces of the dried fishes, 25 kg of rice and a bottle of rice-beer from groom's house. Every packet which is sent to the bride's house should contain odd number of articles. Because, even number of articles are offered on the occasion of ritual related to death.

On the day of marriage, activities start from early morning. Early in the morning at about 4.00 a.m. the invitees and relatives of the groom gather in his house. The villagers also gather in the groom's house. The relatives make a new *Taan* (basket made of bamboo) where 25 kg of rice is packed. Then the remaining 5 pieces of dried fishes kept for the day of marriage and 100 kg of rice-beer are arranged in 5 different sizes of *Taam*. Now-a-day, instead of bamboo basket, plastic buckets are used to carry rice-beer. The same *Kamwa* carries rice in the new *Taam* covered with new white cloth. He is to lead the group to the bride's house. And the group walks in a line. The *Kamwa* is followed by the person who carries rice-beer. They are followed by the persons who carry 31 kg of rice and 2 male pigs. And the last one would be the bridegroom. In the bride's house, at first her maternal uncle or aunty has to open the *Taam* of rice. Then only, the ritual part begins. After that the pig is sacrificed. The liver of the pig is examined to understand the omen and to know the future of the couple by aged and experienced person. Then half part of the sacrificed pig and 1 *Taam* of rice-beer are given to the maternal uncle of the bride. After that, respect is shown to the *Kamwa* by giving Rs. 31.00 from bride's uncle and Rs. 31.00 from bride's parents, along with 5 pieces of pork are given to the *Kamwa* by the parents of the bride. The half part of the meat of the pork and rice-beer are distributed among the close maternal uncle of the bride. Pork and rice-beer is specially offered to the bride's father's and mother's sisters. Only after distributing the articles to the respective persons, the community feast is arranged. After the completion of community feast, all the empty vessels and the *Taam* are carried back to the groom's house. The groom's party returned back to the house along with the bride. On return journey also, the *Kamwa* lead the party, but he is followed by the bride. And the groom would be last on the line. The bride carries along with her *Wantam* (coin necklace), *Khanghum* (made of beads, *Jao* (*dao*), *Repunghaat* (cotton blanket), utensils, 1 bottle of rice-beer, pig meat (from neck portion) and personal dresses. On the next day, a feast is arranged in the groom's house where the kin-members and the villagers are entertained. After completion of one year of marriage, the bride brings chicks and a baby pig from her parental house to her husband's house.

Bride Price

Heavy bride-price was prevalent in earlier times. There are also many cases where even after the marriage; there is no end of demand. The bride's family takes advantage of marriage and occasional demands are made from time to time. The groom's family is to oblige the demand to maintain the cordial relation between two families. In recent years a case is reported where a few days after marriage bride's family demands a buffalo or the cost of a buffalo from the groom's family, which he is to pay.

It was reported by C.P. about her son's marriage.

> *At the time of marriage, girl's side demanded two mithuns and other materials. They even paid Rs. 20,000 for completing the marriage ceremony. After marriage a feast was arranged with pigs and rice beer where all the villagers were entertained. The elderly villager, who was conversant with the system, examined the liver of pigs and predicted all about the future of the couple.*

Another case was reported where M.J. has mentioned about the bride price.

> *In her marriage the husband's family had to give two pigs, 5 buckets of rice beer (representing different quantity and different names) and 5 buckets of rice cooked rice in different quantities, i.e. 11 kg, 9 kg, 7 kg, 5 kg and 3 kg. From her house 1 lota, two plates of brass metal and 1 dao, 1 full bamboo tube of rice beer, rice 1 kg and her own ornaments.*

It is customary that after a few days the bride is to visit her parents with her husband. But in her case as the husband had to leave for service he could not accompany her. Her mother in law went with her and they stayed there for a day.

Love marriage is frequent phenomenon among the Tangsas. After attaining the age of puberty, the Tangsa girls are given a lot of freedom and privileges to select their life partner. Of course, such marriages are later on socially recognized by performing the marriage rituals.

B.J. (23 yrs.) reported that her marriage as follows–It was a love marriage and no ceremony or formalities were observed in their relationship. When she was 4 months pregnant, boy's parents send a Kamwa (mediator) to her parents with the marriage proposal. A bottle of rice-beer was sent with the Kamwa. Her parents accepted rice-beer which indicates their approval. After initial acceptance, rice-beer and money were sent to her parent's house by her in-laws to show their happiness and respect for accepting the proposal.

The marriage ceremony was not celebrated in an elaborate way. As she was 4 months pregnant during that time, they wanted to formalize it early. Among the Tangsas, as per customary law, the delivery of the child has to take place in the house of the husband. Therefore, the marriage ceremony must be held before the approach of delivery period. Because of this law, her in-law did not get sufficient time for the arrangement of the ceremony. Therefore, it was done in a simple way. The formal, elaborate ceremony in which gifts as an honour are given to maternal uncle and relatives was not done.

On the day of marriage, the Kamwa (mediator), her husband's parents, relatives and some of the villagers went to her parent's home. They carried 1 pig and rice-beer. The pig was sacrificed in her parent's house and the liver was examined by some experienced person to understand omen of the future of the couple. Then a small community feast was arranged, where some of the relatives and villagers were entertained. After completion of feast, she along with her husband, kin members, villagers and Kamwa proceeded to her husband's place before sunset. Her parents made arrangement to send rice-beer, rice-beer juice, local rice, cotton shawl, dao and some brass utensils with her as a customary rules and convention. From that day, they started as new life together. On the next day, a small community feast was arranged in her husband's house where the relatives and the villagers were entertained.

Muklom

A slight variation is found in celebrating marriage ceremony among the Mukloms. The person after marriage would prefer to have his own separate establishment. Eldest male member, usually father is treated as head of the family, but important decision relating to the family is taken collectively by adult member. Both the male and female members of a family equally contribute their share in maintaining the family. However, the contribution of womenfolk may be considered more in the sense that they are to engage themselves from dawn to dusk in various domestic works, i.e. pounding of rice, cooking, fetching water, looking after the children besides going to the agricultural fields. But as a patriarchal society, the Tangsas as a whole have a preference for son.

Among the Mukloms the final marriage ceremony is observed in the groom's household and the bride is to come for the ceremony following their traditions and customs. The Muklom marriage ceremony is performed in two ways—(a) *Nakpinh* and (b) *Nakhow*. The first one is more elaborate where large amount of articles are needed and the procedures are lengthy. While the second type of marriage is a bit simple. Depending on the socio-economic condition the respective family decides the ways of marriage.

In the first type of marriage, i.e. *Nak-pinh*, 60 relatives related to the bride are invited on the wedding day. It is a special invitation from the groom's side. In *Nak-kha* only 30 relatives of the brides are invited. The special invitees are selected from the first and second uncle, aunty (both maternal and paternal side), cousin etc. These relatives are provided with either pig or buffalo meat pieces along with rice-beer (each containing 10 kg). Normally, four pigs or buffaloes are required to give to the bride's family. The groom family also has to provide rice (for preparing rice-beer) and sufficient quantity of rice for the marriage, to the bride's family. On the first day of marriage, the male members which includes villagers, close relatives of the bride and elderly ladies proceed directly to the groom's house.

Among the Tangsas marriage is an important social institution. The religion and custom prevalent among them prescribe a set of rule, ceremonies and ritual procedures to formalize the matrimonial ties. These norms and rules are by and large observed by the Tangsas, though there are minor variations on the basis of sub-tribe.

The present study among the Lungchangs and Mukloms reveal that *Kamwa* plays an important role in matchmaking and mediator among the Tangsas. Bride price or giving valuable gifts to the girl's family is well accepted. Among the Mukloms also initial discussion was initiated by the *Kamwa*. It is the responsibility of boy's parents to send *Kamwa* with a bottle of rice-beer. If it is accepted by the girl's family, then they proceed to the next stage of marriage, i.e. formal discussion between the two families with the help of *Kamwa.* If the discussion turns favourable, a token amount of cash (equivalent to Rs. 70.00) is offered to the girl's family. This token amount is known as *Thaang Dang.*

After the fixation of the date of marriage, the groom's family starts arranging for the final marriage ceremony. The significant feature of the marriage ceremony among the Mukloms is that ceremony is observed in the groom's house.

Marriage Ceremony

Among the Mukloms, when date of marriage is fixed, the girl has to come to her maternal uncle's house one day before the marriage. Three days are required to complete the rituals relating to marriage ceremony. The first day of marriage is full of enjoyment and merriment. Every member of the boy's and girl's relatives participates in the management of the marriage rituals. The near relatives of the groom are engaged in performing the rituals. The boy's parents prepare thirty buckets of rice-beer each containing 10 kg of rice. Invitation is specially made to the girl's uncle, aunties and sisters. The male members and the elderly females may directly go to the boy's house whereas; the relatives and the friends of girl's assemble at her uncle's house. The hectic moment at the boy's house starts early in the morning at 6.00 a.m. Relatives of the boy from far away villages may reach the previous day. In the meantime, the bride accompanied by relatives and friends proceed to the groom's house for the marriage ceremony. While entering the gate, the girl is asked to scoop rice three times. These are to be placed in a bowl and the bowl has to be filled up with three scoops only. Then the formal ceremony started. On the first day two pigs are sacrificed. Thirty packets of meat are prepared, which are meant for bride's uncle, sister and other blood relations. Equal number of packets is kept aside for other relatives of the bride which are later on distriuted among the members considering significant relationship and closeness with the bride's family. Some portion of meat from the first pig is prepared and served to the villagers in the boy's house.

In the meantime, uncles, aunties and sisters of the bride are served rice plates with meat called '*Tilkhoong*'. Before taking the meal, they recite hymns and prayers in the name of the clan titles of the bride and groom, wishing a happy conjugal life for the couple. The maternal uncle of the bride tie thread in both hands of the bride and groom for their happy married life (if the ritual is performed by means of '*Nakhow*', the packet of meat is reduced to half, i.e. 15 packets). After the feast also, singing and dancing continues along with drinking of rice-beer. Dance and songs continue till the next day. The second pig is slaughtered for a ritual called *Saamkhingloh.* The meat of this pig is divided into three parts. The first part, i.e. the neck portion is given to the maternal uncle of the bride. The second part comprises one hind leg and fore leg, which is separately kept for bride's parents. This portion of pig is carried to the bride's house by the relatives of the bride who accompanied her to the groom's house. The third part comprising one hind leg and fore leg is cooked and served to the active workers who help the groom's family in the management of marriage ceremony. Then, the bride with her friends and relatives are escorted by the *Kamwa* halfway to her home. In the midway, *Kamwa* performs a small ritual by placing branches of trees on the pathway. Here, a pouch of boiled meat is served to the friends of bride who accompanied her. The *Kamwa* chanted *mantras*, wishing a happy return. After this, the bride is accompanied by her friends and relatives to her house. And the *Kamwa* returns back to the groom's house.

On the same day, third pig called *nowa wakpin* is sent to the bride's house by friends and relatives of the groom as a mark of respect to the bride's family. Next day a grand feast is arranged by the bride's parents where the villagers and close relatives of the groom's parents are invited. Chest portion of the pork (*nowa wakpin*) is given to the groom's relatives and friends, who had carried the pig to the bride's house. Rice-beer, rice, meat etc. are served lavishly to all the members present there. A fourth pig called *hotey wakree* is offered to the bride's maternal uncle, from the groom's side. The groom with friends and relatives carry this pig to the bride's maternal uncle's house and personally handover it to the uncle. This is particularly done to show due respect and honour to maternal uncle. The pig is sacrificed and a grand party is arranged where the guardians, relatives and friends of the bride and groom take part. This type of marriage is very elaborate and only socio-economically sound families may go for it; while the majority of the families perform their marriage by means of '*Nakhow*' system.

After the completion of marriage ceremony, the bride stays at her parent's house, normally for 1 to 2 yrs. But if she becomes pregnant during this period, she is to move to her in-laws house for delivery. Because according to the Tangsa's customs delivery must take place in her husband's house.

A case is reported here where marriage took place among the same clan members:

> *N.N. (35 yrs.) reported that their marriage took place 6 yrs. ago. Both the husband and the wife are from the same village and belong to the same clan. Among the Tangsas marriage among the same clan is strictly prohibited and the offenders are expelled from the society. They were aware about this custom, but they could not avoid the relationship and decided to marry. When their parents and family members came to know about their relationship they strongly opposed it. Even her brother physically assaulted her. They made all their efforts to convince them that such type of marriage would bring misfortune to the family. As she was pregnant during that time there were no other formalities than to formalize the relationship. No formal ritual was performed, but simple feast was arranged to the villagers to announce their relationship. Though they are accepted by the society yet the common villagers do not consider them as an ideal couple.*

The Tangsas reckoned their relationship through the male lines and kinship bond is very strong among them. Their kinship terminology may be called classificatory, as they use certain common terms of address, both for lineal relatives and certain category of collateral relatives.

The relationship between kin members is very strong and is inseparable at all situations. Kin members have specific roles and obligations to one another. They are dependent on each other in every sphere of their life. In religious ceremonies and rituals, their obligation and responsibility is clearly visible.

The kinship terminology may be called classificatory, since every sub-tribe use common terms of address for both collateral and lineal relatives. For example among the Lunchang Tangsas the term 'Ewi' is used to address the father's mother, as well as mother's mother. On the other hand, the Muklom Tangsas address their mother's mother as 'Evih'. The same word is used for father's mother as well. It is significant to note that among the Mukloms, the term 'Evih' is also used to address for grandmother's mothers and fathers. The term of address for father is 'Ewah' among the Mukloms and the mother is 'Ewih'. While among the Lunchang Tangsas, the terms of address for mother are 'Enyung' and father is 'Ewa' which is more or less similar with the Muklom Tangsas.

Among the Lungchang Tangsas, the father's father and the mother's father are addressed by the same term 'Etai'. In the same way, the father's father's sister's husband (FFSH), the sister's husband's father (SHF) and the mother's brother (MB) have the same term of address, i.e. 'Ephu'. 'Ephu' is also used to address one's own brother (elder) and also to his father's elder brother's son (FEBS).

Among the Muklom Tangsas, daughter-in-law addresses her father-in-law as 'Ehocha' and mother-in-law as 'Enichah'. 'Ephoh' is the term to address all elder's brother of the same father or father's brother's son. 'Enoh' is used to refer the younger brothers and sisters of the same clan. The elder sisters are addressed as 'Enah'. It is believed by the Muklom Tangsas that the same term used to address various relatives keep the family relation together.

A brief description of kinship terminology reflects that terms of address are slightly different among the Lungchang and the Muklom Tangsas. The category of relatives included under the same term is also different. This confirms that in certain cases there are minor variations in the sub-tribe level.

The family level relationship among the Tangsas is very cordial. It is reflected in their day-to-day life as well as on various special occasions. In the community and village level also they maintain cordial relation. But among the Tangsas, clan members play more significant role in all the occasions. Various socio-religious ceremonies may also be confined within the boundary of clan members. But this does not mean that village level relationship is loosening. In recent years a significant change emerges in the relations due to occupational change. The educational and occupational opportunities have developed a sense of individuality among the Tangsas.

6
Religious System

The study of religion is a subject matter of interest from wide perspective. It is one of the universal and pervasive institutions in human society. The beliefs, thought and action with which religion is concerned could be found at all levels of culture, primitive or civilized. Religion may be defined as a "set of beliefs, emotional attitudes, and practices by means of which a group of people attempts to cope with ultimate problems of human life." Every society has religious codes which act as regulator of human conduct and behaviour of the individuals in that society. This intimate interrelation between religion and society are reflected in various socio-religious activities of a community. "One might say that all that appears to be social is in fact religious and all that appears religious is in fact social" (Dumont and Pocock, 1957:20). On the level of religion, it has been noted that various festivals have given them an opportunity for developing community sentiments. It is agreed by most of the scholars that the essential function of religion is the regulations, maintenance and sentiments on which the constitution of a society depends. As a part of religion, various festivals are observed by the ethnic communities all over the world. A festival or fist is an event, usually staged by a local community, which centres' on some theme, sometimes on some unique aspects of the community. Festivals are an essential part of the socio-cultural life of the people. They represent a colourful heritage of an ethnic community. Some part of every festival has religious significance. Religion is the institutionalized set of belief men hold about supernatural forces. Thus, there is a very close relationship between society and religion.

The life and culture of the Tangsas are strongly religious oriented. With regard to religion, it was reported "they have their own tribal religion which speaks of Nature worship. They believe that different aspects

Mother Nature rule and guide human destiny". (Baveja). Traditionally, the Tangsas believed in animistic faith and animals were sacrificed to please the deities and spirits. They have their own religious beliefs and practices. But in course of time, the impact of Buddhists, Hinduism and indigenous tribal faiths are visible among the Tangsas. Most of the religious rites and rituals, ceremonies and festivals are associated with the agricultural activities. Though, basically similar religious faiths are maintained by the Tangsas as a whole, yet uniqueness of each sub-tribe is visible in various socio-religious life. Moreover, each village has its own time schedule and highly systematic mechanism for proper organization and celebration of a festival and other cultural events. In most cases, dates are not fixed once for ever and are normally determined by the village community according to their convenience. The *lungwang* (village headman) and his council decide the date and time frame for celebration of each festival. The name of festival differs from one village to another. The village community over a period of time has evolved a systematic mechanism for observation of ceremonies and festivals in their own village.

Pre-harvest and post-harvest festivals are celebrated at the community level. However, certain festivals are confined within the individual family. Throughout the year, various festivals and rituals are performed according to their traditional faith. Their *Jhum* cultivation is supposed to start in December-January and by October-November all the *Jhum* crops were harvested. They cultivate mainly paddy, maize, chilies, tapioca, arum, sweet potatoes and millets in their *jhum* field. These crops are sown in January-February and harvested in June- July. *Jhum* paddy sown in April-May is harvested in October-November. Since 1947, the Tangsas have started wet paddy cultivation in the hills as well as plains in Changlang district. The significant feature of these cropping is that their cultural and religious life is scheduled around these agricultural calendars.

Most of the festivals are marked by offering of prayers to *Lord Rangs Frah* for well-being and betterment of the entire village community and worship with reverence. *Lord Rang Frah* is considered as the supreme pantheon and their religion may be termed as *Rang Frahism*. They also have faith and worship various deities, e.g. *Thungja Chamja* (Lakshmi, custodian of wealth), *Hum Matai* (Family deity). Besides, they have faith in various malevolent and benevolent spirits and are worshipped as and when situation demands. They believe that the displeasure of spirits is the major source of human sufferings. They have faith in body and soul and possession.

The religious philosophy of the Tangsas as a whole is same, but there are slight variations among the sub-tribe level. Here effort has been made to describe the religious beliefs and practices of the Lungchangs and the Mukloms, the two major sub-tribes.

The main festivals celebrated by the Lungchangs are Moh, Parang etc., and that of the Mukloms are Mol, Kungtom and Chemtuk.

Religious Ceremonies of the Lungchang Tangsas

The Lungchangs believe in their traditional tribal religion. Their religious beliefs may easily be traced from the various festivals, ancestral worship, ritual activities etc. They believe in malevolent and benevolent spirits and deities and rituals are performed to propitiate them on various occasions. And this reflects their faith in their animistic tribal religion. To appease the deities, they sacrifice different animals. Pigs and fowls are sacrificed in most of the religious ceremonies, both in the family and community level.

Family Level Rituals

Wunangthat/Wukakak

This ritual is performed at family level to worship home deity (*Hum Matai*). It is performed to secure protection against diseases, evil spirits and enemies of the family. A fowl is sacrificed by the head of the family and the legs of the fowl acts as an omen. By observing the legs, the expert may foresee about the future of the family members. This ritual is performed once or twice a year in presence of all the family members.

Parong

This festival is also referred as *Harong* by the Lungchangs. *Harong* is celebrated in the month of June when *jhum* crops like millet (*konidhan*) are ready for harvesting. Worship is started by sacrificing pigs and fowls to appease the Lord *Hakhusome*. The festival is enjoyed by all the villagers with music and dance. They are enjoying the festival with a sumptuous feast.

Narong/Nahrim/Chamrim

The Narong festival is celebrated by the Lungchangs at the time when wet paddy crops gets ripened and *jhum* crops are ready for harvesting. This festival has socio-economic significance, as nobody is allowed to go for reaping the crops without performing this ritual. It is usually done in the month of November last or December. In this ritual a pig or a fowl are slaughtered and sacrificed in the name of the spirit of the crops. On that day all the villagers irrespective of male, female and children participate in the festival and enjoyed the feast where plenty of foods, meat and drinks are served. It is normally performed near the main canal of the paddy field. This ritual is performed to appease the spirit of the crops for good production and expecting the same for successive crops.

It is also referred that on that particular day three bundles of the paddy straw are brought and placed on the spot earmarked for the ritual in the field. Blood of the animals is sprinkled on the bundle of the paddy. These bundles are brought and kept in a particular spot at home. In the next cropping season, the paddy seeds from this bundle are mixed with the seeds sown in the next season. It is believed that this enhances the productivity of the crops.

Poum Thong

This ritual is performed when a pregnant lady suffers from sickness, prolonged diseases, weakness or any other health related problems. It is believed that evil spirits are responsible for such problems. A pig and a fowl are scarified by the priest to propitiate the spirit.

Naw-Nagot

This ritual is performed at the time of piercing the earlobes of the new born. A pig or a fowl is sacrificed on this occasion. By examining the pig's lever or the fowl's legs the future of the baby may be read.

Marongphut/Jachum

This ritual is performed when a family member faces any accident. It is believed that some spirits are responsible for such accident. A fowl is sacrificed by the priest (*sama*) to appear such spirits.

Moh

During the *Moh* festival, which is celebrated in the month of May, a ritual known as *Him Rom/Hum-Rom* is performed. The presence of all family members is a must in this ceremony. The father or the eldest son is to pour food and rice-beer on every household item, where the beys were fastened in the morning. By chanting certain *mantras*, they pour rice-beer three times over all the objects.

The following rituals are performed by individual family who have faced an incidents recently, i.e. sometimes before this year's *Moh* festival or after the last year's *Moh* festival.

(i) A ritual known as *Mangrei* or *Mangit* is performed to propitiate the soul of a member of family who dies in recent years. It is believed that the departed soul remains within the house till this ritual is performed. Hovering of such departed soul may create problems. So, this ritual is performed by sacrificing a fowl in the name of the deceased person. The real reason behind performing this ritual is to make the soul aware that he/she is no more a member of this family and has left for the *walim* (the other world).

(ii) They celebrate a ritual known as *Him-Mtai* by sacrificing cattle to propitiate the spirit responsible for the welfare and prosperity of the family. While performing this ritual, they observe certain taboos, by refraining oneself from eating certain kinds of food and visiting certain places. They are to observe these taboos, until *Pay-Tasai* is done by sacrificing a pig.

(iii) In case of newly married woman, a ritual is observed in the husband's house to initiate the daughter-in-law. Normally, a pig is sacrificed as an initiation rite and after performing this ritual, she is considered as a member of her husband's family.

(iv) In case of construction of new house, a pig is sacrificed to please the spirit called *Him-Mtai* (home deity). It is believed that home deity may feel offended when the original dwelling house is dismantled.

(v) When a family makes new *Nong* (drum) a pig is sacrificed as a mark of welcoming it to the family.

The survival of a community always depends on agricultural practices. Agricultural practices on the other hand depend on nature. It is a universal practice that each community or tribe perform certain religious rites and celebrate certain festivals which are centered round the agricultural practices.

Community Level Ritual

The Lungchangs celebrate mainly two festivals in a year. These festivals have religious significance and exclusively performed according to their own way. These two festivals are celebrated both at the family level as well as community level. These festivals are:

(1) The Moh Festival
(2) The Parong Festival.

The *Moh* is celebrated by the Lungchangs for a maximum period of 3-5 days, though the main celebration continues for three days. In the *Moh* festivals, the roles of certain members are considered significant. First the role of *Lamshiwa* (leader of the dance, i.e. the person entitled to lead the dancers while dancing) is significant. He is selected from a particular clan and his leadership is continued on suitability of their partnerships in the celebration. Then the *Nong-Rom-tang* (a particular family/house is selected who are to perform a ritual specially dedicated for keeping the *Nongs* for that year). In *Nongbut* (another family ritual) the *Nongs* are brought to a halt on the last day of the dance. The owner is to keep the *Nong* in safety after the concluding ceremony. It is a taboo to take away the *Nong* from this house without following certain norms. They are allowed to take it away only two days prior to the celebration of *Moh* festival. The roles played by these personalities, i.e. *Lamshiwa, Nongrom-Tang* and *Nongbut-Tang* are significant and as it has been referred that their partnership continued on the basis of their suitability of performing *Moh* festival. If the yield of the crops shows a poor quantity/ quality or if any misfortune occurs, then it is believed that these three persons are responsible for it. To overcome it, they have a convention to change the members for the next year. Contrary to that the partnership would continue for the successive years, if they get a good harvest. The *Nong*, being the chief musical instrument for the groups, visiting every household in the village, is the most important feature of their celebration.

The *Moh* festival continues for three days. The first day is known as *Nyapsik Sha*, the second and third day are known as *Rom-Rom-Sha* and *Mohchim Shah,* respectively. The final day is referred as *Nongbut Sha.*

The day before the *Nyapsik Sha*, is referred as *Nongking Sha*. The preparation of *Moh* celebration is done on this day. The *Nongs* are particularly repaired on this day. Necklace, beads, *jangbangs* (caps made of can, which are used during festivals) and clothes to decorate themselves are repaired and cleaned if necessary. The housewives remained busy in cleaning and preparing for the festival.

Nyapsik Sha

This is the first day of festival. With the day break, the male members from each household set out to jungles to fetch *Nyap* (phyrinum pubinar vag) commonly called leaves. The leaves that are fetched for the festivals are known as *Nyap-Sha*. Collection of the *Nyap* is mainly done for the rites and rituals (*Him-rom* or *Nong rom* etc.) that would be done on the second day of the *Moh*. In obtaining the *Nyap-Sha*, the tools like *daos*, knives etc. are not used. It should be obtained by hands only. It is a custom not to give the *Nyap-Sha* to members belonging to other clans. So, if some individuals are unable to procure *Nyap-Sha*, normally request the members from their own clan to collect it on their behalf.

By noon, the men folk dancers, (mostly youth and the middle aged) turned up carrying their *Nongs* and gather at a house called *Lamkhet Him* (the same house is referred as *Nong-rom Him*). The dance is supposed to begin from this house all the time, until decided different way. The dancers, called *Nong-winh* are dressed up at this house. The women folk do not participate in the dance on *Nyapsik Sha*. Every dancer attained in traditional gear begins beating their *Nongs* who dance in the courtyard of *Nong-rom Him*. The *Lamshi-wa* leads the dance and *Nong-winh* follows him. After dancing briefly, they take rest for some time, when the owner of the house serves rice-beer. The members visit each household, dancing for some time. This process of visiting every household in the village, playing *Nong* is known as *Kengho* or the *Keng-Shok*. It is not obligatory on the part of the *Lamshi-wa* to begin the songs and any of the *Run-winh* (dancers) in the group who has knowledge of the songs can begin first. It is then repeated by others in chorus. When it gets dark, the *Nong-wink* retires to respective homes.

Rom-Rom Sha

The second day is called *Rom-Rom-Sha* which is elaborately linked with a series of ritual proceedings. It is considered as a real celebration of *Moh* because the real cause of observing *Moh* lies behind performing it.

Preparations for the *Him-rom* start in every household from the early morning. The head of the family cuts *kom* (round shaped brass metal) into minute three pieces in the presence of all family members. He chants while he cuts the *kom*.

Rice-beer specially prepared for this day is called *Jau-sah*. It is mainly consumed by the male members of the family, which may also be shared by others if they belong to the same clan. They make required number of beys out of sah. The beys are fastened to the various household items, e.g. musical instrument, *Chok khu* (skull of a deer), *Waknghi-khu* (skull of a wild boar or a pig), *Loi-khu* (skull of a buffalo), *Wu-thau* (a structure with a small opening made from woven bamboo splits to keep the fowls), *Wak-khung* (a large wooden block use to give fodder to the pigs), *Kalung* (door), *Rangkai* (a self on the wall to keep utensils), *Kharang* (a shelf above the fire place to dry fire-wood), *Laleichong* (ladder) in the evening.

After that rites are performed by sacrificing a pig or fowl according to their economic condition. Soon after this, members of every household leave for their agricultural fields carrying with them *Wutai-tok* (roasted egg), *Wutai-khong* (shells of the roasted egg), *Wongbaan* (rice soaked in water), *Jan-rei* (rice-beer) and *Kom-khanh-maan* (kom that was cut in the morning). These items are offered to appease *Tungja chamja* in the agricultural field. *Maanrung* (a small bamboo platform) is raised in the agricultural field. After offering all the items in the *maanrung*, they return back to the village. They sing sasai all along to the way back to the village. The observance of this *Pikrom* ritual was prevalent among the *Tangsas* for a long time. Today it has lost its significance due to shifting of *jhum* cultivation to wet cultivation.

At present, as usual the *Runn winh* (dancers) begin the *Keng shok* from the *Nongrom him*. On *Rom-Rom-sha*, the women folk, dressed in their traditional attire come forward for dancing. They need not start their dance from *Nong-rom-Him* and is required to visit each and every house in the village.

Both the groups stop dancing while it gets dark, to attend *Him-rom* at respective houses. The presence of all the family members is a must in this ceremony. The father or the eldest son is to pour food and rice-beer on every household item where the *beys* were fastened in the morning. They chant different words before every object and pour rice-beer three times over all the *beys*.

After *Him-rom*, the *Nongwinh* go back to the same house referred to as *Nongrom-Him*, where the *Nongs* are treated ceremoniously by the owner of the house. Just before reaching the *Nongrom-Him*, the *Lamshi-*

wa beats the shing indicating their arrival, so, that arrangement are made to receive them. They are received at the door-step by the owner of the *Nongrom-Him*, one by one offering them a handful of cooked rice mixed with *chingki* (ginger), *simlang* (black salt locally extracted) and bits of pork. The other persons who are assisting the owner offer them *jau* (rice-beer). The *Lamshi-wa* now beating the *shing* leads the *Nongwinh* to dance three rounds inside the house.

The *Nongrom-wa* selects two of the *Nongs* called *Rom-Nong* and fastens *bey* to both of these *Nongs* which they consider represent all other *Nongs*. A selected elderly person plays the *Rom Nong* who chants three times *Tunglap-Chamlap* (good harvest).

A little later following the *Nong-rom*, the dance is again resumed and this time they are to dance and play *Nongs* inside the house. The significant feature is that they may pass the *Nong* to any member or guests who assemble there. The youths, consisting of boys, girls and even children do not wish to miss this opportunity to dance by playing *Nongs* (the persons who dance need not put their traditional dresses).

The *Nongs* are always assembling at one place before moving from house to house. The *Nongs* are entertained by the host serving rice-beer and meat. The families who could afford may serve cooked food to the *Nongs*.

The youth are especially interested to accompany *Sasai*. Every member of the household is free to take part in singing and dancing following the rule that it should be confine within the house (In earlier occasions *Nongs* are used only by the dancers who dress up with traditional attain and women are not allowed to use *Nong*).

Mohchim Sha

The third and the fourth days are commonly known as *Mohchim Sha*. The dance keeps on going within the house for two consecutive days. The group of dancers, playing *Nongs*, keeps visiting the houses which go on continuously in all these days but in a sequential manner. Beating of *bongs* and *shings* can also be heard in those household who possess it.

The *Sasai* predominates the *Mohchim* days. Different groups of people go with one's own age group who either sing *Sasai* or play *Bongs* while others go for playing *Nongs*. The elderly people assemble around the hearth and sing *Bajaang sai*. The youth hardly turn out for *Basaang sai*, because they do not understand the actual meaning it carries.

The language used in the song is unintelligible to them. Only the old and elderly people who understand the meaning take interest in singing *Baijaang sai*. Some elderly people from nearby village also join the host who continuously sing day and night. The youth, therefore, prefer to sing *Sasai* or to play *Nongs* and *Bongs*. In the meantime, the *Nongwinh* try their best to complete the visit of every household before dawn.

Nangbut Sha

This is the last day of *Moh* festival. The guests started to leave for their home at the break of the day. Before noon, the *Nongwin* (who danced on the first and second day in complete traditional attire) assemble to put off their traditional festival dresses. The *Kengshok*, on the concluding day commences a bit earlier than the previous two days so as to bring the celebration to an end not later than noon. So, when dances begin, the *Lamshi-wa* quicken their pace of movement and just whisks away in front of every house so that they are not delayed. Having danced at all the places, the *Lamshi-wa* finally leads the *Nong-winch* towards the *Nongbut-Him* with the accompanying music of *Nongsai*. The *Lamshi-wa* beats the *Kangrang Hai-shing* just before they get into the *Nongbut-Him*. Then, after dancing for the last three rounds one by one who are received at the step of the house by the owner of the *Nongbut-Him*. Here they are received in the same way as it was done for the second day, i.e. *Rom-Rom-Sha* celebration. The playing of *Nongs* comes to a halt with the playing of *Chomlang-tom* by a selected elderly person. The celebration of *Moh* thus concluded and the *Nongs* are left there in the shelves in the *Nongbut-Him* for at least two days after which the owner of the *Nongs* would collect it from there. It is taboo not to collect it before that and it should not be played after this until the time of next year's celebration.

As it is a harvest festival, the women play an important role in the *Moh* festival. The women started to weave beautiful *lungi*, locally known as *Khat-nei* and *mekhela* (*Neibang*) as the festival day approaches. They are to weave *khat-nei* for all the members of the family, excluding the children. They also repair their necklaces for wearing in the festival. They started to prepare rice-beer (locally called *Jau*) a week before the festival.

During the festival days, on the first, second and fifth day, womenfolk mostly remain busy at home serving rice-beer and food etc. to the dancers and guests. However, on the third and the fourth day, womenfolk in their festive dresses take part in the dances, which continue from house to house.

Parong Festival

Parong festival is also known as *Harong* festival and normally celebrated after few days of *Moh* festival. This festival is also related to agricultural activities and is celrebrated in the month of June. The festival continued for two days. However, in this festival, no musical instruments are used and festival is observed by singing, dancing, eating and drinking rice-beer.

The date of the festival is not fixed like the *Moh* festival. The *gaon burah* (village headman) arrange a meeting where all the youth are invited. After discussion, the date of the festival is fixed considering the convenience of the villagers. In the meeting, responsibilities like collection of donation, fire-wood, rice, rice-beer, utensils etc. are allotted among the youth. Some youths are given the charge of arranging chickens, pigs for the purpose of sacrificing in the festival. In the same way arrangement is made to organize the community feast, where cow or buffalo is a must. Responsibility is also given to different families for preparing rice-beer as large quantity of rice-beer is needed for the community feast.

Parong or *Harong* festival is celebrated for two days in the month of June. The festival starts with a ritual which is performed at the main entrance of the village. In this festival, the role of the priest is most significant (as the priest must belong to a particular clan). A pig and a fowl are sacrificed by the priest. Sacrifice is done to propitiate the land deity (*Ha-Tai*). The lever of the pig and legs of the fowl are examined to know about the future.

On the first day, the youth go to the jungle early in the morning to collect some branches of trees. The branches (*pushei*) are designed by removing barks on one side and from top to bottom; criss-cross sign are designed. Then these branches are fixed on both sides of the village at the main entrance of the village. The sight looks very beautiful. The youth remained busy for preparation of the feasts.

The animals needed for the ritual are brought to the spot. Some elderly persons accompanied by the priest erect a small bamboo platform to keep the offerings. When the arrangement is completed, a pig and a chicken are sacrificed by the priest. Some portion of it like the chicken wings, legs, head and the tail of the pig are offered at the bamboo platform. Sacrifice is done to propitiate the land deity (*Ha-Tai*). The lever of the pig and legs of the fowl are examined to know about the future. The omen is seen by examining the position of the legs of the sacrificed chicken or the shape and size of the lever of the sacrificed pig.

The youth then make the arrangement for community feast. Rice-beer which is prepared by the womenfolk is brought to the spot. The rice and meat are prepared by the youth and the male members. When the arrangements are completed, all the villagers and the guests assemble on the spot. Before serving to the members, the food and meat are offered on the platform by the priest.

After the community feast, youth and elders go from house to house and perform the dance. The dance of the *Parong* or *Harong* festival is very simple. Both male and female dancers, mainly the male members, form a circle by holding each other hands. They wave their hands in front and back together and foot tapping on the floor of the house (in the *Parong* festival, dance is performed on the platform of the house and not on the ground like the *Moh* festival), simultaneously, but in a slow steps. The song is sung maintaining a rhyme, i.e. one person who is conversant to the songs start it, which is followed by the other dancers in chorus. In this way, the group dance from house to house, where they are provided with rice-beer and food in each household. There is no hard and fast rule to visit every household of the village, but the dancers try to complete the round as far as possible.

On the second day, there is no special celebration. The villagers pass their day in eating, drinking and marry making. The villagers are not supposed to do any work on that day.

Belief in Lord Raang Frah

At present, the Lungchang Tangsas believe in a mythological faith and adopted it as their religion called "*Rang Fraism*" under *Rang Frah* Faith Promotion Society, which is now already formed and registered.

In a mythology, it is mentioned that once upon a time, this human world was destroyed by a severe annihilation on earth. Because of those natural calamities, all human beings perished from the earth. Only two orphans who were brother and sister hide themselves beneath the earth, till the danger was over. As they were made aware about the happenings by *Rang Frah* beforehand, they could escape themselves from that disaster. As the time pass on, human races began to multiply again. The Tangsas, including Lungchangs claim themselves to be the descendants of those orphans, who could survive by the grace of almighty *Rang Frah.*

There is a *Rang Frah* Temple in each of the Lungchang village. The villagers used to visit the temple every Sunday and offer their prayer to almighty *Rang Frah.* According to a text book of *Rang Fraism*, the second coming of *Rang Frah*, published by the *Rang Frah* Faith Promotion Society, Arunachal Pradesh (India) 2006 stated that "*Rang-Frataism*, as a religion may be new to certain extent but as a *dharma*, **it is as old as the** creation of human being itself hence external."

An effort has been made to describe the procedure of celebration of Rang Frah Day by the Tangsas at New Changlang village.

Lord *Rang-Frah* is the traditional God of the Tangsa and the Tutsa community of Arunachal Pradesh. He is worshipped and believed to be the creator, destroyer and preserver of this world.

Lord Rang-Frah was worshipped first in an idol form on 4th November, 1997, at New Changlang village, Changlang, where the idol/statue of Lord *Rang-Frah* was installed in a temple. Different sub-tribes of Tangsas, Tutsa and even members from other communities also participated in that ceremony. That was a full moon day and believed to be auspicious one. Since then, every year in the month of *Yakey* (November) on the full moon day, *Rang-Frah Day* is observed by the Tangsas. It is celebrated in village-wise with great enthusiasm, but sometimes the neighbouring villages jointly organize it.

Arrangement for Celebration

The celebration of festival is elaborate and they try to involve each and every person in the celebration. Normally meeting is held at the residence of *gaon burah* where the Secretary/President of Rang Frah Faith Promotion Society, New Changlang, intellectuals and youth are invited. Several meetings are held to come to a final decision.

In these meetings decisions are taken regarding the collection of donation from each family and the tentative expenditures for celebration of the Day. The Longri village which is situated near the New Changlang and falls under the jurisdiction of the same *gaon-burah* jointly celebrated the Day. Different activities are allotted to the youth, e.g. collection of donation, preparation of rice (*dung*), rice-beer (*jau*), *prasad*, collection of fire-wood (*chen*), leaves (*Nyap*), utensils etc. It is also decided that the villagers has to voluntarily contribute their service two days for the celebration. If the amount of money collected for the celebration is not sufficient to meet the estimated expenditures, they may take the decision to withdraw the money deposited in the bank. Some of the villagers voluntarily supply the required materials like bamboo, rice etc.

It has also been noted that many of the government departments have extended their support by providing the necessary requirements. The Electricity Department help in connecting electricity supply, Public Health Engineering Department supply the water; the Block also helps in supplying C.I. Sheet for roofing a shed in the *Mandir* complex.

As decided by the committee the villagers voluntarily extended their service by cleaning the compound and making a temporary shed in front of the *Rangsomhom* (*Mandir*). The temple is decorated with coloured papers. A temporary gate is made which are decorated with bamboo posts and leaves. Required firewood and leaves for wrapping the *prasad* are collected from the jungle. A week, before the celebration, rice-beer (*jau)* is prepared from 50 kg of rice (*wong*), which are normally done by the female members of those families, which are situated near the *mandir* complex.

The youth and young children remained busy in practicing *Ruun-shai* (dancing-singing) and preparing for cultural programme, which will be held in the evening. A pig is also arranged for the feast.

Prior to the day of celebration, some women remained busy in preparing of *Prasad* called *Wongbaanpan* (a kind of *roti* or *chapatti*, made of local rice powder). The rice powders are collected from each household of the village. The *wongbaam* (rice-powder) is mixed with *badam* (groundnut), coconut pieces and packed in leaves (*Nyap*). Then several packets are put into the boiling water of the utensils. When it is considered that powder is totally prepared, then it is taken out of the water. These are then cut into 2-3 inches square pieces. The *prasad* are ready for the celebration and kept in one of the household of the village.

On the day of festival villagers are seen visiting the temple (*Rangsamham*) either individually or in group. The women are found carrying small basket/buckets filled with beautiful flowers of different colours and fruits. Small children accompanied by their guardian/parents also come to attend the ceremony. The villagers pray to *Rang Frah* by offering flowers, fruits and lighting candles and incense sticks. The priest sprinkled water with *Tulsi* leave to the devotees who are present at the temple. The water is collected from tap water and the basil leaves are from *mandir* complex.

Youth are found busy in different activities allotted to them. Some are actively involved in preparation for feast (rice, meat etc.) some are busy in preparing seating arrangement for the gatherings. Some are busy in decorating community hall. The elderly people supervise the entire activities and offer suggestion off and on for the completion of the ceremony.

Now, it is the time for the arrival of *Rang-sama* (*Rang* means sky and *sama* means priest), a lady priest of about 45-50 years. of age from Paulom village, which is nearly 50 km away from New Changlang village. It has been communicated by divine power that *Lord Rang Frah* had entered into her body a few days prior to the celebration. It is believed that they will receive command of *Rang-Frah* through her. So, she is considered to be the main attraction of the day. The whole villagers and gatherings wait for her making two rows at the main gate. The villagers and gatherings receive her at the gate by offering flower garland and uttered *"Rang Frah Ajung"* (*Rang Frah* is great), *Rang-sama Ajung* (*Rang Sama* is great). She enter the *Rangsomhom* (temple) followed by the gatherings. She goes near the idol of *Rang-Frah* and offers prayers, chanting few words. She then looked around the gathering and began to speak. Normally, she wears a black skirt and a traditional *Khatnei* (*mekhela*). She is trembling like an ill person and it is believed that she is possessed. Occasionally, she used to weave her hands in the air. The devotees are standing silently with folded hands praying to *Rang-Sama*. The Secretary General of *Rang Frah* Faith Promotion Society talked about *Rang-sama*. He described how *Rang-sama* is possesed by *Rang Frah*. By observing the symptom, they understand that she is possessed by the *Rang Frah*. He advised the gathering to have faith in *Rang Frah* and *Rang Sama* and take every step to have faith in *Lord Rang Frah*. Possessions plays an important role in certain religious ceremonies of many tribal societies and the same trend is visible among the Tangsas also. During possession the person may predict the future and offer various remedies for illness.

Religious Ceremonies of the Muklom Tangsas

It has already been mentioned that each sub-tribe of the Tangsas have some uniqueness in performing the religious rites and rituals. Though the basic philosophy behind observing the rituals are more or less same yet variations may also easily be traced. Most of their religious ceremonies are centred round the agricultural practices. Here some of the important religious ceremonies performed by the Mukoms are presented on the basis of field investigation.

Rum Moll

The festival is celebrated by the Mukloms in the month of June every year. It is a pre-harvest festival and is celebrated before harvesting *kanidhan*. Duration of festival is three days. Rice-beer is prepared in advance and necessary arrangements are made to perform rituals and entertaining the guests and villagers.

On the first day of the *Ram Moll* festival, known as *Lumkhat*, people get up early in the morning and beat drums to make loud and roaring sound capable enough to reach neighbouring villages. This drum beating is a kind of invitation to all the neighbouring villagers to join *Rum Moll*.

The individual family performs *Nam-Rom* ritual early in the morning to worship the Goddess of wealth (*Lakshmi*). They prepare hook like packets from leaves of *nam phan* plant (palm leave) in which rice is filled up and incantations are cited. These packets are then stuck up in *wak khung* (piggery), *wothil* (cage of fowls), *ngam wak* (the skulls of the hunted animals), *waak* (the skulls of domesticated animals), *kall pak* (top of the fire place). They perform this ritual before the arrival of guests.

Subsequently, rituals are also performed in the house of *Romwa* or *Romte*. *Romwa* is the leader of the festival who belongs to *Rekhung* clan among the Mukloms. All drums and musical instruments are collected and leaves of *nap phaan* are tagged in every item used for the ceremony. At this time also incantations are recited.

After performing these rituals, males and females dress up by putting on colourful costumes, headgears, bracelets, garlands and ornaments. The males also wear traditional weapons and by 3.00 p.m. they assemble in front of the house of *Ramwa*, who is the leader of *Moll* festival. Males and females line up in circle and formally start performing ceremonial dance. Before performing this ritual, no one is allowed to come out of the house to dance. They make three rounds in the *Chingngum*, i.e. the common public ground attached to the residence of *Romwa*. Thereafter, the dance party goes to make three rounds of the entire village. On the way, the dance party is warmly welcomed by members of each household. Rice beer is served to the *Moll* dancers everywhere. After making three rounds of the village, the *Moll* dance party returns to *Chingngum*.

The goddess *Lakshmi* is also worshipped by sacrificing buffalos, pigs and chicken. Meat, fish, rice etc. is cooked and rice-beer is kept ready to be served to the *Moll* party and the guests. After the completion of the *Moll* dance, ritual guests are entertained.

The drums are then taken to the house of *Romwa* and male dancers form a circle. They make three rounds at the public ground. With this the formal part comes to an end and the general public may take part in the dance. The young boys constitute drum party which keeps on performing dances in circle and semi-circle throughout the day and night. The elderly persons, the girls, women and the visitor constitute *runwa*, which is accompanied by songs. They normally sing those songs which reflect their traditional cultural norms, glory and mythology about the origin of their community. The dance, music and cultural performances continue for three days. On the last day of festival, the villagers meet and decide the date of harvesting *kanidhon* (normally after 14 to 15 days) on the fourth day of the festival; the villagers take complete rest and normally do not perform any work. Thus, the festival comes to end.

Ronghoon

Ronghoon is celebrated by the Muklom in July-August, when the harvesting of millet/rice crop is over and grain stock is brought home. This festival is celebrated every year when bumper crop is harvested. In case if a village is in the grip of famine, drought and crop yield is very poor or nil, people do not prefer to celebrate this festival. This festival is synonymous to a festival called *Chamtuk*, and hence in the villages where *chamtuk* is observed separately as full-fledged festival in those villages *Ranghoon* is not observed. But, sometimes the festival of *Ranghoon* is clubbed together with *chamtuk.*

As soon as the dates of *Ronghoon* are fixed up by village council, rice-beer is prepared on large scale. On the first day of the festival, the community members from each family/household go to the forest to collect leaves of *nap phan, bala, sapmol.* They also collect *supshang* (thorny bushes) to make broom. With this broom they clean the house and then throw it out and never use it again. Before they move to the forest to collect these things they started to beat drum in a selected house of the village. After returning from the forest again they are trying to beat the drum on that particular house only. Everyone fastens the collected *nap phan* leave in the *khuta* (pillar) of their household. On that day in the evening recently harvested millet or rice crop is taken to house by each family, which symbolizes arrival of wealth or Goddess *Lakshmi* into the house.

Generally, they start beating drum from 3 p.m. to 4 a.m. on the first day. In this festival animals are not sacrificed at individual family level. The animals are sacrificed at a place earmarked for offering of community level prayers. This ritual is performed under the guidance of priests. Normally, cows, buffaloes and pigs are sacrificed on this occasion. The number of animals sacrificed may go up to 4-5, so, that there is no dearth of meat on this occasion. Rituals are performed by using rice and leaves of *nap phan* plant to seek blessings from the Goddess of wealth.

After sacrificing animals, meat is equally distributed among all households in a village. Meat of the animals is cooked along with other food items. Guests are entertained with meat, rice, rice-beer etc. in every household. So, the activities of *Ronghoon* festival are concluded in the night. The third day is observed as rest day.

Chamtuk

Chamtuk is an agricultural festival of the Mukloms. This festival is celebrated twice in a year. First it is observed in the month of June before the harvesting of millet crops, and for the second time it is observed in October before harvesting of the *jhum* paddy crop. The purpose of this festival is to express gratitude to *Lord Rang Frah* and the Goddess of wealth.

As soon as the date of *Chamtuk* festival is fixed they started to prepare rice-beer in huge quantity. On the first day they get up early in the morning and collect the leaves of various crops which are ripened and ready for harvest are brought to home. These leaves are kept in a *Chikhuk* (basket). At this time the head of the family ceremoniously spread away cooked rice outside the house/in the courtyard and offer prayer to the Goddess of wealth to bless the family and ensure peace, prosperity, happiness and good health.

The sacrificial ceremony is performed at the highest point of the village. At the time of sacrificing animals some aged persons of the community recite some incantations. These meats is cooked and shared by the villagers with plenty of rice-beer and it is arranged as community feast in the village. The head of the animal is hung up on a pole or the tree called *Manrung Bang* tree at the highest point of the village. Before putting this head on the pole, the chin, the teeth and the minor organs are separated and placed on the lowest point of the village. These are tied on a pole of *Manrung Bang* tree. Thus, with the community feast and rituals, this festival comes to an end. The following day is observed as rest day, people are supposed to stay at home and take rest.

Thal Moll

It is a festival, which is celebrated by the Mukloms for three days in the period between April-June every year. Interestingly, no sacrifices are offered in this festival. On this occasion plenty of rice-beer is prepared. The songs and dances continue for 3 days, visits are exchanged and the festival is celebrated with traditional songs and dances which mark this occasion.

On the third day brothers visit their married sister's home to perform a ritual. He ties thread of the bark of *Remey* tree in the left hand of his nephew and the thread of the bark of *Riben* tree in the left of hand of his niece. But today due to lack of *Riben* tree they use the bark of *Remey* tree for both boys and girls to tie their hands. After tying thread the maternal uncle *chews chunkho* (a type of spice) and spit in the left hand of nephew/niece for their good health. After the completion of this ritual they take rest on the fourth day as holiday. On the fifth day all the villagers go to river bank with plenty of rice-beer, rice etc. for celebrating a feast. They started fishing in the river and collected enough fishes. These fishes are cooked and shared by the villagers along with plenty of rice beer, rice, etc. as a community feast. After completion of cooking they eat some food and fishes on the spot along with the fellow members. While a portion of the food and fishes are left in the river with a belief that along with that food they are leaving the evil spirit of the village there. They never return to the village in group. Thus, the festival comes to an end formally.

The Muklom Tangsa also has faith in Lord *Rang Frah*. But, they rely mainly on possession. According to Mukloms, the possessed person is considered as purest form of Lord *Rang Frah*. They are considered next to Lord *Rang Frah* and it is believed that some powers of Lord are present inside the possessed person. There are two types of possession. In one process, the power of God directly enters in the body of a person, i.e. he/she is possessed by the God. Secondly, there are persons who have true faith in God and wish to become possessed. In that process one is to take proper training and follow some rules and regulations. He must prove his faith in God.

The person is to maintain some restrictions in their day-to-day life. They are not allowed to take rice-beer or intoxicated items. They cannot take meat or fish or even their family members cannot have these things inside their home. In their day-to-day life, they are to maintain a strict routine. Everyday, in the morning and evening, they are to offer prayer to God at their sacred place. They may pray either by lighting a lamp or incense sticks before the God.

They have also attained the power to heal other person's misery. For minor problems like pain they normally message the part of the body. In major problems, like gall bladder stone or appendix, they use medicine to cure the patient. They are to do these free of cost. Thus, it is believed that when a person is possessed, he/she gets some extraordinary power by which she/he can serve the community.

To understand any cultural phenomena, background knowledge is always a necessity. The scatter and insular existence on hilltop for fear of head hunting, non-communication with fellow tribal population had made their village confine within one sub-tribe. As a result most of the ceremonies and festivals are confined within a sub-tribe level and such situation helps in the development of certain uniqueness within the sub-tribe level. However, by nature they are gregarious and have an encyclopedic memory. Therefore, with the opening of communication and growing interaction among the sub-tribes, there is a tendency to celebrate many of the festivals together. The *Khu-Mol* festival is one such occasion where the sub-tribes of the Tangsas join together to express their common cultural heritage.

Khu-Mol

Khu-Mol is a festival of harvest. It is celebrated to harvest the paddy and also to sow paddy in a newly cultivated *jhum* land in the month of April to June every year. It is celebrated when the paddy becomes almost ripen, a festival which is performed to eat the newly harvested paddy ceremoniously and to welcome the New Year. It is celebrated to ward off pests from plant and appeasement of deities who control the mother earth to get bumper crops.

It is a festival of both joy and sorrow because during this festival pig/buffalo is sacrificed to perform the ritual to appease the God and Goddesses for healthy living, prosperity, wealth and multiplication of domestic animals. On the other hand, it is a festival of sorrow as it is performed by every grieved family to offer last food to the departed soul who died in the previous year. Mother of the person supposed to carry hair and is to observe death anniversary ceremoniously so that they may start the *Moh- Mol* festival. They are to complete the entire process three days before the commencement of festival.

A brief description of the religious beliefs and practices reveal that the Tangsas as a whole have faith in their traditional religious beliefs and practices. Most of their rituals and practices are centred round the agricultural practices. Animal sacrifices are considered must in most of their traditional religious ceremonies. But, in recent years they are influenced by Lord *Rang Frah* whom they consider as their supreme God and Rang Frah Faith Promotion Society is taking various measures to influence the Tangsas to develop faith in this religion. Though the very philosophy of various rituals and ceremonies are same among the Tangsas as a whole, yet a slight difference is noticed both in the nomenclature and procedure of performing the religious rituals and ceremonies in the sub-tribe level. It has also been revealed that with the advancement of communication and contact there is a growing tendency to celebrate the festivals and ceremonies jointly in a large scale.

In the forgoving chapters an effort has been made to describe the social system of the Tangsas. Human society is unique as it has a definite system to perform its roles and function. The society consists of various units and each unit is contributing its respective share for the proper functioning of a society. Since the emergence of human being they developed some sort of system for their existence. There is no doubt that human society as a formal institution is later development yet it is also true that they have some sort of mechanism to carry out their life.

Scholar like Parson conceives of society as a system surrounded by other related system. A society is said to be in equilibrium when it maintains the boundaries with other related components. Unless society functions as a system there is every possibility of its extinction. In the context of studying their relationship with other components one may presume that any ordered set of relationship between components is defined as a system. Thus, when social scientist deals with relationship between anything defined as a part there is a system which should be described. While describing social system, a social scientist may describe only a model of social reality. This model represents in effect the anthropologist's hypothesis about "how the social system works". For the smooth functioning of the system, various institutions/organizations emerge through which system works. Elliot and Merrill (1950:14) has stated "social organization is a state of being, a condition in which various institutions, in a society are functioning in accordance with their recognized or implied purposes". Social organization would consist of interrelations between particular types of group that makes social life possible to move. The family, the marriage system, kinship system, the clan, dormitory etc. are some of the examples. Herskovits stated that social organization can be studied from two broad institutions, namely those that grow out of kinship and those that result from the free associations of individuals. It is thus evident that social organization consists of various components, the form of which is ascertained by pattern of the interrelationship existing between these constituents. It is also evident that the nature, status and role of the constituents differ from one community to another. This happens because of the socio-ecological variation of a given community and society. Thus, while attempt is made to understand a society, it is considered essential to describe social process. R. Brown (1959) assumes that normally in every social system the parts dovetail in such a fashion so as to entail harmonious working of the system.

To understand the social system of the Tangsas of Arunachal Pradesh an effort has been made to describe the various institutions/organizations, e.g. economic systems, the family, marriage and religious system so that one may get a real picture of the system. The study reveals that the Tangsas have a unique social system because of its geographical location and traditional socio-cultural norms. Thus, it is hoped that an analysis of their social system/process no doubt reflect various dimensions of their colourful social life which are still unknown to others. This may help the scholars who are working on such subject.

7
Fertility Determinants

Marriage and fertility performance are very closely related. Marital status assumed demographic importance, because marriage gives men and women a civil status which legalizes reproduction and hence directly affects the fertility of the population. Marriage is socially and ritually preformed for the continuity of their family line. Fertility is determined by both biological and socio-cultural factors. It is necessary to know what proportion of population is in reproductive period. Thus, a detailed analysis of their fertility performances is considered significant to understand the socio-demographic characteristic of a particular community.

Lungchang Tangsas

Fertility is one of the fundamental determinants of the population growth, and represents an essential feature in ones approach to the understanding of human society. In this chapter the fertility performance of the Lungchang Tangsa women of the New Changlang, Old Changlang and Rangkatu villages of Changlang District of Arunachal Pradesh are presented in a tabular form. The data were collected with the help of household survey schedules. The schedule contains detail household census like total population, age and sex, age at menarche, age at marriage, marriage spatial distance and data related to demographic structure.

New Changlang

Table 7.1 shows the distribution of females on the basis of different age groups in New Changlang village. It was observed that the highesı frequency of females falls within the age group of 19–23 yrs., i.e. 13 (14.94%). It is followed by the age group 9–13 yrs., i.e. 11 (12.65%). The least frequency, i.e. 1 number (1.15%) falls in six different age groups which may be considered as upper age.

Table 7.1: Distribution of Females on the Basis of Different Age Group in New Changlang

Sl. No.	*Age group (yrs.)*	*No. of females*	*Percentage*
1.	9–13	11	12.65
2.	14–18	10	11.49
3.	19–23	13	14.94
4.	24–28	9	10.34
5.	29–33	9	10.34
6.	34–38	9	10.34
7.	39–43	8	9.20
8.	44–48	1	1.15
9.	49–53	2	2.30
10.	54–58	6	6.90
11.	59–63	1	1.15
12.	64–68	4	4.60
13.	69–73	1	1.15
14.	74–78–83	–	–
15.	84–88	1	1.15
16.	89–93	1	1.15
17.	94 +	1	1.15
	Total	**87**	**100.00**

Table 7.2 shows the distribution of women according to age at menarche. Table 7.2 shows that the female experienced by first

Table 7.2: Distribution of Lungchang Girls according to Age at Menarche in New Changlang

Sl. No.	*Age at Menarche (yrs.)*	*No. of Girls*	*%*	*Mean*	*S.D*	*S.E*
1.	9	–	–			
2.	10	1	1.45			
3.	11	4	5.79			
4.	12	3	4.35	13.61	1.62	± 0.19
5.	13	17	24.64			
6.	14	32	46.38			
7.	15	12	17.39			
	Total	**69**	**100.00**			

Table 7.3: Distribution of Women according to Age at Marriage in New Changlang

Sl. No.	Age at marriage (yrs.)	No. of women	%	Mean	SD	SE
1.	17	5	11.36			
2.	18	8	18.18			
3.	19	4	9.09			
4.	20	9	20.45			
5.	21	1	2.27			
6.	22	4	9.09	20.86	3.17	± 0.48
7.	23	4	9.09			
8.	24	3	6.83			
9.	25	3	6.83			
10.	26	1	2.27			
11.	27-28	–	–			
13.	29	1	2.27			
14.	30	1	2.27			
	Total	**44**	**100.00**			

menstruation at the age of 13, 14 and 15 yrs. is a bit high and the number of females is accordingly 17 (24.64%), 32 (46.38%) and 12 (17.39%). This shows that the frequency of menarche age is high at the age of 14 yrs. The number of female found in the age 10, 11 and 12 yrs. are a bit low, i.e. 1 (1.45%), 4 (5.79%) and 3 (4.35%), respectively. This trend of early menstruation among the Lungchang girls is reflected in the present generation. The mean age at menarche is 13.61 yrs. with the S.D. of 1.62 and S.E. is ± 0.19.

The distribution of women according to age at marriage of New Changlang village is shown in Table 7.3. It reveals that the marriage age of Tangsa girls of the village varies between 17 to 30 yrs. Out of 44 married women, the highest number of women, i.e. 9 (20.45%) got married at the age of 20 yrs. Next 8 (18.18%) women who got married at the age of 18 yrs. 1 woman (2.27%) each who got married at the age of 26, 29 and 30 yrs. So, the table reveals that their suitable age at marriage is 17-20 yrs. Their mean age at marriage is 20.86 with standard deviation of 3.17 and standard error is ± 0.48.

The distribution of women according to their age at marriage by education is given in Table 7.4. It is revealed that in the age group of 15-19 yrs. maximum number of women who got married falls in the category of Primary School (Up to IV) level, i.e. 7, which is followed by 3 women

Table 7.4: Distribution of Females Age at Marriage by Education in New Changlang

Sl. No.	*Age at marriage (yrs.)*	*Primary (Up to IV)*	*Middle (V-VII)*	*H.S (VIII-X)*	*H.S.S (XI-XII)*	*Nurse*	*Others*	*Total*
1.	15–19	7	3	3	3	–	–	16
2.	20–24	9	1	5	4	1	2	22
3.	Above 25	3	–	–	3	–	–	6
	Total	**19**	**4**	**8**	**10**	**1**	**2**	**44**

each falls in the category of Middle School (V–VII), H.S (VII–X) and H.S.S. (XI–XII), respectively.

In the age group 20–24 yrs. the maximum number of women who got married falls again in the category of Primary School (Up to IV) level, i.e. 9. It is followed by 5 and 4 women falls in the category of H.S. (VIII–X), and H.S.S. (XI–XII) level, respectively. This is followed by 2 women falls in the category of others. It is followed by 1 woman each falls in the category of Middle School (V–VII) level and working as Nurse.

In the age group 25 and above years, 3 women each who got married falls in the category of Primary School (Up to IV) level and H.S.S. (XI–XII) level.

Table 7.5 shows the distribution of Lungchang population of New Changlang village by age difference at marriage. It is clear from table that maximum number of male, i.e. 5 (6.25%) out of the 36 male got married at the age of 26 yrs. and the lowest number of male, i.e. 1 (1.25%) each got married at the age of 18, 20, 33 and 34 yrs., respectively.

Whereas, maximum number of females, i.e. 8 (10.00%) out of the 44 females got married at the age of 18 yrs. The lowest number of females, i.e. 1 (1.25%) got married at the age of 21, 29 and 30 yrs., respectively. Therefore, it is clear that in comparison to the Lungchang males, maximum number of Lungchang females got married in the early age.

Table 7.6 shows the data collected on marriage area of New Changlang village according to spatial distance. Table 7.6 shows that the Lungchangs prefer more in practicing intra village marriage. The frequency of marriage within the village is 23, i.e. 52.27 per cent. The second highest frequency, i.e. 6 (13.64%) marriages took place between 16 to 20 km distances. Again same number of marriage, i.e. 6 (13.64%) took place above 100 km away from the studied village.

Table 7.5: Distribution by Age Difference at Marriage in New Changlang

Sl. No.	Age group (yrs.)	Male	%	Female	%	Total	%
1.	17	–	–	5	6.25	5	6.25
2.	18	1	1.25	8	10.00	9	11.25
3.	19	3	3.75	4	5.00	7	8.75
4.	20	1	1.25	8	10.00	9	11.25
5.	21	2	2.50	1	1.25	3	3.75
6.	22	2	2.50	5	6.25	7	8.75
7.	23	4	5.00	5	6.25	9	11.25
8.	24	2	2.50	2	2.50	4	5.00
9.	25	3	3.75	4	5.00	7	8.75
10.	26	5	6.25	–	–	5	6.25
11.	27	2	2.50	–	–	2	2.50
12.	28	3	3.75	–	–	3	3.75
13.	29	–	–	1	1.25	1	1.25
14.	30	2	2.50	1	1.25	3	3.75
15.	31	–	–	–	–	–	–
16.	32	4	5.00	–	–	4	5.00
17.	33	1	1.25	–	–	1	1.25
18.	34	1	1.25	–	–	1	1.25
	Total	**36**	**45.00**	**44**	**55.00**	**80**	**100.00**

Table 7.6: Marriage Area according to Spatial Distance in New Changlang

Sl. No.	Spatial distance (km)	No. of marriage	%
1.	Below 1	–	–
2.	1–5	23	52.27
3.	6–10	4	9.09
4.	11–15	2	4.55
5.	16–20	6	13.64
6.	21–25	1	2.27
7.	26–40	–	–
8.	41–45	1	2.27
9.	46–50	–	–
10.	51–55	1	2.27
11.	56–100	–	–
12.	Above 100	6	13.64
	Total	**44**	**100.00**

The distribution of women according to number of conception is shown in Table 7.7. All the 44 married women had experienced conception. Table reveals that number of conception ranges from 1 to 11. All the 11 women (25.00%) in the age up to 30 yrs. are found to have a range of 1 to 2 conceptions. 6 women (13.64%) have conceived once whilst 5 women (11.36%) has conceived twice.

In the age group 31-44 yrs., recorded 16 women (36.36%), their conception ranges from 2 to 11. Here, maximum of 6 women (13.64%) has 2 and 3 conception. In the last age group of 45 and above years, recorded 17 women (38.64%), their conception ranges were from 1 to 9. Here, maximum of 4 women (9.09%) have 9 conceptions. The table reveals that the mothers of higher age group show the highest number of conception.

Table 7.8 shows the age specific distribution of mothers according to age at first child birth. The table shows that the age of mothers at the time of first child birth varies from 17 to 34 yrs. The highest number of women, i.e. 14 (31.82%) reported to have made their first child birth in the age group of 20–22 yrs. It is followed by the age group of 17–19 yrs. and 23–25 yrs., i.e. 12 (27.27%) in each group. The frequency decreases as the age group increases. The mean age at first child birth is 22.02 ±0.53 with a standard deviation of 3.50.

The distribution of pregnant and pregnancy outcome of mothers according to their present age is shown in Table 7.9. Table 7.8 shows that there are all total 44 mothers with all totals of 171 numbers of pregnancies. The highest number of mothers, i.e. 12 falls under the age group of 35–44 yrs. with 37 numbers of pregnancies. And the 9 mothers fall in the age group of 55–64 yrs. with the highest number of pregnancies, i.e. 53. The highest number of live births, i.e. 47 (27.49%) out of 149 live birth is recorded in the age group of 55–64 yrs., i.e. by 9 mothers. The second highest live birth, i.e. 33 (19.30%) is recorded in the category of 35–44 yrs. by 12 mothers.

The total of 15 still births had been recorded in the village. The highest number still births, i.e. 5 had been found in the category of 55–64 yrs. 65–74 yrs. age group by 9 and 3 women, respectively. The next highest still birth, i.e. 3 is recorded in the age group of 35–44 yrs. and the minimum number, i.e. 1 each is recorded in the age group of 45–54 yrs. and 85–94 yrs. No case of artificial abortion was recorded.

Table 7.7: Distribution of Women according to Number of Conception in New Changlang

Sl. No.	No. of conception	Up to 30 yrs.		31- 44 yrs.		45 + yrs.		Total	
		No. of women	%	No. of women	%	No. of women	%	No. of women	%
1.	1	6	13.64	–	–	1	2.27	7	15.90
2.	2	5	11.36	6	13.64	1	2.27	12	27.27
3.	3	–	–	6	13.64	2	4.55	8	18.18
4.	4	–	–	2	4.55	3	6.82	5	11.36
5.	5	–	–	–	–	1	2.27	1	2.27
6.	6	–	–	–	–	3	6.82	3	6.82
7.	7	–	–	1	2.27	2	4.55	3	6.82
8.	8	–	–	–	–	–	–	–	–
9.	9	–	–	–	–	4	9.09	4	9.09
10.	10	–	–	–	–	–	–	–	–
11.	11	–	–	1	2.27	–	–	1	2.27
	Total	**11**	**25.00**	**16**	**36.36**	**17**	**38.64**	**44**	**100.00**

Table 7.8: Distribution of Women according to Age at First Child Birth in New Changlang

Sl. No.	Age group (yrs.)	No. of women	%	Mean	S.D	S.E
1.	17–19	12	27.27			
2.	20–22	14	31.82			
3.	23–25	12	27.27	22.02	3.50	± 0.53
4.	26–28	4	9.09			
5.	29–31	1	2.28			
6.	32–34	1	2.28			
	Total	**44**	**100**			

The distribution of mothers according to age at marriage and mortality experience of the New Changlang village is shown in Table 7.10. Out of 44 mothers the highest number of mothers, i.e. 22 got married in the age group of 20–24 yrs. and also experienced the highest number of live births, i.e. 70. Next is followed by 17 women with 59 live births in the age group of 15–19 yrs. and 5 mothers with 20 live births falls in the age group of 25 yrs. and above.

Table 7.9: Distribution of Pregnant/Pregnancy Outcome according to Age in New Changlang

Sl. No.	*Present age (yrs)*	*No. of mothers*	*No. of pregnancies*	*Carrying child*	*Pregnant Outcome*							
					L.B		*S.B*		*Spontaneous abortion*		*Total no. of Foetal wastage*	
					No.	*%*	*No.*	*%*	*No.*	*%*	*No.*	*%*
1.	15–24	3	4	–	4	2.34	–	–	–	–	–	–
2.	25–34	11	26	4	21	12.28	–	–	1	0.58	1	0.58
3.	35–44	12	37	–	33	19.30	3	1.74	1	0.58	4	2.34
4.	45–54	3	18	–	17	9.94	1	0.58	–		1	0.58
5.	55–64	9	53	–	47	27.49	5	2.92	1	0.58	6	3.51
6.	65–74	3	24	–	19	11.11	5	2.92	–	–	5	2.92
7.	75–84	1	3	–	3	1.74	–	–	–	–	–	
8.	85–94	1	5	–	4	2.34	1	0.58	–	–	1	0.58
9.	95–104	1	1	–	1	0.58	–	–	–	–	–	–
	Total	**44**	**171**	**4**	**149**	**87.13**	**15**	**8.77**	**3**	**1.74**	**18**	**10.53**

Table 7.10: Distribution of Mothers according to Age at Marriage and Mortality Experience in New Changlang

Sl. No.	*Age group (yrs.)*	*No. of mothers*	*Total live births*	*Infant mortality (0-1 yr.)*	*Child mortality (1.1-5 yrs.)*	*Juvenile (5.1-14)*	*14.1+ yrs.*
1.	Up to-14	–	–	–	–	–	–
2.	15-19	17	59	–	2	–	–
3.	20-24	22	70	4	1	–	1
4.	25 and above	5	20	4	2	1	–
	Total	**44**	**149**	**8**	**5**	**1**	**1**

Table 7.10 also reflects the total of 15 mortalities in the village which is categorized in three divisions. There were 8 infant mortalities with 4 each in the age group of 20–24 and 25 and above years of mothers. 5 child mortality with 2 each in the age group of 15–19 and 25 yrs. and 1 in the age group of 20–24 yrs. There is 1 juvenile mortality falls in the age group of 25 and above years. There is also 1 adulthood death which falls in the age group of 20–24 yrs. of mothers.

Table 7.11 shows the distribution of mother's education and their mortality experience. Out of the total of 44 mothers, the highest number of mothers, i.e. 21 falls in the category of illiterate and also experienced the highest number of live births, i.e. 91 out of the total 149 live births. It is followed by 9 mothers falls in the category of Middle School level (V–VII) with 19 live births, 8 mothers in category H.S level (VIII–X) with 16 live births, 4 mothers in the category Primary School level (Up to IV) with 20 live births, 2 mothers in the category of H.S.S. level (XI–XII) with 3 live births.

Table 7.11: Distribution of Mothers Education and Mortality Experience in New Changlang

Sl. No.	*Literacy*	*No. of mothers*	*Total live birth*	*Infant mortality (0-1 yr.)*	*Child mortality (1.1-5 yrs.)*	*Juvenile (5.1-4 yrs.)*	*14.1+ yrs.*
1.	Illiterate	21	91	8	5	1	1
2.	Primary (Up to IV)	4	20	–	–	–	–
3.	Middle (V–VII)	9	19	–	–	–	–
4.	H.S. (VIII–X)	8	16	–	–	–	–
5.	H.S.S. (XI–XII)	2	3	–	–	–	–
	Total	**44**	**149**	**8**	**5**	**1**	**1**

Table 7.11 also reflects of 15 cases of mortality in the village. Out of which 8 are found to be in the infant mortality experienced by the illiterate mother's. Five cases of child mortality and 1 case each of juvenile mortality and adulthood death were also experienced by the illiterate mothers. It can be said that education plays an important role in the life of women.

Table 7.12: Distribution of Women according to Age at Menopause in New Changlang

Sl. No.	*Age group (yrs.)*	*No. of woman*	*%*	*Mean*	*S.D.*	*S.E.*
1.	Up to 40	–	–			
2.	41–43	1	5.88			
3.	44–46	11	64.71	45.71	1.64	± 0.40
4.	47–49	5	29.41			
	Total	**17**	**100.00**			

Note: Out of 44 women only 17 women had experienced menopause.

Table 7.12 shows that the distribution of women according to the age at menopause. The range of menopause varies between 40 to 49 yrs. The highest number is recorded with 11 (64.71%) women who had attained menopause in the age group of 44–46 yrs. Next are 5 women (29.41%) in 47–49 yrs. and 1 woman (5.88%) in the age group of 41–43 yrs. The mean age at menopause is 45.71 ± 0.40 with a S.D. of 1.64.

Old Changlang Village

The fertility performance of females is analysed separately in this chapter.

Table 7.13 shows the distribution of Lungchang females on the basis of different age groups. In this table females below 9 yrs. of age are not included. The table reveals that maximum number of females falls in the age groups of 14–18 yrs. with 24 (13.87%) females out of the total 173 females. The second maximum number of females falls in the age group of 9–13 yrs., i.e. 23 (13.29%) females. This is followed by 19 (10.98%) females each falls in the age group of 29–33 yrs. and 34–38 yrs., respectively, which is followed by 15 (8.67%) females in the age group of 19–23 yrs., 14 (8.09%) females in 39–43 yrs., 13 (7.51%) females in 44–48 yrs., 12 (6.64%) females in 24–28 yrs., 9 (5.20%) females in 59–63 yrs., 7 (4.05%) females in 54–58 yrs., 6 (3.47%) females in 64–68 yrs., 5 (2.89%) females in 49–53 yrs., 4 (2.31%) females in 69–73 yrs.,

Table 7.13: Distribution of females on the Basis of Different Age Group in Old Changlang

Sl. No.	*Age group (yrs.)*	*No. of females*	*Percentage*
1.	9–13	23	13.29
2.	14–18	24	13.87
3.	19–23	15	8.67
4.	24–28	12	6.64
5.	29–33	19	10.98
6.	34–38	19	10.98
7.	39–43	14	8.09
8.	44–48	13	7.51
9.	49–53	5	2.89
10.	54–58	7	4.05
11.	59–63	9	5.20
12.	64–68	6	3.47
13.	69–73	4	2.31
14.	74–78	2	1.16
15.	79–83	1	0.58
	Total	**173**	**100.00**

2 (1.16%) females in 74–78 yrs. and 1 (0.58%) females in 79–83 yrs. So, we can say that the oldest woman in the village falls in the age group of 79–83 yrs. The table reveals that the life span of Lungchang females is very long.

Table 7.14 shows the distribution of women menstruating at different age. It is observed from the table that the age at menarche varies from 11 to 15 yrs. The table also reveals that the maximum number of girls attained menarche at the age of 14 yrs., which is 88 (58.28%) in number. However, concentration of women in 13 yrs. is also appreciably high, i.e. 44 (29.14%) in number. The mean age at menarche age is calculated as 13.70 ± 0.06 with a S.D. of 0.72.

Table 7.14: Distribution of Lungchang Girls according to Age at Menarche in Old Changlang

Sl. No.	*Age at Menarche*	*No. of Girls*	*%*	*Mean*	*S.D*	*S.E*
1.	9	–	–			
2.	10	–	–	13.70	0.72	± 0.06
3.	11	2	0.66			
4.	12	4	2.65			
5.	13	44	29.14			
6.	14	88	58.28			
7.	15	13	8.61			
	Total	**151**	**100.00**			

The distribution of Lungchang women according to age at marriage is shown in Table 7.15. Their marriage age varies between 17 to 32 yrs. There are all total 87 married women recorded in the village. The highest number of women got married in the age of 20 yrs. with 13 (14.94%) women.

Table 7.15: Distribution of Women according to Age at Marriage in Old Changlang

Sl. No.	Age at marriage	No. of women	%	Mean	SD	SE
1.	17	3	3.45			
2.	18	3	3.45			
3.	19	11	12.64			
4.	20	13	14.94			
5.	21	6	6.89			
6.	22	8	9.19			
7.	23	9	10.34			
8.	24	10	11.49	22.69	3.44	± 0.37
9.	25	8	9.19			
10.	26	3	3.45			
11.	27	5	5.75			
12.	28	2	2.29			
13.	29	2	2.29			
14.	30	1	1.15			
15.	31	2	2.29			
16.	32	1	1.15			
	Total	**87**	**100.00**			

Next is followed by 11 (12.64%) women who got married at the age of 19 yrs. 10 (11.49%) women got married at the age of 24 yrs., while 9 (10.34%) got married at the age of 23 yrs. This is followed by 8 (9.19%) women each got married at the age of 22 and 25 yrs., respectively. 6 (6.89%) women got married at the age of 21 yrs. and 5 (5.75%) got married at the age of 27 yrs. While 3 (3.45%) women each got married at the age of 17 yrs., 18 yrs. and 26 yrs. 2 (2.29%) women each got married at the age of 28 yrs., 29 yrs. and 31 yrs. 1 (1.15%) woman each got married at the age of 30 and 32 yrs. Therefore, the table reveals that the suitable age at marriage of the Lungchang girls of Old Changlang village is 19 to 25 yrs.

Their mean age at marriage is 22.69 ± 0.37 with the S.D. of 3.44.

Table 7.16 shows the distribution of Lungchang females according to their age at marriage by education. The table reveals that there are 9 women who falls in the illiterate category, which is followed by 5 females

Table 7.16: Distribution of Females' Age at Marriage by Education in Old Changlang

Sl. No.	Age at marriage (yrs.)	Illiterate	Primary (Up to IV)	Middle (V-VII)	H.S. (VIII-X)	H.S.S. (XI-XII)	Graduate	Total
1.	15–19	9	2	2	4	–	–	17
2.	20–24	25	12	4	4	1	–	46
3.	Above 25	13	4	3	1	2	1	24
	Total	**47**	**18**	**9**	**9**	**3**	**1**	**87**

who fall in the category of Higher Secondary level. It is followed by 3 and 2 females fall in the category of Primary and Middle School level accordingly.

In the age group 20–24 yrs., again the maximum number of females who got married falls in the category of illiterate and the number is 25 which is followed by 12 females in the Primary level, 4 females in High Secondary level, 4 females in Middle School level and 1 females in Higher Secondary level, respectively.

In the age group 25 yrs. and above, maximum number of females who got married falls in the illiterate category, i.e. 13. It is followed by 4 females in Primary level, 3 females in Middle level, 2 females in Higher Secondary level and 1 each in High School and Graduate level.

Table 7.17 shows the distribution of Lungchang population of Old Changlang village by age difference at marriage. From the table it is clear that maximum number of males, i.e. 12 (6.70%) out of 92 (51.40%) males got married at the age of 28 yrs. The lowest number of male, i.e. 1 (0.56%) each got married at the age of 21 yrs., 37 yrs., 38 yrs., 39 yrs. and 43 yrs. Whereas, out of the 87 (48.60%) females, maximum number of females, i.e. 13 (7.26%) got married at the age of 20 yrs. and the lowest number of females, i.e. 1 (0.56%) each got married at the age of 30 and 32 yrs., respectively. Therefore, from the table it is clear that in comparison to the males maximum number of females got married at the early age.

The distribution of the marriage area of the Old Changlang village according to spatial distance is given in Table 7.18. The table shows that the total number of marriages is recorded 108. Out of 108 marriages 72 marriages (77.76%) took place within the spatial distance of below 1 km, which mean that marriages occur within the same village. 12 marriages (12.96%) have been recorded in the category of the spatial distance above 100 km. 9 marriages (9.72%) has been taken within the spatial distance

Table 7.17: Distribution of Lungchang by Age Difference at Marriage in Old Changlang

Sl. No.	*Age group (yrs.)*	*Male*	*%*	*Female*	*%*	*Total*	*%*
1.	17	–	–	3	1.68	3	1.68
2.	18	–	–	3	1.68	3	1.68
3.	19	–	–	11	6.14	11	6.14
4.	20	–	–	13	7.26	13	7.26
5.	21	1	0.56	6	3.35	7	3.91
6.	22	8	4.47	8	4.47	16	8.14
7.	23	2	1.12	9	5.03	11	6.14
8.	24	7	3.91	10	5.59	17	9.49
9.	25	3	1.68	8	4.47	11	6.14
10.	26	3	1.68	3	1.68	6	3.35
11.	27	10	5.59	5	2.79	15	8.38
12.	28	12	6.70	2	1.12	14	7.82
13.	29	9	5.03	2	1.12	11	6.14
14.	30	11	6.14	1	0.56	12	6.70
15.	31	3	1.68	2	1.12	5	2.79
16.	32	9	5.03	1	0.56	10	5.59
17.	33	3	1.68	–	–	3	1.68
18.	34	4	2.23	–	–	4	2.23
19.	35	3	1.68	–	–	3	1.68
20.	36	–	–	–	–	–	–
21.	37	1	0.56	–	–	1	0.56
22.	38	1	0.56	–	–	1	0.56
23.	39	1	0.56	–	–	1	0.56
24.	40-41-42	–	–	–	–	–	–
25.	43	1	0.56	–	–	1	0.56
	Total	**92**	**51.40**	**87**	**48.60**	**179**	**100.00**

of 11–15 km. Which is followed by 4 marriages (4.32%) within 51–55 km, 3 marriages (3.24%) within 96-100 km, 2 marriages (2.16%) each in the category of 16–20 km and 31–35 km and 1 (1.08%) each in the category of 1–5 km, 6–10 km, 21–25 km and 41–45 km, respectively.

From Table 7.18 it may be said that there is no such restriction or preference for marriage area.

Table 7.19 shows the distribution of women according to number of conception. All the 85 married women had experienced conception. The table reveals that number of conception ranges from 1 to 7.

All the 16 (18.82%) in the age up to 30 yrs. are found to have a range of 1 to 3 conceptions. Seven women (8.24%) have conceived twice, while 2 women (2.36%) have 3 conceptions.

In the age group 31–44 yrs., recording 27 women (31.76%), their conception ranges from 1 to 6. Here maximum of 16 women (18.82%)

Table 7.18: Marriage Area according to Spatial Distance in Old Changlang

Sl. No.	*Spatial distance*	*No. of marriages*	*Percentage*
1.	Below 1	72	77.76
2.	1–5	1	1.08
3.	6–10	1	1.08
4.	11–15	9	9.72
5.	16–20	2	2.16
6.	21–25	1	1.08
7.	26–30	–	–
8.	31–35	2	2.16
9.	36–40	–	–
10.	41–45	1	1.08
11.	46–50	–	–
12.	51–55	4	4.32
14.	56–95	–	–
21.	96–100	3	3.24
22.	Above 100	12	12.96
	Total	**108**	**100.00**

Table 7.19: Distribution of Women according to number of Conception in Old Changlang

Sl. No.	*Number of conceptions*	*Up to 30 yrs.*		*31–44 yrs.*		*45 yrs. +*		*Total*	
		No. of women	*%*	*No. of women*	*%*	*No. of women*	*%*	*No. of women*	*%*
1.	1	7	8.24	1	1.18	2	2.36	10	11.76
2.	2	7	8.24	7	8.24	7	8.24	21	24.71
3.	3	2	2.36	16	18.82	9	10.59	27	31.76
4.	4	–	–	1	1.18	6	7.06	7	8.24
5.	5	–	–	1	1.18	6	7.06	7	8.24
6.	6	–	–	1	1.18	8	9.41	9	10.59
7.	7	–	–	–	–	4	4.71	4	4.71
	Total	**16**	**18.82**	**27**	**31.76**	**42**	**49.41**	**85**	**100.00**

have conceived thrice. It is followed by 7 women (8.24%) who have conceived twice. It is recorded that 1 woman has conceived once. While the remaining 3 women conceived 4, 5 and 6 times, respectively.

In the last age group of 45 and above years, recording 42 women (49.41%), their conception ranges from 1 to 7. Here maximum of 9 women (10.59%) have conceived thrice. It is followed 8 women (9.41%) with 6 conceptions, 7 women (8.24%) having 2 conceptions, 6 women (7.06%) each having 4 and 5 conceptions, 4 women (4.71%) having 7 conceptions and 2 women (2.36%) having 1 conception.

The table reveals that the mothers of higher age group show the highest number of conceptions.

Table 7.20: Distribution of Women according to Age at First Child Birth in Old Changlang

Sl. No.	*Age group (yrs.)*	*No. of women*	*%*	*Mean*	*S.D*	*S.E*
1.	17–19	6	6.90			
2.	20–22	31	35.63			
3.	23–25	27	31.03	23.68	3.46	± 0.37
4.	26–28	15	17.24			
5.	29–31	5	5.75			
6.	32–34	3	3.45			
	Total	**87**	**100.00**			

Table 7.20 shows the age specific distribution of mothers according to age at first child birth. The age of mothers at the time of first child birth varies from 17 to 34 yrs. The highest number of women, i.e. 31 (35.63%) is reported to have their first child birth in the age group of 20–22 yrs. It is followed by the age group of 23–25 and 26–28 yrs., i.e. 27 women (31.03%) and 15 women (17.24%), respectively. The frequency decreases as the age group increases. The mean age at first child birth is 23.68 ± 0.37 with the S.D. of 3.46.

Table 7.21 shows the pregnant and pregnancy outcome of mothers according to their present age. The table shows that there are all total 87 mothers with all totals of 292 numbers of pregnancies. The table reveals that the highest number of mothers falls in the age group of 35–44 yrs., i.e. 26 (29.88%) mothers with the highest number of pregnancies, i.e. 78 (26.71%). The highest number of live birth is also recorded in this category with 73 numbers (25.00%). The next highest number of mothers falls in the category of 25–34 and 55–64 yrs., i.e. 16 mothers (18.39%) in each group with 36 (12.33%) and 62 (21.23%) number of pregnancies, respectively. Whereas 62 (21.23%) pregnancies is the second highest number of pregnancies with second highest number of live births, i.e. 60 (20.55%). The third highest number of mothers falls in the category of 45–54 yrs., i.e. 15 mothers (17.24%) with third highest number of pregnancies, i.e. 57 (19.52%) and 55 (18.83%) live births. There are 8 (9.19%) mothers with 41 (14.04%) number of pregnancies and 36 (12.33%) live births in the category of 65–74 yrs., 3 (3.45%) mothers each fall in the category of 15–24 yrs. and 75–84 yrs. with 5 (1.71%) and

Table 7.21: Distribution of Pregnant and Pregnancy Outcome of Mothers according to Present Age in Old Changlang

Sl. No.	Present age (yrs)	No. of mothers	No. of pregnancies	Carrying child	Pregnancy outcome							
					LB		SB		Spontaneous abortion		Total No. of Foetal wastage	
					No.	%	No.	%	No.	%	No.	%
1.	15–24	3	5	1	4	1.37	–	–	–	–	–	–
2.	25–34	16	36	8	28	9.59	–	–	–	–	–	–
3.	35–44	26	78	3	73	25.00	1	0.34	–	–	1	0.34
4.	45–54	15	57	–	55	18.83	1	0.34	1	0.34	2	0.68
5.	55–64	16	62	–	60	20.53	1	0.34	1	0.34	2	0.68
6.	65–74	8	41	–	36	12.33	4	1.37	1	0.34	5	1.71
7.	75–84	3	13	–	11	3.77	2	0.68	–	–	2	0.68
8.	85 +	–	–	–	–	–	–	–	–	–	–	–
	Total	**87**	**292**	**12**	**267**	**91.44**	**9**	**3.08**	**3**	**1.03**	**12**	**4.11**

13 (4.45%) pregnancies with 4 (1.37%) and 11 (3.77%) live births, respectively.

The total of 9 (3.08%) still birth is recorded in the village. Out of which 4 (1.37%) has been found in the category of 65–74 yrs. 2 (0.68%) still birth is recorded in the 75–84 yrs. While 1 (0.34%) still birth each recorded in the category of 35–44 yrs., 45–54 yrs. and 55–64 yrs., respectively.

Total number of 12 (4.11%) foetal wastage is recorded, out of which 9 (3.08%) are still birth and 3 (1.03%) are spontaneous abortion cases.

The table also reflects that there are 12 (13.79%) women who are pregnant. Out of which 8 (9.19%) women fall in the category of 25–34 yrs., 3 (3.45%) women in the category of 35–44 yrs. and 1 (1.15%) in the category of 15–24 yrs.

The distribution of mother's age at marriage and mortality experience of Old Changlang village has been shown in Table 7.22. The highest number of mothers, i.e. 46 (54.12%) out of the 85 mothers got married in the age group of 20–24 yrs. and also experienced the highest number of live births, i.e. 142 (53.18%) out of the 267 live births. It is followed by 22 (25.88%) mothers who got married in the age group of 25 and above years and also experienced the second highest number of live births, i.e. 59 (22.10%). Last one is followed by 17 (20.00%) mothers who got married in the age group of 15–19 yrs. with 66 (24.72%) numbers of live births.

Table 7.22: Distribution of Mothers according to Age at Marriage and Mortality Experience in Old Changlang

Sl. No.	*Age group (yrs.)*	*Number of mothers*	*Total live births*	*Infant mortality (0-1 yrs.)*	*Child mortality (1.1-5 yrs.)*	*Juvenile (5.1-14 Yrs.)*	*14.1+yrs.*
1.	Up to–14	–	–	–	–	–	–
2.	15–19	17	66	1	2	1	1
3.	20–24	46	142	–	2	2	1
4.	25 and above	22	59	–	1	–	–
	Total	**85**	**267**	**1**	**5**	**3**	**2**

The table also reflects that mortality in the village is divided in 3 categories. Five child mortality is recorded in the village out of which 2 each falls in the age group of 15–19 yrs. and 20–24 yrs. 1 child mortality is recorded in the age group of 25 and above years. 3 juvenile mortality is also recorded in the village with 1 falls in the 15–19 yrs. of age group and 2 falls in the 20–24 yrs. of age group. 2 adulthood death is found in the village out of which 1 falls in the age group of 15–19 yrs. and 1 falls in the age group of 20–24 yrs.

Table 7.23 shows the distribution of mothers' education and mortality experience. The highest number of mothers, i.e. 46 (54.12%) out of the total 85 mothers are illiterate and also experienced the highest number of live births, i.e. 171 (64.04%) out of the total 267 live births. Next is followed by 18 (21.18%) mothers in the category of primary level (Up to–IV) with the second highest number of live births, i.e. 51 (19.10%). It is followed by 9 (10.59%) mothers fall in the category of High school level (VIII–X) with 17 (6.37%) live births. 8 (9.41%) mothers fall in the category of Middle school level (V–VII) with 20 (7.49%) live births. While 3 (3.53%) mothers fall in the category of Higher Secondary level (XI–XII) with 6 (2.25%) number of live births. Only 1 (1.18%) woman falls in the category of Graduate-level with 2 (0.75%) live births.

Table 7.23: Distribution of Mothers Education and Mortality Experience in Old Changlang

Sl. No.	*Literacy*	*No. of mothers*	*Total live birth*	*Infant mortality (0-1 yr.)*	*Child mortality (1.1-5 yrs.)*	*Juvenile (5.1- 4 yrs.)*	*14.1+ yrs.*
1.	Illiterate	46	171	1	5	3	1
2.	Primary (Up to IV)	18	51	–	–	–	1
3.	Middle (V–VII)	8	20	–	–	–	–
4.	H.S. (VIII–X)	9	17	–	–	–	–
5.	H.S.S. (XI–XII)	3	6	–	–	–	–
6.	Graduate	1	2	–	–	–	–
	Total	**85**	**267**	**1**	**5**	**3**	**2**

Note: Out of 87 women, 85 women had given birth to child, while 1 woman had not given birth to child, 1 woman is pregnant (newly married).

The table also reflects that 11 mortalities were there in the village. Out of which 1 is infant mortality recorded in the illiterate category. Five were child mortality, also recorded in the illiterate category. Three were juvenile mortality again found in the illiterate category. Two were adulthood death among which 1 is recorded in the illiterate category and the other 1 is recorded in the primary (Up to–IV) category.

Table 7.24 shows the distribution of women according to age at menopause. The range of the age at menopause of the Lungchang women of Old Changlang village varies between 44–49 yrs. The highest number of women, which is 19 (57.58%), attains their menopause in the age group of 44–46 years. It is followed by the age group 47–49 yrs., the number of which is 14 (42.42%). Their mean age at menopause is 46.27 ± 0.26 yrs. with the S.D. of 1.48.

Table 7.24: Distribution of Women according to Age at Menopause in Old Changlang

Sl. No.	*Age group (yrs.)*	*No. of woman*	*Percentage*	*Mean*	*S.D.*	*S.E.*
1.	Up to 43	–	–			
2.	44–46	19	57.58	46.27	1.48	± 0.26
3.	47–49	14	42.42			
	Total	**33**	**100.00**			

Note: Out of 87 women, 33 had experienced menopause.

Rangkatu Village

The fertility performance of females has been reported in this chapter.

Table 7.25: Distribution of Females of Different Age Group in Village Rangkatu

Sl. No.	*Age group (yrs.)*	*No. of females*	*Percentage*
1.	9–13	33	18.54
2.	14–18	17	9.55
3.	19–23	21	11.80
4.	24–28	23	12.92
5.	29–33	12	6.74
6.	34–38	17	9.55
7.	39–43	18	10.11
8.	44–48	10	5.62
9.	49–53	6	3.37
10.	54–58	4	2.25
11.	59–63	5	2.81
12.	64–68	1	0.56
13.	69–73	3	1.69
14.	74–78	3	1.69
15.	79–83	4	2.25
16.	84–88	1	0.56
	Total	**178**	**100.00**

Note: Below 9 yrs. of age girls are not included.

The table reveals that the life span of the Lungchang females of the village is very long.

Table 7.25 shows the distribution of Lungchang females on the basis of different age group of Rangkatu village. It was observed that the maximum number female fall in the age group of 9–13 yrs. with 33 females (18.54%) out of total 178 females. However, in this table the females from 9 to 88 yrs. had been included only. The next is followed by 23 females (12.92%) and 21 females (11.80%) in the age group of 24–28 and 19–23 yrs., respectively. While 18 (10.11%) females in 39–43 age group, 17 (9.55%) females each in 14–18 yrs. and 34–38 yrs., 12 (6.74) females in 29–33 yrs., 10 (5.62%) in 44–48 yrs., 6 (3.37%) in 49–53 yrs., 5 (2.81%) in 59–63 yrs., 4 (2.25%) each in 64–68 and 79–83 yrs.,3 (1.69%) each in 69–73 and 74–78 yrs., 1 (0.56%) each in 64–68 and 84–88 yrs. It can be said that the oldest female in the village falls in the age group of 84–88 yrs.

Table 7.26: Distribution of Lungchang Girls according to Age at Menarche in Rangkatu

Sl. No.	*Age at Menarche (Yrs.)*	*No. of Girls*	*%*	*Mean*	*SD*	*SE*
1.	Up to 10	–	–			
2.	11	1	0.68			
3.	12	17	11.65			
4.	13	33	22.60	13.86	1.09	± 0.09
5.	14	55	37.67			
6.	15	31	21.23			
7.	16	9	6.17			
	Total	**146**	**100**			

Table 7.26 shows the distribution of Lungchang girls according to age at menarche of Rangkatu village. It was observed that 146 girls had experienced their menstruation within the age group of 11–16 out of total 226 females in the village.

The highest number of the girls had attained menarche in the age group of 14 yrs. with 55 girls (37.67%) out of 146. Next is followed by 33 (22.60%) and 31 (21.23%) in the age group of 13 and 15 yrs., respectively. While 17 girls (11.65%) experienced menarche at the age of 12 yrs., 9 (6.17%) in 16 yrs. and a single girl experienced in 11 yrs. The mean age at menarche is recorded 13.86 yrs. and S.E is ± 0.09 with the S.D of 1.09.

Table 7.27 distribution of women according to age at marriage of Rangkatu village shows that the marriage age of Lungchang girls of the village

Table 7.27: Distribution of Women according to Age at Marriage in Rangkatu

Sl. No.	Age at marriage	No. of women	%	Mean	SD	SE
1.	16	2	1.89			
2.	17	4	3.77			
3.	18	12	11.32			
4.	19	15	14.15			
5.	20	13	12.26			
6.	21	13	12.26			
7.	22	9	8.49			
8.	23	8	7.55	21.97	3.34	± 0.32
9.	24	6	5.66			
10.	25	7	6.60			
11.	26	3	2.83			
12.	27	2	1.89			
13.	28	6	5.66			
14.	29	–	–			
15.	30	2	1.89			
16.	31	2	1.89			
17.	32	1	0.94			
18.	33, 34	–	–			
19.	35	1	0.94			
	Total	**106**	**100.00**			

varies between 16 yrs. to 35 yrs. There are total of 106 married women found in the village, where the highest number of women recorded in the age group of 19 yrs. with 15 women (14.15%). Next are 13 women (12.26%) each who had married in the age group of 20 yrs. and 21 yrs., respectively. Twelve women (11.32%) are found married in 18 yrs. This reveals that the suitable age at marriage of the Lungchang girls is 18–21 yrs.

Table 7.27 also reveals that 6 women had got married in the age group of 30–35 yrs., i.e. 2 (1.89%) women each in 30 and 31 yrs. and a single woman each in the age group at 32 and 35 yrs.

The mean age at marriage is 21.97 with S.D. of 3.34 and S.E. is ± 0.32.

Table 7.28 shows the distribution of females according to their age at marriage by education. The table reveals that in the age group 15–19 yrs., maximum number of women, i.e. 20, who got married falls in the category of illiterate. It is followed by 6 females in the category of Middle (V–VII) School level. It is again followed by 4, 3 and 1 women in the category of Primary (Up to IV), High School (VII–X) and Higher Secondary School (XI–XII) level, respectively.

Table 7.28: Distribution of Females' Age at Marriage by Education in Rangkatu

Sl. No.	Age at marriage	Illiterate	Primary (Up to IV)	Middle (V-VII)	H.S. (VIII-X)	H.S.S. (XI-XII)	Total
1.	15–19	20	4	6	3	1	34
2.	20–24	38	2	4	3	1	48
3.	25 and Above	19	–	3	2	–	24
	Total	**77**	**6**	**13**	**8**	**2**	**106**

In the age group of 20–24 yrs. maximum number of women who got married falls in the category of illiterate, i.e. 38 in number. This is followed by 4, 3, 2 and 1 females who fall in the category of Middle School (V–VII), High School (VIII–X), Primary School (Up to IV) and Higher Secondary School (XI–XII) level, respectively.

In the age group 25 yrs. and above maximum number of women who got married also falls in the category of illiterate, i.e. 19. It is followed by 3 and 2 women who fall in the category of Middle School (V–VII) and High School (VIII–X) level, respectively.

Table 7.29: Distribution of Lungchang by Age Difference at Marriage in Rangkatu

Sl. No.	Age group (yrs.)	Male	%	Female	%	Total	%
1.	16	–	–	2	0.97	2	0.97
2.	17	–	–	4	1.93	4	1.93
3.	18	–	–	14	6.76	14	6.76
4.	19	2	0.97	14	6.76	16	7.73
5.	20	3	1.45	12	5.80	15	7.25
6.	21	3	1.45	13	6.28	16	7.73
7.	22	4	1.93	9	4.35	13	6.28
8.	23	7	3.38	8	3.86	15	7.25
9.	24	5	2.42	6	2.90	11	5.31
10.	25	14	6.76	7	3.38	21	10.14
11.	26	9	4.35	3	1.45	12	5.80
12.	27	5	2.42	2	0.97	7	3.38
13.	28	17	8.21	6	2.90	23	11.11
14.	29	11	5.31	–	–	11	5.31
15.	30	8	3.86	2	0.97	10	4.83
16.	31	3	1.45	2	0.97	5	2.42
17.	32	4	1.93	1	0.48	5	2.42
18.	33	2	0.97	–	–	2	0.97
19.	34	2	0.97	–	–	2	0.97
20.	35	1	0.48	1	0.48	2	0.97
21.	36	1	0.48	–	–	1	0.48
	Total	**101**	**48.79**	**106**	**51.21**	**207**	**100.00**

Table 7.29 shows the distribution of Lungchang population of Rangkatu village by age difference at marriage. From the table it is clear that maximum number of male, i.e. 17 (8.21%) out of 101 male got married at the age of 28 yrs. and the minimum number of male, i.e. 1 (0.48%) each got married at the age of 35 and 36 yrs., respectively.

Whereas, out of 106 females, maximum number of females, i.e. 14 (6.76%) each got married at the age of 18 and 19 yrs., respectively. The minimum number of females', i.e. 1 (0.48%) each got married at the age of 32 and 35 yrs., accordingly.

So, the above table reveals that in comparison to the males females got married at the early age.

Table 7.30: Marriage Area according to Spatial Distance in Rangkatu

Sl. No.	*Spatial distance*	*No. of marriages*	*Percentage*
1.	Below 1	71	66.98
2.	1–5	20	18.87
3.	6–10	1	0.94
4.	11–15	3	2.83
5.	16–20	4	3.77
6.	21–35	–	–
7.	36–40	1	0.94
8.	41–55	–	–
9.	56–60	1	0.94
10.	61–65	–	–
11.	66–70	1	0.94
12.	71–100	–	–
13.	Above 100	4	3.77
	Total	**106**	**100.00**

Table 7.30 shows the distribution of the marriage area of the Rangkatu village according to spatial distance. It is revealed that the total number of marriage recorded 106. Out of 106 marriages 71 marriages (66.98%) had been taken place within the spatial distance of below 1 km. Here the marriage below 1 km indicates the marriages within the same village. Twenty (18.87%) marriages had been taken place within the 1–5 km. 4 (3.77%) within16–20 km, 3 marriages (2.83%) within 11–15 km, 1 (0.94%) marriage each in the category 6–10 km, 36–40 km, 56–60 and 66–70 km, respectively. There are 4 (3.77%) marriages which took place in the category of the spatial distance of above 100 km.

From the table we can say that there is no such restriction on preference for area regarding the marriages.

Table 7.31: Distribution of Women according to Number of Conception in Rangkatu

Sl. No.	*No. of conception*	*Up to 30 yrs.*		*31- 44 yrs.*		*45 + yrs.*		*Total*	
		No. of women	*%*	*No. of women*	*%*	*No. of women*	*%*	*No. of women*	*%*
1.	1	10	9.80	2	1.96	2	1.96	14	13.73
2.	2	9	8.82	5	4.90	3	2.94	17	16.67
3.	3	5	4.90	16	15.69	2	1.96	23	22.55
4.	4	2	1.96	7	6.86	9	8.82	18	17.65
5.	5	1	0.98	6	5.88	6	5.88	13	12.75
6.	6	–	–	3	2.94	3	2.94	6	5.88
7.	7	–	–	1	0.98	4	3.92	5	4.90
8.	8	–	–	–	–	5	4.90	5	4.90
9.	9	–	–	–	–	–	–	–	–
10.	10	–	–	–	–	1	0.98	1	0.98
	Total	**27**	**26.47**	**40**	**39.22**	**35**	**34.31**	**102**	**100**

Note: Out of 106 married women 102 had experienced conception. 4 had not experienced conception yet.

Table 7.31 shows that the distribution of women according to number of conception. It is evident from the table that out of 106 married women 102 of them had experienced conception. The number of conception ranges from 1 to10. All the 27 women (26.47%) in the age group up to 30 yrs. are found to have a range of 1 to 5 conception. The highest number of women which is 10 in number (9.80%) under the category has conceived once. In the age group of 31–44 yrs. recording 40 women (39.22%), their conception ranges from 1 to7. Here, maximum of 16 women (15.69%) have conceived thrice. In the last age group of 45 and above years, recording 35 women (34.31%), the maximum of 9 women (8.82%) had the conception of 4 numbers. The table revels that the mothers of the higher age group shows the highest number of conception.

Table 7.32 shows the age specific distribution of mothers according to their age at first child birth. The age of mothers at the time of first child birth varies from 17 to 37 yrs. The highest number of women, i.e. 37 (36.27%) reported to have made their first child birth in the age group 20–22 yrs. It is followed by 23 (22.55%) and 21 (20.59%) women who falls in the age group of 23–25 yrs. and 17–19 yrs., respectively. The frequency decreases as the age group increases. The Mean Age at first child birth is 22.76 with S.D. of 4.06 and the S.E is ± 0.40.

The pregnant and pregnancy outcome of mothers, according to their present age is shown in Table 7.33. Table shows that there are all total

Table 7.32: Distribution of Women according to Age at First Child Birth in Rangkatu

Sl. No.	*Age group (yrs.)*	*No. of women*	*Percentage*	*Mean*	*S.D.*	*S.E.*
1.	17–19	21	20.59			
2.	20–22	37	36.27			
3.	23–25	23	22.55			
4.	26–28	11	10.79	22.76	4.06	± 0.40
5.	29–31	5	4.90			
6.	32–34	4	3.92			
7.	35–37	1	0.98			
	Total	**102**	**100.00**			

102 mothers with all totals of 393 numbers of pregnancies. It reveals that the highest number of mothers fall in the age group of 35–44 yrs., i.e. 34 mothers (33.33%) with a highest number of pregnancies, i.e. 129 (32.82%). The highest number of live birth is also recorded in this category with 124 numbers (31.55%) out of 374 live births. The next highest number of mothers falls in the category of 25–34 yrs., i.e. 24 (23.53%) with 65 (16.54%) number of pregnancies and 57 (14.50%) live births.

The third highest number of mothers falls in the category of 45–54 yrs., i.e. 15 (14.71%) mothers with second highest number of pregnancies, i.e. 68 (17.30%). The second highest live birth is also recorded in this category with 68 (17.30%). There were 9 (8.82%) mothers with 46 (11.70%) number of pregnancies with 45 (11.45%) live birth in the category 55–64 yrs., 8 (7.84%) mothers each in the category 15–24 and 75–84 yrs. with 16 pregnancies (3.31%) and 48 (11.70%) pregnancies and with 13 (3.31%) and 46 (11.70%) live births, respectively. Three mothers (2.94%) in the category 65–74 yrs. with 15 (3.82%) pregnancies with 15 (3.82%) live births and a single woman in the category 85–94 yrs. having 6 (1.53%) numbers of pregnancies with 6 (1.53%) live births. Total of 5 (1.27%) still birth has been recorded in the village. Four of them have been in the category of 35–44 yrs. while 1 (0.25%) still birth is recorded in the category of 25–34 yrs.

The table reflects that there was total number of 9 women who were pregnant. Out of these numbers 5 women were in the 25–34 yrs. of age group, 3 in 15–24 yrs. and 1 woman in 35–44 yrs.

Total number of 10 cases of foetal wastage is recorded, i.e. 5 still births and 5 were spontaneous abortion.

Table 7.33: Distribution of Pregnant and Pregnancy Outcome of Mothers according to their Present Age in Rangkatu

Sl. No.	Present age (yrs)	No. of mothers	No. of pregnancies	Carrying child	Pregnancy outcome							
					L.B		S.B		Spontaneous abortion		Total foetal wastage	
					No.	%	No.	%	No.	%	No.	%
1.	15–24	8	16	3	13	3.31	–	–	–	–	–	–
2.	25–34	24	65	5	57	14.50	1	0.25	2	0.51	3	0.76
3.	35–44	34	129	1	124	31.55	4	1.02	–	–	4	1.02
4.	45–54	15	68	–	68	17.30	–	–	–	–	–	–
5.	55–64	9	46	–	45	11.45	–	–	1	0.25	1	0.25
6.	65–74	3	15	–	15	3.82	–	–	–	–	–	–
7.	75–84	8	48	–	46	11.70	–	–	2	0.51	2	0.51
8.	85–94	1	6	–	6	1.53	–	–	–	–	–	–
Total		**102**	**393**	**9**	**374**	**95.16**	**5**	**1.27**	**5**	**1.27**	**10**	**2.54**

Table 7.34: Distribution of Mothers according to Age at Marriage and Mortality Experience in Rangkatu

Sl. No.	*Age group (yrs.)*	*Number of mothers*	*Total live births*	*Infant mortality (0-1 yrs.)*	*Child mortality (1.1-5 yrs.)*	*Juvenile (5.1-14)*	*14.1+yrs.*
1.	Up to–14	–	–	–	–	–	–
2.	15–19	33	120	5	2	–	1
3.	20–24	47	160	5	1	1	1
4.	25 and above	22	94	6	2	1	7
	Total	**102**	**374**	**16**	**5**	**2**	**9**

Table 7.34 shows the distribution of mothers' age at marriage and mortality experience of Rangkatu village. The highest number of mothers got married in the age group of 20–24 yrs. with 47 mothers (46.08%) out of the total 102 mothers and also experienced the highest number of live birth, i.e. 160 (42.78%) out of the total 374 live births. Next is followed by 33 mothers (32.35%) with 120 live births (30.09%) in the age group of 15–19 yrs., and 22 mothers (21.57%) with 94 live births (25.13%) in the category 25 yrs. and above.

The table also reflects the total of 23 mortality in the village, which is divided in 3 categories. There were 16 infant mortality with 6 numbers were in above 25 yrs. of age group. While 5 infant mortalities were recorded, each in the age group of 15–19 and 20–24 yrs. were also been recorded. It is also revealed 5 child mortality with 2 each in the age group of 15– 19 yrs. and 25 yrs. and above. The analysis also indicates 1 child mortality in the age group of 20–24 yrs. At the same time 2 cases of juvenile mortality have been found with 1 each in 20–24 yrs. and above 25 years. The table also reflects 9 number of Adulthood death with 7 in the category 25 yrs. and above and 1 each in the category of 15–19 and 20–24 yrs. 5 child mortality with 2 each in 15 –19 and 25 and above years age group and 1 in the age group of 20–24 yrs. 2 juvenile mortality with 1 each in 20–24 and 25 and above years. The tables also reflects 9 number of adult hood deaths with 7 in the category 25 and above and 1 each in the category of 15–19 and 20–24 yrs.

Table 7.35 shows the distribution of mother's education and mortality experience. The highest number of mother's, i.e. 74 out of the total of 102 mothers' is illiterate and also experienced the highest number of live births, i.e. 296 out of the total 374 live births. Next is followed 12 mothers' with the second highest number of illiterate, i.e. 36 falls in the Middle School (V–VII) category. Eight mothers' with 19 numbers of live births falls in the High School (VIII–X) level. Six mothers with 19 live births falls in the Primary School (I–IV) level and 2 mothers with 4 numbers of live births falls in the Higher Secondary School (XI–XII) level.

Table 7.35: Distribution of Mothers' Education and Mortality Experience in Rangkatu

Sl. No.	*Literacy*	*No. of mothers*	*Total live birth*	*Infant mortality (0-1 yrs.)*	*Child mortality (1.1-5 yrs.)*	*Juvenile (5.1- 4 yrs.)*	*14.1+yrs.*
1.	Illiterate	74	296	15	4	2	8
2.	Primary (Up to IV)	6	19	–	–	–	1
3.	Middle (V–VII)	12	36	1	1	–	–
4.	H.S. (VIII–X)	8	19	–	–	–	–
5.	H.S.S. (XI–XII)	2	4	–	–	–	–
	Total	**102**	**374**	**16**	**5**	**2**	**9**

The table also reflects that 32 mortalities were found in the village. Out of which 16 infant mortalities has been recorded in the village. Fifteen of them out of these 16 fall in the illiterate category and 1 falls in the Middle School (V–VII) category. Five child mortalities were found in the village, out of which 4 falls in the illiterate and 1 fall in the Middle School (V–VII) level. Two juvenile mortalities are recorded in the illiterate category. Nine adulthoods mortality are found in the village out of which, 8 falls in the illiterate category and 1 falls in the Primary (I–IV) level.

Table 7.36: Distribution of Women according to Age at Menopause

Sl. No.	*Age group (yrs.)*	*No. of women*	*%*	*Mean*	*SD*	*SE*
1.	Up to 43	–	–			
2.	44–46	11	37.93	46.86	1.45	±0.27
3.	47–49	18	62.07			
	Total	**29**	**100**			

Note: Out of 106 women, only 29 women had experienced menopause.

Table 7.36 shows the distribution of women according to age at menopause shows that the range of the age at menopause of the Lungchang women of Rangkatu village. It has revealed that range of age at menopause varies between 44–49 yrs. The table also indicates that out of the total 106 women only 29 women had attained their menopause. Out of the total 29 women who had attained menopause, highest number is recorded in the age group of 47–49 yrs. with 18 women (62.07%) and next in the age group of 44–46 yrs. with 11 women (37.93%). The mean age at menopause is recorded 46.86 ± 0.27 yrs. with the S.D. of 1.45.

Mukloms Tangsas

The fertility determinants of Mukloms have been collected from three villages and presented as follows:

Laktong Village

Table 7.37 shows the distribution of Muklom females on the basis of different age group. The total number of females is 42. However, in this table female from 9 to 73 yrs. of age has been included. Maximum number of females, i.e. 9 (21.43%), falls in the age group of 29–33 yrs. The second highest number of females, i.e. 6 (14.29%) falls in each of the age groups of 9–13 and 19–23 yrs., which is followed by the 5 (11.90%) female members fall in the age group of 14–18 yrs., which is again followed by 4 (9.52%) in the age group 39–43 yrs., 3 (7.14%) in 34–38 yrs., 2 (4.76%) in 24–28, 44–48, 64–68 and 69–73 yrs. and 1 in 49–50 yrs., respectively. Thus, it may be said that the oldest female in the village falls in the age group of 69–73 yrs., the percentage of which is 4.76 and the number is 2. The table reveals that the life span of the Muklom females is long.

Table 7.37: Distribution of Females on the Basis of Different Age Group in Laktong

Sl. No.	*Age group (yrs.)*	*No. of females*	*Percentage*
1.	9– 13	6	14.29
2.	14–18	5	11.90
3.	19–23	6	14.29
4.	24–28	2	4.76
5.	29–33	9	21.43
6.	34–38	3	7.14
7.	39–43	4	9.52
8.	44–48	2	4.76
9.	49–53	1	2.38
10.	54–63	–	–
11.	64–68	2	4.76
12.	69–73	2	4.76
	Total	**42**	**100.00**

Note: Below 9 yrs. of age girls are not included.

The distribution of Muklom girls (Taole 7.38) according to age at menarche of Laktong village shows that 35 females had experienced their menstruation. It is observed from the table that the age at menarche varies from 12 yrs. to 16 yrs. The table also reveals that maximum number of girls, i.e. 17 (48.57%) attain menarche at the age of 14 yrs. However, concentration of females, i.e. 13 (37.14%) in 15 yrs. is also appreciably high. Three (8.57%) female members of the village have attain their menarche at the age of 13 yrs. 1 (2.86%) female in each group has attain their menarche at the age of 12 yrs. and 16 yrs., respectively.

Table 7.38: Distribution of Muklom Girls according to Age at Menarche in Laktong

Sl. No.	*Age at Menarche*	*No. of Girls*	*%*	*Mean*	*SD*	*SE*
1.	9–11	–	–			
2.	12	1	2.86			
3.	13	3	8.57	14.28	0.78	±0.13
4.	14	17	48.57			
5.	15	13	37.14			
6.	16	1	2.86			
	Total	**35**	**100.00**			

The mean menarcheal age is calculated as 14.28 yrs., with a standard deviation of 0.78 and standard error is ±0.13.

Table 7.39: Distribution of Women according to Age at Marriage in Laktong

Sl. No.	*Age at marriage*	*No. of women*	*Percentage*	*Mean*	*SD*	*SE*
1.	16	–	–			
2.	17	1	4.35			
3.	18	1	4.35			
4.	19	3	13.04			
5.	20	2	8.70			
6.	21	2	8.70	23.30	3.56	±0.74
7.	22	–	–			
8.	23	2	8.70			
9.	24	2	8.70			
10.	25	1	4.35			
11.	26	4	17.39			
12.	27	2	8.70			
13.	28	2	8.70			
14.	29	1	4.35			
	Total	**23**	**100.00**			

Table 7.39 shows the distribution of Muklom women according to age at marriage. It was observed that age at marriage varies between 17–29 yrs. There are all total 23 Muklom married women in the village. The table reveals that the highest number of women, i.e. 4 (17.39%) got married in the age of 26 yrs., which is followed by the 3 women (13.04%) who got married at the age of 19 yrs. 2 (8.70%) women in each group who got married at the age of 20, 21, 23, 24, 27 and 28 yrs., respectively. 1 (4.35%) woman in each group is found to got married at the age of 17, 18, 25 and 29 yrs., respectively.

The mean age at marriage of Muklom women is 23.30 and the standard error is ±0.74 with the standard deviation of 3.56.

Table 7.40 shows the distribution of female according to their age at marriage by education. The table reveals that in the age group 15–19 yrs. there are 5 women, out of which, maximum number of women who got married falls in the category of illiterate, i.e. 4. And only 1 woman falls in the category of High School (VIII–X) level.

Table 7.40: Distribution of Women according to Age at Marriage by Education in Laktong

Sl. No.	*Age at marriage*	*Illiterate*	*Primary (Up to IV)*	*Middle (V-VII)*	*H.S. (VIII-X)*	*H.S.S. (XI-XII)*	*Total*
1.	15–19	4	–	–	1	–	5
2.	20–24	4	–	2	–	2	8
3.	25 & Above	7	–	1	1	1	10
	Total	**15**	**–**	**3**	**2**	**3**	**23**

In the age group 20–24 yrs. 8 women got married. Here, maximum of 4 women fall in the illiterate category. Two women in each fall in the Middle School level (V–VII) and Higher Secondary level (XI–XII), respectively.

Ten women got married in the age group of above 25 yrs., out of which, maximum number of women, i.e. 7 women fall in the illiterate category. Only 1 woman each falls in the Middle (V–VII) High School (VIII–X) and Higher Secondary (XI–XII).

Table 7.41 shows the distribution of Mukloms of Laktong village by age difference at marriage. From the table it is clear that maximum number of male, i.e. 4 (9.52%) out of 19 (45.24%) males got married at the age of 30 yrs. The lowest number of male, i.e. 1 (2.38%) got married at the age of 22, 26, 31 and 34 yrs.

Whereas, out of 23 (54.76%) females, maximum number of women i.e. 4 (9.52%) got married at the age of 26 yrs.

Table 7.41: Distribution of Muklom by Age Difference at Marriage in Laktong

Sl. No.	Age group (yrs.)	Male	%	Female	%	Total	%
1.	16	–	–	–	–	–	–
2.	17	–	–	1	2.38	1	2.38
3.	18	–	–	1	2.38	1	2.38
4.	19	–	–	3	7.14	3	7.14
5.	20	–	–	2	4.76	2	4.76
6.	21	–	–	2	4.76	2	4.76
7.	22	1	2.38	–	–	1	2.38
8.	23	2	4.76	2	4.76	4	9.52
9.	24	2	4.76	2	4.76	4	9.52
10.	25	–	–	1	2.38	1	2.38
11.	26	1	2.38	4	9.52	5	11.90
12.	27	2	4.76	2	4.76	4	9.52
13.	28	2	4.76	2	4.76	4	9.52
14.	29	3	7.14	1	2.38	4	9.52
15.	30	4	9.52	–	–	4	9.52
16.	31	1	2.38	–	–	1	2.38
17.	32–33	–	–	–	–	–	–
18.	34	1	2.38	–	–	1	2.38
	Total	**19**	**45.24**	**23**	**54.76**	**42**	**100.00**

The table reveals that in comparison to males maximum number of females got married at the early age.

Table 7.42: Marriage Area according to Spatial Distance in Laktong

Sl. No.	Spatial Distance (km)	No. of Marriages	Percentage
1.	Below 1	4	17.39
2.	1–5	1	4.35
3.	6–10	5	21.74
4.	11–15	3	13.04
5.	16–20	4	17.39
6.	21–25	–	–
7.	26–30	2	8.70
8.	31–40	–	–
9.	41–45	1	4.35
10.	46–100	–	–
11.	Above 100	3	13.04
	Total	**23**	**100**

Table 7.42 shows the distribution of the marriage area of the Laktong village according to spatial distance. The table shows that there are all total 23 marriages recorded. Out of 23 marriages, 5 (21.74%) marriages have taken place within the spatial distance of 6–10 km. 4 (17.39%) marriages in each category is recorded in the category of the spatial distance of below 1 km and 16–20 km. 3 (13.04%) marriages each have been found within the spatial distance of 11–15 km and above 100 km which is followed by 2 (8.70%) marriages found in the category of 26–30 km. Only 1 (4.35%) marriage each found in the spatial distance of 1–5 km and 41–45 km.

From Table 7.42 we can say that there is no such restriction on preference for area regarding the marriage.

Table 7.43 shows the distribution of women according to number of conception. It is evident from the table that all the 23 married women have experienced the conception. The number of conception ranges from 1 to 8.

All the 6 women (26.09%) in the age group up to 30 yrs. are found to have a range of 1 to 3 conceptions. The highest number of women, i.e. 4 (17.39%) under the category has conceived twice.

Table 7.43: Distribution of Women according to Number of Conceptions in Laktong

Sl. No.	*No. of conception*	*Up to 30 yrs.*		*31–44 yrs.*		*45+ yrs.*		*Total*	
		No. of women	*%*	*No. of women*	*%*	*No. of women*	*%*	*No. of women*	*%*
1.	1	1	4.35	–	–	1	4.35	2	8.70
2.	2	4	17.39	2	8.70	–	–	6	26.09
3.	3	1	4.35	5	21.74	–	–	6	26.09
4.	4	–	–	3	13.04	3	13.04	6	26.09
5.	5	–	–	–	–	–	–	–	–
6.	6	–	–	–	–	1	4.35	1	4.35
7.	7	–	–	–	–	1	4.35	1	4.35
8.	8	–	–	–	–	1	4.35	1	4.35
	Total	**6**	**26.09**	**10**	**43.48**	**7**	**30.43**	**23**	**100**

In the age group of 31–44 yrs. recording 10 women (43.48%) whose conception ranges from 2–4. Here maximum of 5 women (21.74%) have conceived thrice. In the age group of 45 yrs. and above, 7 women (30.43%) were recorded. The maximum of 3 women (13.04%) has conceived four times. Table 7.45 reveals that the mothers of the higher age group show the highest number of conception.

Table 7.44: Distribution of Women according to Age at First Child Birth in Laktong

Sl. No.	*Age group (yrs.)*	*No. of women*	*Percentage*	*Mean*	*S.D*	*S.E*
1.	17–19	2	8.70			
2.	20–22	7	30.43			
3.	23–25	4	17.39	24.26	3.64	±0.76
4.	26–28	7	30.43			
5.	29–31	3	13.04			
	Total	**23**	**100**			

Table 7.44 shows the age specific distribution of mothers according to age at first child-birth. It is revealed that the age of mothers at the time of first childbirth varies from 17 to 31 yrs. The highest number of women, i.e. 7 (30.43%) women each reported to have made their first child-birth in the age group 20–22 and 26–28 yrs., respectively. It is followed by 4 (17.39%) women in the age group 23–25 yrs. The table also indicates that 3 (13.04%) and 2 (8.70%) women in the age groups 29–31 yrs. and 17–19 yrs. accordingly. The mean age at first childbirth is 24.26±0.76 with the S.D. of 3.64.

The pregnant and pregnancy outcome of mothers according to their present age is presented in Table 4.45. The table reveals that there are all

Table 7.45: Distribution of Pregnant and Pregnancy Outcome of Mothers according to their Present Age in Laktong

Sl. No.	*Present age (yrs)*	*No. of mothers*	*No. of preg-nancies*	*Carrying child*	*Pregnancy*							
					L.B		*S.B*		*Spontaneous abortion*		*Total no. of Foetal wastage*	
					No.	*%*	*No.*	*%*	*No.*	*%*	*No.*	*%*
1.	15–24	2	4	–	4	4.65			–	–	–	–
2.	25–34	8	26	4	22	25.58			–	–	–	–
3.	35–44	6	20	2	18	20.39			–	–	–	–
4.	45–54	3	16	–	16	18.60			–	–	–	–
5.	55–64	–	–	–	–	–			–	–	–	–
6.	65-74	4	20	–	18	20.93	18	20.93	2	2.32	2	2.32
	Total	**23**	**86**	**6**	**78**	**90.70**			**2**	**2.32**	**2**	**2.32**

total 23 Muklom mothers with total number of 86 pregnancies. It is found that the maximum number of mothers, i.e. 8 (34.78%) falls in the age group of 25–34 yrs. with a highest number of pregnancies, i.e. 26 (30.23%).

The highest number of live births is also recorded in this category with 22 numbers (25.58%) out of 78 live births. The next highest number of mothers falls in the category of 35–44 yrs., i.e. 6 with third highest number of pregnancies, i.e. 20 (23.25%) and 18 (20.93%) live births. The third highest number of mothers fall in the category of 65–74 yrs., i.e. 4 (17.39%) with second highest number of pregnancies, i.e. 20 (23.25%) and 18 live births (20.93%). This is followed by 3 mothers (13.04%) in the category of 45–54 yrs. with 16 pregnancies (18.60%) and 16 live births (18.60%). There are 2 mothers in the category of 15–24 yrs. with 4 (4.65%) numbers of pregnancies and 4 live births (4.65%). There is no artificial abortion.

Table 7.45 reflects that there were all total 6 women who were pregnant. Out of 6 pregnant women, 4 women fall in the age group of 25–34 yrs. and 2 fall in the age group of 35–44 yrs. Two cases of foetal wastage were recorded. All were spontaneous abortion.

Table 7.46: Distribution of Mothers according to Age at Marriage and Mortality Experience in Laktong

Sl. No.	*Age group (yrs.)*	*Number of mothers*	*Total live births*	*Infant mortality (0-1 yrs.)*	*Child mortality (1.1-5 yrs.)*	*Juvenile (5.1-14)*	*14.1+ yrs.*
1.	Up to 14	–	–	–	–	–	–
2.	15 – 19	5	16	–	–	–	–
3.	20 – 24	8	27	–	–	–	1
4.	25 and above	10	35	1	–	–	2
	Total	**23**	**78**	**1**	**-**	**-**	**3**

Table 7.46 shows the distribution of mother's age at marriage and mortality experience of Laktong village. The highest number of mothers got married in the age group of 25 and above years. Ten mothers out of 23 also experienced the highest number of live births, i.e. 35 out of all total 78 live births. This is followed by 8 mothers who got married in the age group of 20–24 yrs. with the second highest live births, i.e. 27. Last one is followed by 5 mothers who got married in the age group of 15–19 yrs. with 16 numbers of live births.

Table 7.46 also reflects that one case of mortality is recorded in the village, which falls in the category of infant mortality and is experienced by the mother in the age group of 25 yrs. and above. Table also recorded 3 number of adulthood death out of which 2 adulthood deaths falls in the age group of 25 yrs. and above and 1 in the age group of 20–24 yrs.

Table 7.47 shows the distribution of mothers' education and mortality experience. Out of the total 23 mothers, the highest number of mothers, i.e. 15 falls in the category of illiterate and also experienced the highest number of live births, i.e. 56 out of the total 78 live births. Next is followed by 3 mothers in each category within the educational status of Middle (V–VII) and XI–XII standard and experienced 9 and 6 live births, respectively. Two mothers with the educational status of High (VIII–X) school level experienced 7 live births.

Table 7.47: Distribution of Mothers' Education and Mortality Experience in Laktong

Sl. No.	*Literacy*	*No. of mothers*	*Total live birth*	*Infant mortality (0-1 yrs.)*	*Child mortality (1.1-5 yrs.)*	*Juvenile (5.1- 4 yrs.)*	*14.1+ yrs.*
1.	Illiterate	15	56	–	–	–	3
2.	Primary (Up to IV)	–	–	–	–	–	–
3.	Middle (V–VII)	3	9	–	–	–	–
4.	H.S. (VIII–X)	2	7	1	–	–	–
5.	H.S.S. (XI–XII)	3	6	–	–	–	–
	Total	**23**	**78**	**1**	**–**	**–**	**3**

Table 7.47 reflects that 4 mortalities were reported in the village. One case of infant mortality is recorded in the category of High School level (VIII–X). Three adulthood deaths are recorded in the illiterate category.

Table 7.48 shows distribution of Muklom women according to age at menopause. From the table it is clear that the range of the age at menopause varies from 44–49 yrs.

Table 7.48: Distribution of Women according to Age at Menopause in Laktong

Sl. No.	*Age group*	*No. of women*	*%*	*Mean*	*S.D.*	*S.E.*
1.	Up to 43	–	–			
2.	44–46	5	71.43	45.86	1.35	±0.51
3.	47–49	2	28.57			
	Total	**7**	**100.00**			

The maximum number of women, which is 5 (71.43%), has attained their menopause in the age group of 44–46 yrs. And 2 (28.57%) women have attained their menopause in the age group of 47–49 yrs. The mean age at menopause is 45.86 with the standard deviation of 1.35 and the standard error is ±0.51.

Simrang Village

The fertility performance of females has been incorporated in this chapter. The maximum number of females falls in the age group of 14–18 yrs. with 23 females (26.74%) out of the total 86 females, which is followed by 12 (13.95%) females fall in each of the age group 19–23 and 34–38 yrs. (Table 7.49). It is followed by 11 (12.79%) females in 9–13 yrs., 8 females in the 39–43 yrs., 4 (4.65%) females in the 29–33 yrs. of age group accordingly. 3 (3.49%) females fall in each of the age group 24–28, 44–48 and 64–68 yrs., respectively. Two (2.32%) females each in each age group 59–63 and 74–78 yrs. accordingly. One (1.16%) female in each age group 49–53, 54–58 and 69–73 yrs., respectively.

Table 7.49: Distribution of Females on the Basis of Different Age Groups in Village Simrang

Sl. No.	*Age Group (yrs.)*	*No. of Females*	*Percentage*
1.	9–13	11	12.79
2.	14–18	23	26.74
3.	19–23	12	13.95
4.	24–28	3	3.49
5.	29–33	4	4.65
6.	34–38	12	13.95
7.	39–43	8	9.30
8.	44–48	3	3.49
9.	49–53	1	1.16
10.	54–58	1	1.16
11.	59–63	2	2.32
12.	64–68	3	3.49
13.	69–73	1	1.16
14.	74–78	2	2.32
15.	79–93	–	–
	Total	**86**	**100.00**

Note: In this table females below 9 yrs. of age are not included.

Table 7.49 reveals that the life span of Muklom females of Simrang village is long.

Table 7.50 shows the distribution of women menstruating at different age. It is observed from the table that the age at menarche varies from 12–15 yrs. The table also reveals that the maximum number of girls attain menarche at the age of 14 yrs., which is 33 (47.14%) in number. However, concentration of women in 13 yrs. is also appreciably high, i.e. 20 (28.57%) in number. It is followed by 14 (20.00%) women in 15 yrs. and 3 (4.29%) women in 12 yrs., respectively. The mean menarcheal age is calculated as 13.83±0.09 yrs.

Table 7.50: Distribution of Muklom Girls according to Age at Menarche in Village Simrang

Sl. No.	Age at Menarche	No of Girls	%	Mean	S.D.	S.E.
1.	9–11	–	–			
2.	12	3	4.29			
3.	13	20	28.57	13.83	0.75	±0.62
4.	14	33	47.14			
5.	15	14	20.00			
6.	16	–	–			
	Total	**70**	**100**			

The distribution of Muklom women of Simrang village according to their age at marriage has been presented in Table 7.51.

Table 7.51: Distribution of Women according to Age at Marriage in Village Simrang

Sl. No.	Age at Marriage	No. of women	%	Mean	S.D.	S.E.
1.	16	1	2.63			
2.	17	2	5.26			
3.	18	5	13.16			
4.	19	5	13.16			
5.	20	4	10.53			
6.	21	2	5.26			
7.	22	4	10.53	21.37	3.83	±0.62
8.	23	1	2.63			
9.	24	5	13.16			
10.	25-26	–	–			
11.	27	4	10.53			
12.	28	2	5.26			
13.	29	–	–			
14.	30	2	5.26			
	Total	**37**	**100**			

Note: Non-Tangsas are not included.

Their marriage age varies from 16 to 30 yrs. There are all total 37 married women in the village. The highest number of women, i.e. 5 (13.16%) got married at the age of 18, 19 and 24 yrs. It is followed by 4 (10.53%) each got married at the age of 20, 22 and 27 yrs., respectively. Two (5.26%) each got married at the age of 17, 21, 28 and 30 yrs. One (2.63%) woman each got married at the age of 16 and 23 yrs., respectively. Their mean age at marriage is 21.37 yrs. and S.E. is ±0.62 with the S.D. of 3.83.

Table 7.52 shows the distribution of female according to their age at marriage by education. The table reveals that in the age group 15–19 yrs. maximum number of women who got married falls in the category of illiterate, i.e. 10. It is followed by 2 women who fall in the Primary (Up to IV) category. It is followed by 1 woman each fall in the category of Middle School (V–VII) level and High School Level (VIII–X).

Table 7.52: Distribution of Women according to Age at Marriage by Education in Simrang

Sl. No.	*Age at Marriage*	*Illite-rate*	*Primary (up to IV)*	*Middle (V-VII)*	*H.S. (VIII-X)*	*H.S.S. (XI-XII)*	*Graduate and P.G.*	*Total*
1.	15–19	10	2	1	1	–	–	14
2.	20–24	8	4	2	1	1	–	16
3.	25 and Above	6	2	–	–	–	–	8
	Total	**24**	**8**	**3**	**2**	**1**	**–**	**38**

In the age group 20–24 yrs. again the maximum number of females who got married falls in the illiterate category which is 8 in number. It is followed by 4 women in the category of Primary, 2 in Middle School level and 1 each in High School and Higher Secondary School level.

In the age group 25 and above year's maximum number of females who got married, fall in the illiterate category, i.e. 6 in number. 2 women fall in the Primary level.

Table 7.53 shows the distribution of Muklom population of Simrang village by age difference at marriage. From the table it is clear that maximum number of male, i.e. 5 (6.85%) out of 35 (47.95%) got married at the age of above 25 yrs. Whereas, out of the 38 (52.05%) females maximum number of women, i.e. 5 (6.85%) each got married at the age of 18, 19 and 24 yrs., respectively. Table 7.53 reveals that the females got married early in comparison to the male's age at marriage. As the age at marriage increases the frequency of males also increases whereas the frequency of females decreases with the increasing of age at marriage.

Table 7.53: Distribution of Muklom by Age Difference at Marriage in Simrang

Sl. No.	Age Group	Male	%	Female	%	Total	%
1.	16	–	–	1	1.37	1	1.37
2.	17	–	–	3	4.11	3	4.11
3.	18	–	–	5	6.85	5	6.85
4.	19	1	1.37	5	6.85	6	8.22
5.	20	–	–	4	5.48	4	5.48
6.	21	2	2.74	3	4.11	5	6.85
7.	22	2	2.74	3	4.11	5	6.85
8.	23	2	2.74	1	1.37	3	4.11
9.	24	2	2.74	5	6.85	7	9.59
10.	25	5	6.85	–	–	5	6.85
11.	26	2	2.74	–	–	2	2.74
12.	27	4	5.48	4	5.48	8	10.96
13.	28	3	4.11	2	2.74	5	6.85
14.	29	1	1.37	1	1.37	2	2.74
15.	30	4	5.48	1	1.37	5	6.85
16.	31	2	2.74	–	–	2	2.74
17.	32	1	1.37	–	–	1	1.37
18.	33	2	2.74	–	–	2	2.74
19.	34	–	–	–	–	–	–
20.	35	2	2.74	–	–	2	2.74
	Total	**35**	**47.95**	**38**	**52.05**	**73**	**100.00**

Table 7.54 shows the distribution of the marriage area of the Simrang village according to spatial distance. The table shows that the total number of marriages recorded is 38 where 26 (68.42%) are found within the spatial distance below 1 km. Marriage below 1 km means marriage within the same village. Six (15.79%) marriages are found within the spatial distance of 46–50 km. 2 (5.26%) marriages are recorded within 41–45 km. One (2.63%) marriage each recorded within the spatial distance of 21–25 km, 51–55 km, 71–75 km and above 100 km, respectively.

Table 7.54: Marriage Area according to Spatial Distance in Simrang

Sl. No.	Spatial Distance (km)	No. of Marriages	Percentage
1.	Below 1	26	68.42
2.	21–25	1	2.63
3.	41–45	2	5.26
4.	46–50	6	15.79
5.	51–55	1	2.63
6.	71–75	1	2.63
7.	100 +	1	2.63
	Total	**38**	**100.00**

Table 7.55 shows the distribution of women according to number of conception. Out of the 38 married women, 37 had experienced conception.

Table 7.55: Distribution of Women according to Number of Conception in Simrang Village

Sl. No.	*No. of conception*	*Up to 30 years*		*31–44 years*		*45+ years*		*Total*	
		No. of women	*%*	*No. of women*	*%*	*No. of women*	*%*	*No. of women*	*%*
1.	1	4	10.81	–	–	1	2.70	5	13.51
2.	2	1	2.70	3	8.11	–	–	4	10.81
3.	3	2	5.40	5	13.51	2	5.40	9	24.32
4.	4	1	2.70	5	13.51	1	2.70	7	18.92
5.	5	–	–	5	13.51	2	5.40	7	18.92
6.	6	–	–	–	–	1	2.70	1	2.70
7.	7	–	–	–	–	1	2.70	1	2.70
8.	8	–	–	–	–	1	2.70	1	2.70
9.	9	–	–	–	–	–	–	–	–
10.	10	–	–	1	2.70	1	2.70	2	5.40
	Total	**8**	**21.62**	**19**	**51.35**	**10**	**27.03**	**37**	**100.00**

Table 7.55 reveals that the number of conception ranges from 1 to 10. Out of 8 (21.62%) women in the age group up to 30 yrs., 4 (10.81%) women had 1 conception. Two (5.40%) had conceived thrice. One (2.70%) woman each had 2 conceptions and 4 conceptions, respectively.

In the age group 31–44 yrs., recording 19 (51.35%) women, their conception ranges from 2 to 10. Here, maximum of 5 (13.51%) women each had experienced 3, 4 and 5 conceptions. While 3 (8.11%) women had conceived twice and 1 (2.70%) woman experienced 10 conceptions.

In the age group 45 yrs. and above, 10 (27.03%) women were recorded whose conceptions range from 1 to 10. Here, maximum of 2 (5.40%) women each had experienced 3 and 5 conceptions, respectively.

Table 7.56: Distribution of Women according to Age at First Childbirth in Simrong

Sl. No.	*Age group (yrs.)*	*No. of women*	*%*	*Mean*	*S.D.*	*S.E.*
1.	17–19	9	24.32			
2.	20–22	10	27.03			
3.	23–25	10	27.03	22.57	3.66	±0.60
4.	26–28	5	13.51			
5.	29–31	3	8.11			
	Total	**37**	**100.00**			

Table 7.56 shows the distribution of mothers according to their age at first childbirth. The table shows that the age of mothers at the time of first childbirth varies from 17 to 31 yrs. The highest number of women, i.e. 10 (27.03%) reported to have their first child birth in the age group of 20–22 and 23–25 yrs. It is followed by 9 (24.32%) women in the age group of 17–19 yrs. There are 5 (13.51%) women in the age group of 26–28 yrs. and 3 (8.11%) in the age group of 29–31 yrs. had their first childbirth. The frequency decreases as the age group increases. The mean age at first childbirth is 22.57±0.60 yrs. with the S.D. of 3.66.

Table 7.57 shows the pregnant and pregnancy outcome of mothers according to their present age. It is seen that there are all total 37 mothers with all totals of 144 numbers of pregnancies. The table also reveals that the highest number of mothers falls in the age group 35–44 yrs., i.e. 16 mothers with the highest number of pregnancies, i.e. 68. The highest number of live births is also recorded in this category with 67 (46.53%) numbers.

The second highest number of mothers falls in the category of 25–34 yrs., i.e. 7 mothers with the second highest number of pregnancies, i.e. 20 with 20 (13.89%) live births which is again the second highest number of live births. Four mothers each fall in the age groups 15–24 and 65–74 yrs. with 4 and 18 numbers of pregnancies, with 3 (2.08%) and 16 (11.11%) live births. Three mothers with 13 numbers of pregnancies and 13 (9.03%) live births have been recorded in the age group 45–54 yrs. It is also revealed 2 mothers with 18 pregnancies and 18 live births in the age group 75–84 yrs. One mother with 3 pregnancies and 1 (0.69%) live birth are found in the age group of 55–64 yrs. Two (1.39%) numbers of stillbirths are recorded in the age group 65–74 yrs. Two cases of foetal wastage are also found in the 55–64 yrs. of age group, which is due to spontaneous abortion.

Table 7.57 also reflects that 2 women are pregnant in the village, out of which 1 fall in the 15–24 yrs. and 1 in the 35–44 yrs. of age group. Only 2 cases of foetal wastage are recorded.

Table 7.58 shows the distribution of mother's age at marriage and mortality experience of the Simrang village. The highest number of mothers, i.e. 15 out of the 36 mothers got married at the age group of 20–24 yrs. and also experienced the highest number of live births, i.e. 56 in number. It is followed by 14 mothers who got married in the age group of 15–19 yrs. and the number of live births is 54. While 7 mothers got married in the age of 25 yrs. and above with 28 numbers of live births.

Table 7.57: Distribution of Pregnant and Pregnancy outcome of Mother's according to Their Present Age in Simrang Village

Sl. No.	Present age (yrs)	No. of mothers	No. of pregnancies	Carrying child	Pregnancy outcome							
					L-B		S-B		Spontaneous Abortion		Total No. Foetal wastage	
					No.	%	No.	%	No.	%	No.	%
1.	15 – 24	4	4	1	3	2.08	–	–	–	–	–	–
2.	25 – 34	7	20	–	20	13.89	–	–	–	–	–	–
3.	35 – 44	16	68	1	67	46.53	–	–	–	–	–	–
4.	45 – 54	3	13	–	13	9.03	–	–	–	–	–	–
5.	55 – 64	1	3	–	1	0.69	–	–	2	1.39	2	1.39
6.	65 – 74	4	18	–	16	11.11	2	1.39	–	–	2	1.39
7.	75 – 84	2	18	–	18	12.50	–	–	–	–	–	–
	Total	**37**	**144**	**2**	**138**	**95.83**	**2**	**1.39**	**2**	**1.39**	**4**	**2.78**

Table 7.58: Mother's Age at Marriage and Mortality Experience in Simrang

Sl. No.	Age Group	No. of Mothers	Total Live Birth	Infant Mortality (0–1 yrs.)	Child Mortality (1.1–5 yrs.)	Juvenile Mortality (5.1–14 yrs.)	14.1 + yrs.
1.	Up to 14	–	–	–	–	–	–
2.	15–19	14	54	1	–	–	–
3.	20–24	15	56	–	4	–	–
4.	25 +	7	28	2	2	1	3
	Total	**36**	**138**	**3**	**6**	**1**	**3**

Note: Out of total 38 married women, 1 is newly married woman and is pregnant, while 1 woman had not given birth to child.

Table 7.58 also reflects that mortality in the village is explained in 3 categories, viz. infant mortality, child mortality and juvenile mortality. Three infant mortalities are recorded in the village. Out of which 2 falls in the age of 25 and above years and 1 fall in the 15–19 yrs. of age group. Six child mortalities are found in the village, where 4 falls in the 20–24 yrs. of age group and 2 falls in the 25 and above years of age group. One juvenile mortality are recorded in the 25 and above years of age group. Three-adulthood deaths are recorded in the 25 and above years of age group.

Table 7.59 shows the distribution of mother's education and mortality experience. The highest number of mothers, i.e. 22 out of 36 mothers is illiterate and also experienced the highest number of live births, i.e. 97 out of the total 138 live births. Next is followed by 8 mothers in the

Table 7.59: Distribution of Mother's Education and Mortality Experience in Laktong

Sl. No.	Literacy	Number of Mothers	Total Live Births	Infant Mortality (0-1 yrs.)	Child Mortality (1.1-5 yrs.)	Juvenile Mortality (5.1-14 yrs.)	14.1 + yrs.
1	Illiterate	22	97	3	6	1	3
2.	Primary (up to IV)	8	24	–	–	–	–
3.	Middle School (V–VII)	3	8	–	–	–	–
4.	H.S. (VIII–X)	2	4	–	–	–	–
5.	H.S.S. (XI–XII)	1	5	–	–	–	–
	Total	**36**	**138**	**3**	**6**	**1**	**3**

Note: Out of 38 married women, 1 woman had not experienced conception, while 1 woman who is newly married is pregnant, and both of them are illiterate.

Primary school (up to IV) category with the second highest number of live births, i.e. 24. While 3 mothers fall in the Middle school (V–VII) level with 8 numbers of live births. There are 2 mothers in the High School level (VIII– X) with 4 numbers of live births. Only 1 mother is in the Higher Secondary School (XI–XII) level with 5 numbers of live births. The table also reflects that there are only 13 mortalities recorded in the village. Out of which 3 were infant mortality in the illiterate category. There are six child mortalities and a lone case of juvenile mortality again fall in the illiterate category. The table also recorded 3 adulthood death is in this category only.

Table 7.60: Distribution of Muklom Women according to Age at Menopause in Simrang Village

Sl. No.	*Age at Menopause*	*No. of Women*	*%*	*Mean*	*S.D.*	*S.E.*
1.	41–43	–	–			
2.	44–46	3	30.00	47.1	1.37	±0.43
3.	47–49	7	70.00			
	Total	**10**	**100**			

Note: Out of 38 married women, only 10 women attained menopause.

Table 7.60 shows the distribution of women according to their age at menopause. The table reflects that the range of the age at menopause of the Mukloms women of Simrang village varies between 44 to 49 yrs. The highest number of women, i.e. 7 (70.00%) attained their menopause in the age group of 47–49 yrs. It is followed by 3 (30.00%) women who attained their menopause in the age group of 44–46 yrs. Their mean age at menopause is 47 yrs. 1±0.43 with the S.D. of 1.37.

Yanman Village

The fertility performance of females has been analysed in this chapter.

Table 7.61 shows the distribution of Muklom females of Yanman village on the basis of different age groups. Here, in this table females below 9 yrs. of age are not included. The table reveals that the maximum number of females falls in the age group of 9–13 yrs. with 37 (20.56%) females out of the total 180 females. The next maximum number of females falls in the age group of 14–18 yrs., i.e. 31 (17.22) which is followed by 17 females (9.44%) fall in the age group of 19–23 yrs. It is

Table 7.61: Distribution of Muklom Females on the Basis of Different Age Groups

Sl. No.	Age Group (Yrs.)	No. of Females	Percentage
1.	9–13	37	20.56
2.	14–18	31	17.22
3.	19–23	17	9.44
4.	24–28	10	5.56
5.	29–33	16	8.89
6.	34–38	15	8.33
7.	39–43	11	6.11
8.	44–48	15	8.33
9.	49–53	6	3.33
10.	54–58	1	0.56
11.	59–63	9	5.00
12.	64–68	3	1.67
13.	69–73	4	2.22
14.	74–78	2	1.11
15.	79–83	2	1.11
16.	84–98	–	–
17.	99–103	1	0.56
	Total	**180**	**100.00**

also found those 16 females (8.89%) in 29–33 yrs., 15 (8.33%) females in each of the age groups 34–38 and 44–48 yrs., respectively. The table reveals that the life span of Muklom females is very long.

Table 7.62: Distribution of Muklom Girls According to Age at Menarche in Yanman

Sl. No.	Age at Menarche	No. of Girls	Percentage	Mean	S.D.	S.E.
1.	9–11	–	–			
2.	12	5	3.38			
3.	13	31	20.94	14.07	0.3'9	±0.03
4.	14	68	45.95			
5.	15	37	25.00			
6.	16	7	4.73			
	Total	**148**	**100.00**			

Table 7.62 shows the distribution of women menstruating at different age. It is observed from the table that the age at menarche varies from 12–16 yrs. The table also reveals that the maximum number of girls attain menarche at the age of 14 yrs. the number of which is 68 (45.95%). However, concentration of women in 13 and 15 yrs. is also appreciably

high, i.e. 37 (25%) and 31 (20.94%), respectively. The mean menarcheal age is calculated as 14.07 ± 0.03 yrs. with the standard deviation of 0.39.

Table 7.63 shows the distribution of females of Yanman village according to age at marriage. Their marriage age varies between 16–32 yrs. There are all total 98 married women in the village. The highest number of women, i.e. 14 (14.29%) got married at the age of 21 yrs. The second highest number of women, i.e. 13 (13.27%) got married at the age of 18 yrs. 12 (12.24%) women each got married at the age of 19 and 20 yrs., respectively. This is followed by 8 (8.16%) women who got married in 17 yrs. 7 (7.14%) women each got married in 22 and 24 yrs., 6 (6.12%) women got married in 25 yrs., 5 (5.10%) women got married in 16 yrs., 4 (4.08%) were married in 30 yrs., 3 (3.06%) women got married in 23 and 27 yrs., and 1 (1.02%) woman each got married in 26, 28, 29 and 27 and 32 yrs., respectively. Their mean age at marriage is 21.11± 0.37.

Table 7.63: Distribution of Women according to Age at Marriage in Yanman

Sl. No.	*Age at Marriage*	*No. of Women*	*Percentage*	*Mean*	*S.D.*	*S.E.*
1.	16	5	5.10			
2.	17	8	8.16			
3.	18	13	13.27			
4.	19	12	12.24			
5.	20	12	12.24			
6.	21	14	14.29			
7.	22	7	7.14			
8.	23	3	3.06			
9.	24	7	7.14	21.11	3.64	±0.37
10.	25	6	6.12			
11.	26	1	1.02			
12.	27	3	3.06			
13.	28	1	1.02			
14.	29	1	1.02			
15.	30	4	8.08			
16.	31	–	–			
17.	32	1	1.02			
	Total	**98**	**100.00**			

Table 7.64 shows the distribution of females according to their age at marriage by education. The table reveals that in the age group of 15–19 yrs. maximum number of women who got married falls in the category of illiterate, i.e. 27, which is followed by 7 women in the primary (up to

IV) category. There are two females each fall in the Middle (V–VII) H.S. (VIII–X) and H.S. (VIII–X) category, respectively.

Table 7.64: Distribution of Females' Age at Marriage by Education in Yanman

Sl. No.	*Age at Marriage*	*Illiterate*	*Primary (Up to IV)*	*Middle (V-VII)*	*H.S. (VIII-X)*	*H.S.S. (XI-XII)*	*Total*
1.	15–19	27	7	2	2	–	38
2.	20–24	35	1	1	6	–	43
3.	25 & above	14	2	–	1	–	17
	Total	**76**	**10**	**3**	**9**	**–**	**98**

In the age group 20–24 yrs., again the maximum number of females who got married falls in the illiterate category which is 35 in number. It is followed by 6 females in the H.S. (VIII) level and 1 in each of the Primary (up to IV) and Middle (V–VII) school level, respectively.

In the age group 25 and above years maximum number of females who got married falls in the illiterate category, i.e. 14 in number. It is followed by 2 females in the primary category and 1 in the H.S. (VIII–X) category, respectively.

Table 7.65 shows the distribution of Muklom females by age difference at marriage. From the table it is clear that maximum number of male, i.e. 15 (8.06%) out of the 88 (4731) males got married at the age of 25 yrs. And the lowest number of male, i.e. 1 (0.54%) and each got married at the age of 34, 40 and 45 yrs., respectively.

Whereas, out of the 98 (52.69%) females maximum number, i.e. 14 (7.53%) got married at the age of 21 yrs. and the lowest number of female, i.e. 1 (0.54%) each got married at the age of 26, 28, 29 and 32 yrs., respectively.

Table 7.65 reveals that in comparison to the male maximum number of females got married in the early age.

Table 7.66 shows the distribution of the marriage area of the Yanman village. Out of total 98 marriages, 72 (73.47%) marriages have been taken place within the spatial distance below 1 km, i.e. within the same village. Ten marriages (10.20%) has been recorded in the spatial distance between 6–10 km. It is followed by 6 (6.12%) marriages within the spatial distance of 11–15 km whereas, 4 (4.08%) marriages recorded in the spatial distance above 100 km. It is followed by 3 (3.06%) marriages within 21–25 km, 2 (2.04%) in the 26–30 km and 1 (1.02%) marriages in the 16–20 km.

Table 7.65: Distribution of Age Difference at Marriage in Yanman

Sl. No.	*Age Group (Yrs.)*	*Male*	*%*	*Female*	*%*	*Total*	*Total %*
1.	15						
2.	16	–	–	5	2.69	5	2.69
3.	17	–	–	8	4.30	8	4.30
4.	18	–	–	13	6.99	13	6.99
5.	19	2	1.08	12	6.45	14	7.53
6.	0	8	4.30	12	6.45	20	10.75
7.	21	3	1.61	14	7.53	17	9.14
8.	22	6	3.23	7	3.76	13	6.99
9.	23	8	4.3[illegible]	3	1.61	11	5.91
10.	24	6	3.23	7	3.76	13	6.99
11.	25	15	8.06	6	3.23	21	11.29
12.	26	6	3.23	1	0.54	7	3.76
13.	27	5	2.69	3	1.61	8	4.30
14.	28	4	2.15	1	0.54	5	2.69
15.	29	4	2.15	1	0.54	5	2.69
16.	30	10	5.38	4	2.15	14	7.53
17.	31	4	2.15	–	–	4	2.15
18.	32	2	1.08	1	1.054	3	1.61
19.	33	–	–	–	–	–	–
20.	34	1	0.54	–	–	1	0.54
21.	35	2	1.08	–	–	2	1.08
22.	36–39	–	–	–	–	–	–
23.	40	1	0.54	–	–	1	–
24.	41–44	–	–	–	–	–	–
25.	45	1	0.54	–	–	1	0.54
	Total	**88**		**98**	**52.69**	**186**	**100.00**

Table 7.66: Marriage Area according to Spatial Distance in Yanman

Sl. No.	*Spatial Distance (km)*	*No. of Marriages*	*Percentage*
1.	1–5	72	73.47
2.	6–10	10	10.20
3.	11–15	6	6.12
4.	16–20	1	1.02
5.	21–25	3	3.06
6.	26–30	2	2.04
7.	31–100	–	–
8.	100 +	4	4.08
	Total	**98**	**100.00**

From above table it is clear that there is no such restriction regarding the marriage and spatial distance.

Table 7.67: Distribution of Women according to Number of Conception in Yanman

Sl. No.	No. of conceptions	Up to 30 years		31-44 years		45+ years		Total	
		No. of Women	%	No. of Women	%	No. of Women	%	No. of Women	%
1.	1	7	7.22	–	–	3	3.09	10	10.31
2.	2	5	5.15	3	3.09	2	2.06	10	10.31
3.	3	2	2.06	3	3.09	4	4.02	9	9.28
4.	4	2	2.06	10	10.31	10	10.31	22	22.68
5.	5	1	1.03	14	14.43	7	7.22	22	22.68
6.	6		–	4	4.12	9	9.28	13	13.40
7.	7	–	–	2	2.06	1	1.03	3	3.09
8.	8	–	–	2	2.06	5	5.15	7	7.22
9.	9	–	–	–	–	–	–	–	–
10.	10	–	–	–	–	1	1.03	1	1.03
11.	11	–	–	–	–	–	–	–	–
	Total	**17**	**17.00**	**38**	**39.00**	**42**	**43.00**	**100**	**100.00**

Table 7.67 shows the distribution of women according to the number of conception. It is clear from above table that out of the 98 married Muklom women 97 had experienced conception and 1 is newly married. Table reveals that number of conception ranges from 1 to 10.

All the 17 (17.53%) women in the age group up to 30 yrs. are found to have a range of 1 to 5 conceptions. Seven (7.022%) had conceived once and 5 women had (5.15%) conceived twice. Two (2.06%) women had conceived thrice and 2 (2.06%) women had four times. One (1.03%) woman had 5 conceptions.

In the age group 31–44 yrs., recording 38 (39.17%) women, their conception ranges from 1 to 8. Here, maximum number of women, i.e. 14 (14.43%), had 5 conceptions. It is followed by 10 (10.31%) women who had four numbers of conceptions and 4 (4.12%) women had 6 numbers of conceptions.

Three (3.09%) women had conceived twice and another 3 (3.09%) had trice, respectively. It is also reported that 2 (2.06%) women had 7 conceptions and another 2 (2.06%) had 8 conceptions.

In the last age group 45 and above years recording 42 (43%) women, their conception ranges from 1 to 10. Here maximum of 10 (10.31%) women had 4 (4.12%) number of conceptions. It is followed by 9 (9.28%) women who had 6 conceptions. Seven (7.22%) women had 5 number of conceptions. Five (5.15%) women had 8 number of conceptions. Four

(4.12%) women had conceived thrice. Three (3.09%) and 2 (2.06%) women had conceived once and twice accordingly. And 1 (1.03%) woman had 7 conceptions while another 1 (1.03%) woman had 10 conceptions.

Table 7.67 reveals that the mother of the higher age group has the highest number of conceptions.

Table 7.68: Distribution of Women according to Age at First Child Birth in Yanman

Sl. No.	Age Group (Yrs)	No. of Women	Mean	S.D.	S.E.
1.	17–19	14			
2.	20–22	33			
3.	23–25	26	23.38	3.99	± 0.41
4.	26–28	13			
5.	29–31	5			
6.	32–34	6			
	Total	**97**			

Note: Newly married-1.

Table 7.68 shows the age specific distribution of Muklom mothers according to their age at first child birth. The age of mothers at the time of first child birth varies from 17–34 yrs. The highest number of women, i.e. 33 (34.02%) each reported to have made their first child birth in the age group of 20–22 yrs., which is followed by the age group of 23–25 yrs. with 26 (26.80%) women. It is followed by 14 (14.43%) women in the age group 17–19 yrs. The frequency decreases as the age group increases. The mean age at first child birth is 23.38±0.41 yrs.

Table 7.69 shows the pregnant and pregnancy outcome of the Muklom mothers according to their present age. The table shows that there are all total 97 numbers of mothers with all totals of 416 pregnancies. The table reveals that the highest number of mothers, i.e. 25 (25.78%) falls in the age group of 25–34 yrs. with the third highest number of pregnancies, i.e. 85 (20.43%). The third highest number of live births, i.e. 80 (19.23%) is also recorded in this category. The second highest number of mothers, i.e. 24 (24.79%) fall in the age group of 35–44 yrs. with the highest number of pregnancies, i.e. 117 (28.12%).

The highest number of live birth is also recorded in this category, i.e. 115 (27.64%). The third highest number of mothers fall in the age group of 45–54 yrs., i.e. 20 (20.62%) with the second highest number of pregnancies and live births, i.e. 93 (22.35) and 92 (22.11), respectively. There are 10 (10.31%) mothers with 50 (12.02%) number of pregnancies

Table 7.69: Distribution of Pregnant and Pregnancy Outcome of Mothers according to Their Present Age in Village Yanman

Sl. No.	*Present Age (yrs)*	*No. of Mothers*	*No. of Pregnancies*	*Carrying child*	*Pregnancy outcome*							
					LB		*SB*		*Spontaneous abortion*		*Total No. of Foetal Wastage*	
					No.	*%*	*No.*	*%*	*No.*	*%*	*No.*	*%*
1.	15–24	6	9	–	9	2.16	–	–	–	–	–	–
2.	25–34	25	85	3	80	19.23	2	0.48	–	–	2	0.48
3.	35–44	24	117	–	115	27.64	2	0.48	–	–	2	0.48
4.	45–54	20	93	–	92	22.11	–	–	1	0.24	1	0.24
5.	55–64	10	50	–	50	12.02	–	–	–	–	–	–
6.	65– 74	7	39	–	38	9.13	–	–	1	0.24	1	0.24
7.	75–84	4	17	–	17	4.08	–	–	–	–	–	–
8.	85–94	–	–	–	–	–	–	–	–	–	–	–
9.	95–104	1	6	–	6	1.44	–	–	–	–	–	–
	Total	**97**	**416**	**3**	**407**	**97.84**	**4**	**0.96**	**2**	**0.48**	**6**	**1.44**

and 50 (12.02%) live births falls in the age group of 55–64 yrs. 7 (7.22%) mothers in the 65–74 yrs. of age group with 39 (9.37%) numbers of pregnancies and 38 live births as well. Four (4.12%) mothers in the age group 75–84 yrs. with 17 (4.08%) number of pregnancies and 17 (4.08%) live births also. There is 1 (1.03%) mother in the age group 95–104 with 6 (1.144%) pregnancies and live birth as well.

The total number of 4 (0.96%) still births is recorded from the village. Out of which 2 (0.48%) number of stillbirth is recorded in the 25–34 yrs. of age group and 2 (0.48%) in the 35–44 yrs. of age group.

Two (0.48%) spontaneous abortion is recorded in the village out of which 1 (0.24%) recorded in each of the 45–54 and 65–74 yrs. of age groups. So, there are all total 6 cases of foetal wastages are recorded in the village.

Table 7.69 also reflects that 3 (3.09%) women in the village are pregnant and fall in the age group of 25–34 yrs. There is no artificial abortion in the village.

Table 7.70 shows the distribution of mothers' age at marriage and mortality experience of the Yanman village. The highest number of mothers, i.e. 43 (44.33%) out of the 97 mothers got married in the age group of 20–24 yrs. and also experienced the highest number of live births, i.e. 181 (44.47%). It is followed by 37 (38.14%) mothers who got married in the age group 15–19 yrs. with the second highest number of live birth, i.e. 156 (38.33%). It is followed by 17 (17.52%) who got married in the age group 25 and above years with 70 (17.20%) live births.

Table 7.70: Distribution of Mothers according to Age at Marriage and Mortality Experience in Yanman

Sl. No.	*Age Group (Yrs.)*	*No. of Mothers*	*Total Live Births*	*Infant Mortality (0-1 yrs.)*	*Child Mortality (0-5 yrs.)*	*Juvenile Mortality (5.1-14 yrs.)*	*14.1+ yrs.*
1.	Up to 14	–	–	–	–	–	–
2.	15–19	37	156	8	3	–	–
3.	20– 24	43	181	16	5	–	–
4.	25 and above	17	70	5	1	2	3
	Total	**97**	**407**	**29**	**9**	**2**	**3**

Table 7.70 also reflects that mortality in the village is presented in three categories viz. infant mortality, child mortality and juvenile mortality. 29 (7.12%) infant mortality is recorded in the village out of which 16 (3.93%) fall in the 20–24 yrs. of age group. While 3 (0.74%) in the

15–19 yrs. of age group and 1 (0.24%) in the 25 and above age group. Two (0.49%) juvenile mortality is also recorded in the village which fall in the 25 and above years of age. There are 3 (0.74%) adulthood death which is recorded in the 25 and above age group.

Table 7.71 shows the distribution of mother's education and mortality experience. The highest number of mothers, i.e. 75 out of the total of 97 is illiterate and also experienced the highest number of live births, i.e. 325 in number. The second highest is followed by 10 mothers fall in the primary (up to IV) category with second highest number of live births, i.e. 46 in numbers. Nine mothers fall in the H.S. (VII–X) category with 27 numbers of live births. Three mothers in the middle (V–VII) school level recorded 9 numbers of live births.

Table 7.71: Distribution of Mothers Education and Mortality Experience in Yanman Village

Sl. No.	*Literacy*	*Number of Mothers*	*Total Live Births*	*Infant Mortality (0-1 years)*	*Child Mortality (1.1-5 yrs.)*	*Juvenile Mortality (5.1-14) years*	*14.1 + yrs.*
1.	Illiterate	75	325	23	8	2	3
2.	Primary (up to IV)	10	46	4	1	–	–
3.	Middle (V–VII)	3	9	1	–	–	–
4.	H.S. (VIII–X)	9	27	1	–	–	–
	Total	**97**	**407**	**29**	**9**	**2**	**3**

Table 7.71 also reflects that 43 numbers of mortality were recorded in the village. Out of which 29 are infant mortality. And among the 29 mortalities 23 numbers are recorded in the illiterate category, 4 in the primary (up to IV) category and 1 each in Middle (V–VII) and H.S. (VIII–X) category respectively. Out of the 9 child mortality 8 numbers are recorded in the illiterate category and 1 in the primary (up to IV) category. Two juvenile deaths were found in the illiterate category. In the same way 3 adulthood death has been recorded in the illiterate category.

Table 7.72 shows the distribution of women according to age at menopause. Table 7.72 reveals that the age at menopause of the Muklom women of the Yanman village varies between 41–49 yrs. The highest number of women, which is 23 (62.16%), attained their menopause in the age group of 44–46 yrs. It is followed by 11 (29.73%) women who attained menopause in the age group of 47–49 yrs. It is followed by the age group of 41–43 yrs., with 3 (8.11%) number. Their mean age at menopause is 45.65 ± 0.28 yrs.

Table 7.72: Distribution of Women according to Age at Menopause in Yanman Village

Sl. No.	Age Group	No. of women	Percentage	Mean	S.D.	S.E.
1.	Up to 40	–	–			
2.	41–43	3	8.11	45.65	1.73	±0.28
3.	44–46	23	62.16			
4.	47 –49	11	29.73			
	Total	**37**	**100.00**			

8
Fertility Determinants of the Tangsas

Fertility means the actual reproductive performance of a woman or a group of women. It directly increases the population whereas mortality reduces the population. It is basically a biological process. The word 'fertility' comes from the Latin word "*fertile*" meaning to bear. So, fertility means to conceive and bear the offspring. It is one of the fundamental determinants of the population growth and represents an essential feature of one's approach to understand human society.

Several socio-cultural, economic, genetic, and physiological as well as environmental factors influence fertility. Hence, fertility behaviour of different population groups is different, as each group exhibits different socio-cultural traits.

North East India is a homeland of a number of tribal populations. Each of these groups has its own socio-cultural characteristics, which influences the fertility behaviour of the group. It is, therefore, necessary to work on the fertility pattern of different population groups separately.

Distribution of the Lungchang females of the three villages, namely New Changlang, Old Changlang and Rangkatu of Changlang district has been presented in Tables 7.1, 7.13 and 7.26. It is apparent from table that the highest population frequency was in the age group of 19–23 yrs. followed by 9–13 yrs. in the New Changlang village. In the Old Changlang village the highest frequency was in the age group of 14–18 yrs. followed by 9–13 yrs. age, whereas in case of the Rangkatu village the highest frequency is in the age group of 9–13 yrs. followed by 24–28 age groups. However, the mean age at menarche for the study population in New Changlang was found to be 13.61 ±0.91. While in Old Changlang it was 13.70 ±0.06, and in Rangkatu it was13.86 ±0.09 yrs. (Tables 7.2, 7.14, and 7.26). The mean age at marriage were found to be highest among the Lungchangs in all the three villages ranging from 20.86 ±0.48, 22.69 ±0.37 21.97 ±0.32, (Tables 7.3, 7.15 and 7.27). It is also revealed that higher age at marriage is recorded in the illiterate group (Tables 7.4, 7.16, and 7.28). Sex differences at age at marriage revealed that significant number of females got married at an early age, i.e. 17 yrs. (Tables 7.5, 7.17 and 7.29). From the study, it is also clear that the Lungchangs prefer more in practicing intra-village marriage, but at the same time there is no such restriction or preference for such marriage among them (Tables 7.6, 7.18 and 7.30).

The study also indicates that the mothers of higher age groups show the highest number of conception than the lower age group. The mean ages at first child birth in the three villagers, namely New Changlang, Old Changlang and Rangkatu are more or less similar (22.02±0.53, 23.68 ±0.37 and 22.76±0.42 yrs.). In all the three villages the frequency decreases as the age group increases (Tables 7.8, 7.20 and 7.32).

Analysis of pregnancy outcome revealed (Tables 7.9, 7.21, and 7.33) a trend of less pregnancy towards the lower age group; the occurrence of live birth also showed almost same result. Regarding the foetal wastage a very few cases of spontaneous abortion was observed in all the three villages. In New Changlang and Rangkatu villages higher age at marriage shows higher mortality than in the lower age at marriage, whereas a reverse picture is observed in the Old Changlang village, i.e. lower age at marriage is associated with higher mortality (Tables 7.9, 7.21 and 7.33).

Comparison of general distribution of mother's education and mortality experiences revealed that illiterate mothers experience more mortality than the literate mothers. It can be said that education plays an important role in the life of the Lungchang women (Tables 7.11, 7.23, 7.35).

Distribution of women according to age at menopause is shown in Tables 7.12, 7.24 and 7.36. It is found that that the range varies between 40–49 yrs. in all the three Lungchang villages. The mean age at menopause in New Changlang, Old Changlang and Rangkatu, is 45.71±0.40, 46.27±0.26 and 46.86±0.27 yrs., respectively. However, the present study shows almost 33 yrs. of reproductive life span among the Lungchang women of Arunachal Pradesh.

Distribution of Muklom females of the three villages, namely Laktong, Simrang (New Thamlom) and Yanman of Changlang district of Arunachal Pradesh has been presented in Tables 7.37, 7.49 and 7.61. It is apparent from table that the maximum numbers of females' fall in the age group of 9–13 yrs. age group (14.29% and 20.56%) in the Laktong and Yanman village whereas in Simrang village the highest frequency is observed in the age group of 14–18 yrs. with a frequency of 26.74%. It is also revealed from the table that the mean age of menarche does not show significant variation village-wise and the ranges vary from 14.28±0.13 yrs. in Laktong, 13.83± 0.09 yrs. in Simrang and 14.07 ± 0.03 yrs. in Yanman (Tables 7.38, 7.50, 7.62). The mean age at marriage in the Simrang and Yanman village is more or less similar (21.37±0.62 and 21.11±0.37 yrs.), respectively, whereas a deviating tendency is observed in the Laktong village where mean age at marriage is (23.30 ± 0.74 yrs.) (Tables 7.51, 7.63, and 7.39). Examination of mean age at marriage and literacy status revealed slightly higher age at marriage in Laktong and Yanman villages, whereas in the Simrang village lower age at marriage is observed among the illiterate group (Tables 7.40, 7.64, and 7.51). The analysis of age at marriage indicates that the maximum number of males and females prefer to marry at a later age, i.e. after 20 yrs. of age (Tables 7.41, 7.53 and 7.65). From the study it is also clear that among the Mukloms most of the marriages took place within their own villages which no doubt indicates preference of intra-village alliances though in reality there is no such preference or prohibition for such marriage among them (Tables 7.42, 7.54 and 7.66). It may be interpreted that due to the location of the villages in the interior areas or lack of proper communication they are to confine the marriages within their own villages.

From the study it is clear that the mother of the higher age groups show the highest number of conception than the lower age group. The number of conceptions ranges from 1 to 10 (Tables 7.43, 7.53 and 7.67). The mean age at first child birth in all the three villages, i.e. Laktong, Simrang and Yanman are more or less similar, i.e. 24.26 ± 0.76 in Laktong, 22.57 ± 0.60 in Simrang and 23.38 ± 0.41 yrs. in Yanman, respectively (Tables 7.44, 7.56 and 7.68).

Analysis of pregnancy outcome (Tables 7.45, 7.57 and 7.69) revealed a trend of less pregnancy towards the lower age group and occurrence of live birth also showed almost same result in all the three villages inhabited by Muklom Tangsa. A very few cases of foetal wastage was recorded while no case of artificial abortion was observed among them.

The distribution of the mother's age at marriage and mortality experience among the Mukloms of three villages show that higher age at marriage shows higher mortality than in the lower age at marriage (Tables 7.46, 7.58 and 7.70).

Comparison of general distribution of mothers' education and mortality experience revealed that illiterate mother experience more mortality than the literate mothers which definitely indicate role of education in the life of the Mukloms of Arunachal Pradesh (Tables 7.47, 7.59 and 7.71).

Distribution of women, according to age at menopause (Tables 7.48, 7.60 and 7.72) shows that among the Mukloms the range varies from 41–49 yrs. The mean age at menopause is 45.86±0.51 in Laktong, 47.1±0.43 in Simrang and 45.65±0.28 yrs. in Yanman, respectively. However, the present study shows almost 37 yrs. of reproductive life span among the Muklom women of Arunachal Pradesh.

The completed fertility, the net reproductive index and sex-ratio of the Offspring has also been analysed in this chapter.

Table 8.1: Completed Fertility and the Net Reproductive Index of Ever Married Women of New Changlang

Total number of women	44
Total number of live born	277
Total number of male born	143+8
Total number of female born	134+6
Average live born/mother	6.25
Net reproductive index	3.04

Table 8.1 shows the complete fertility and net reproductive index of ever married women of New Changlang village. Total number of women who had completed fertility is 44. The average live-birth per mother is 6.25 yr. The net reproductive index is 3.04.

Table 8.2: Sex-Ratio of New Changlang Village

Sex-Ratio of	*Male*	*Female*	*Sex-ratio*
Primary	151	140	107.9
Secondary	143	134	106.7

Table 8.2 shows the two sex-ratio of the population. The primary sex-ratio is found to be 107.85 and secondary sex-ratio is 106.71. It shows slight differences from the appropriate 1:1 ratio that means there is a strong selection within the population.

Table 8.3: Completed Fertility and the Net Reproductive Index of Ever Married Women of Old Changlang Village

Total number of women	87
Total number of live born	305
Total number of male born	157
Total number of female born :	155
Average live born/mother	3.50
Net reproductive index	1.07

Table 8.3 shows the complete fertility and net reproductive index of ever married women of Old Changlang village. It is revealed that total number of women who have completed fertility is 87. The average live birth is 3.50 and the net reproductive index is 1.07.

Table 8.4: Sex-Ratio of Old Changlang Village

Type of sex	*Sex-ratio*
Primary	101.29
Secondary	100.65

From Table 8.4, it is seen that the primary sex-ratio of Old Changlang village is 101.29 and secondary sex-ratio is 100.65. Very slight difference is observed from appropriate 1:1 ratio. It means that there is a strong selection within the population.

Table 8.5: Completed Fertility and the Net Reproductive Index of Ever Married Women of Rangkatu Village

Total number of women	102
Total number of live born	244
Total number of male born	126
Total number of female born	118
Average live born/mother	2.3
Net reproductive index	1.1

Table 8.5 shows the complete fertility and net reproductive index of ever married women of Rangkatu village. The analysis reveals that total number of women who have completed fertility is 102 and average live birth per mother is 2.3. The net reproductive index is 1.1.

Table 8.6 shows the two sex-ratio of the population of Rangkatu village. The primary sex-ratio is found to be 175.00, whereas the secondary sex-ratio is 106.78. The crude primary sex-ratio as well as secondary

Table 8.6: Sex-Ratio of Rangkatu Village

Type of sex	*Male*	*Female*	*Sex-ratio*
Primary sex (Still birth)	129	120	175.00
Secondary sex ratio	126	118	106.78

sex-ratio shows differences from the appropriate 1:1 ratio. This means there is a strong selection within the population.

Table 8.7: Completed Fertility and the Net Reproductive Index of Ever Married Women of Laktong Village

Total number of women	40
Total number of live born	146
Total number of male born	79
Total number of female born	67
Average live born/mother	3.67
Net reproductive index	1.67

Table 8.7 shows the complete fertility and the net reproductive index of ever married women of the Laktong village. It is revealed that the total number of women who have completed fertility is 40. The live birth per mother is 3.65 and the reproductive index is 1.67.

Table 8.8: Sex-Ratio of Laktong Village

Sex type	*Sex-ratio*
Primary	117.01
Secondary	117.91

Table 8.8 shows the primary and secondary sex-ratio of the population of Laktong village. It is clear that the primary sex-ratio is 117.01 and secondary sex-ratio is 1117.91. It means there is a strong selection in the population.

Table 8.9: Completed Fertility and the Net Reproductive Index of Ever Married Women of Simrang Village

Total number of women	37
Total number of live born	144
Total number of male born	68+2
Total number of female born	76+1
Average live born/mother	3.08
Net reproductive index	2.06

Table 8.9 shows the complete fertility and the net reproductive index of ever married women of the village Simrang. The analysis reveals that the total number of women who have completed fertility is 37. The average live birth per mother is 3.08. The net reproductive index is 2.06.

Table 8.10: Sex-Ratio of Simrang Village

Sex type	*Sex-ratio*
Primary	90.51
Secondary	80.94

Table 8.10 shows the sex-ratio of the population of Simrang village. It is clear that the primary sex-ratio of the population is 90.51 and the secondary sex-ratio is 80.94. It means that there is a strong selection within the population.

Table 8.11: Completed Fertility and the Net Reproductive Index of Ever Married Women of Yanman Village

Total number of women	105
Total number of live born	461
Total number of male born	247 +4
Total number of female born	214 +2
Average live born/mother	4.38
Net reproductive index	2.03

Table 8.11 shows the complete fertility and net reproductive index of ever married women of the village Yanman. The total number of women who have completed fertility is 105. The average live birth is 4.38 and the net reproductive index is 2.03.

Table 8.12: Sex-Ratio of Yanman Village

Sex type	*Sex-ratio*
Primary	111.11
Secondary	110.74

Table 8.12 shows the sex-ratio of the population of Yanman village. It is clear that the primary sex-ratio is 111.11 and the secondary sex-ratio is 110.74. There is a strong selection within the population.

Table 8.13: Completed Fertility and the Net Reproductive Index of Ever Married Women of Lungchang

Total number of women	233
Total number of live born	826
Total number of male born	422 + 12
Total number of female born	404 + 9
Average live born/mother	3.80
Net reproductive index	1.73

Table 8.14: Sex-Ratio of Offspring of Lungchang

Sex type	*Sex-ratio*
Primary	102.66
Secondary	104.42

Table 8.15: Completed Fertility and the Net Reproductive Index of Ever Married Women of Muklom Tangsas

Total number of women	182
Total number of live born	751
Total number of male born	394
Total number of female born	357
Average live born/mother	4.13
Net reproductive index	1.95

Table 8.16: Sex-Ratio of Offsprings of Mukloms

Sex type	*Sex-ratio*
Primary	111.11
Secondary	110.36

Tables 8.15 and 8.16 show the two sex-ratios among the Lungchangs and the Mukloms under study. The overall analysis reveals that the crude primary sex-ratio as well as secondary sex-ratio show little difference from appropriate 1:1 ratio. That means there is a sexual selection within the population.

Tables 8.13 and 8.15 show the completed fertility and the net reproductive index of ever married women of the Lungchang and Muklom Tangsa women. Total number of women who had completed fertility among the Lungchangs is 233 women whereas among the Mukloms it is 182 women. The average live birth per mother is 3.80 among the Lungchangs and 4.13 among the Mukloms. The net reproductive index is 1.73 and 1.95, respectively among the two groups of Tangsa women. The analysis reveals slight differences among the two groups of the Tangsas.

9
Summary and Conclusion

In the preceding chapters an effort has been made to project the salient features of socio-demographic profile of the Tangsas of Arunachal Pradesh. The present chapter has been devoted entirely to summarize the findings with certain concluding remarks to highlight the topic under study.

North East India, a macro-geographic region of the country, is characterized by intermingling of different racial, linguistic and cultural groups. Each group is unique having its culture which on the other hand helps them to maintain their own ethnic identity. Indian Civilization is known for centuries because of its philosophy, i.e. unity in diversity. The historians and early travellers have acknowledged it and recorded in their writings. The acceptance of cultural pluralism, no doubt, has given a scope to each ethnic group for contributing its share in the making a nation. Arunachal Pradesh is one of the largest states of North East India, and, Tangsa is a distinct tribe reflecting its own characteristics. Thus, a study of socio-demographic features of a tribe, like Tangsas, may reveal diverse characteristics.

Demography deals with statistical analysis and description of population. It considers distribution, vital statistics like age, sex, birth rate, death rate and mortality. It is concerned with fertility potential, morbidity and longevity, marriage values and norms associated with procreation, illness and death. Demography of a population is no doubt a biological factor. But socio-cultural factors play a significant role in understanding these biological factors. Thus, ethnographic present is pre-requisite for understanding socio-demographic situation of a population.

It has already been emphasized that the study was confined among the Tangsas. Their main concentration is in the district of Tirap, Changlang and Lohit. The present work was confined among the Tangsas of

Changlang district. The Tangsas are one of the major tribes of Arunachal Pradesh. They are divided into a number of sub-tribes, each speaking distinct language, but having close affinities with each other. The scholars were in the opinion that their place of origin was somewhere in the Hukang Valley, in the Highland of Burma (now Myanmar). It was the collective opinion that they have not migrated to this place together and at the same time. It is confirmed by the fact that each sub-tribe has distinct socio-cultural characteristics. Moreover, the Tangsas, though a large group could never project as a powerful tribe because of inter-group rivalry and lack of unity in the broader level. There are various instances where the rivalry between the Mukloms and Tutsa and Lungchangs and others could be traced.

There was no unanimous opinion about the number of sub-tribes among the Tangsas. Though occasionally, they opined that there are 32 sub-tribes, yet the survey conducted by the Anthropological Survey of India could trace only 15 sub-tribes of the Tangsas. In the present project, two sub-tribes of the Tangsas, i.e. the Lungsangs and the Mukloms have been considered, selecting six villages. The data on Lungsang Tangsas have been collected from New Changlang, Old Changlang and Rangkatu villages. On the other hand, the data on Muklom Tangsas have been collected from Laktong, Simrang (New Thamloam) and Yanman villages. The villages were selected considering the distance and location from district headquarters, Changlang. It was emphasized that the Tangsas, as a whole, may be identified in the tribal map of India, but some distinct features in the sub-tribe level is also visible.

The main objective of the present study was to (a) project the socio-cultural life of the Tangsas and (b) to examine certain aspects of demographic features, particularly fertility performance. To fulfil these basic objectives, various parameters have been identified and data were collected accordingly. Biological and social-cultural factors are equally responsible to project the demographic situation of a community.

Age and sex are biological variables, and are related to fertility and mortality rates. These are of great socio-cultural significance. Age and sex composition influence the social organization and life of the people. The factors affecting longevity may include heredity, constitution and environment. The first two factors are biological in origin, while the third is of sociological in nature. Apart from the natural physical surrounding in which one lives, the factors arising from his ways of living, e.g. habit of eating, drinking, occupation and types of social organization influence the mortality level. The age and sex structure of the Tangsas indicate overall high life span of the Tangsas. The analysis of data among the Lungchang Tangsas shows a slight female deficiency. But, it is also significant to note that even in the age group of 95-99 years a single female was recorded. The overall analysis of Muklom Tangsas revealed a slight male deficiency. In Laktong village, a slight female deficiency is revealed, whereas in the Simrang and Yanman villages a slight male deficiency is recorded. The deficiency, either on female or male, is not so significant and it is not possible to come to a definite conclusion on the basis of the present data.

The socio-economic lives of the Tangsas indicate that the Tangsas as a whole are dependent on agriculture. They cultivate shifting/*jhum* and wet/settled cultivation. In recent years, due to the impact of modern education, there is a tendency to go for different salaried job. Regarding land–holding pattern, they have homestead land, wet cultivable land and other type of land. Traditionally, the main livelihood pattern of the Tangsas was shifting or *jhum* cultivation. But a change has been observed in the economic life of the Tangsas. Now-a-days, major section of the Tangsas has opted for wet cultivation. In the opinion of the Tangsas shifting cultivation need hard physical labour and the production is less in comparisons to wet cultivation. This does not mean that they have totally shifted to wet cultivation. They still cultivate some of the seasonal varieties of crops in the *jhum* field. The present study reveals that the Lungchangs and the Mukloms do not cultivate paddy in the *jhum* field. But the Tutsas, the Havis have still cultivated paddy in their *jhum* field. The Lungchangs and the Mukloms particularly cultivate maize, tapioca, big yam, chillis, cabbage and other seasonal vegetables in their *jhum* field. Most of the Tangsas including the Lungchangs and the Mukloms have other types of land, which they occasionally give on lease or cultivate it for their own production.

Among the Tangsas in general and the Lungchangs and the Mukloms in particular there exist two unique modes of land operation, i.e. (a) Lease out and (b) Lease in. Tangsas who have large land holding, usually give lease to outsiders for tea or orange cultivation. Similarly, those who do not have sufficient land normally take land on lease for cultivation. According to the villagers, though they have given their land for lease for tea cultivation, yet they are not benefited out of it as they are force to give a higher percentage to the extremist group.

The Tangsas rear different types of domestic animals. The increasing number of bullocks in all the villages is a new phenomenon which may be due to shift to wet cultivation. Among the Lungchangs, out of 179 families, 90 have bullocks, the percentage being 50.3. While among the Mukloms, out of 153 families 59 have bullocks, the percentage being 38.6. Pigs are reared by almost all the families, as pigs are mostly required both for religious and home consumption. Occasionally, they sell pigs to meet their economic need. They keep the pigs either in enclosure or tied with a rope in the compound. The villagers are not allowed to keep the pigs free and to make this rule more rigid they added an additional taboo on it. If somebody violets the rule, they are to pay fine for it. Some families also rear goats, but it is not so significant, whereas fowls are reared by most of the families and ducks are reared by few. Cows and buffalos are left on off in the jungle and the owner keeps an eye on their movement. To identify their own cattle, they put small marks on the ears by knife in various ways. During *Moh* and *Mall* festivals, it is the responsibility of the owners to see that all the animals return back to their respective households. Only milch cows are kept within their own compound.

The possession of material items indicates the influence of urbanization and better economic condition of the Tangsas. It is significant to note the absence of bicycle among the villagers. According to the villagers due to the hilly areas cycling is not convenient. Only a few families of New Changlang village have their own bicycle.

The family is the basic economic unit. All the members of the family take some part in the economic activities. Family is also a unit which maintain link between individual and community. Though traditionally, the Tangsas were in favour of joint family system, yet the present study reveals the increasing number of nuclear family. The percentage of nuclear family among the Lungchangs is 45.8 and among the Mukloms it is 53.6. Patrilineal and pratilocal type is the normal form of family organization among the Tangsas. Descent among the Tangsas is traced through the father and the residence is pratilocal. It regulates the transmission of property from one generation to the next through the male line. A case was referred where in the absence of sons; the father divided his property among his daughters. Though they have a preference for male child, yet now-a-days, parents try to give education to their children irrespective of sexes. Family is a productive unit and everybody extend their helping hand in maintaining the family. Family among the Tangsas also plays a major role of socialization and enculturation. The family-level relationship among the Tangsas is very cordial.

Attachment of kinship is a great strength for *jhum* cultivating Tangsas. Kin members are considered an inseparable part in the life of the Tangsas, but the clan members seem to play a significant role in the socio-religious life of the Tangsas. Various socio-religious ceremonies are confined within the boundary of clan members. The role of clan members is also distinctly visible in the life cycle rituals. In case of death pyre is lit by the oldest person belonging to the deceased's clan. Role and responsibilities of maternal uncle is reflected in most of their socio-religious life. During marriage due respect is shown to the maternal uncle by offering the major share of meat of sacrificial animals. The kinship terminology among the Tangsas is classificatory in nature and there exist differences in kin terms among the Lungchangs and the Mukloms. This indicates the linguistic difference on the sub-tribe level.

Among the Tangsas unnatural death is considered a curse. The Mukloms consider the birth of twins as the worst curse for the family and took various measures to kill the twins. The twins are taken to the jungle, where they were strangulated to death with a rope. In recent years, a slight change is noticed and it was reported that there was a case where a twin survives.

Marital status assumes demographic importance. Marriage is considered a sacrament among the Tangsas. Though different types of marriage are recorded, yet negotiated type of marriage is considered as ideal. Earlier heavy bride price was prevalent among the Tangsas. In recent years, a change is noticed in the type of materials and amount of money considered as bride price. It was also observed that there is a slight difference among the Lungchangs and Mukloms with regards to the performance of marriage ceremony. The role of *kamwa* (mediator) is evident in both the groups. Among the Lungchangs, the actual marriage ceremony is performed at the bride's house and the groom is to come to the bride's house. On the other hand among the Mukloms, the actual marriage ceremony is performed at grooms place. The bride is to come to the groom's house along with the female members, following the existing customs and traditions of the tribe. Such type of practices is prevalent among many tribes of North East India. The research conducted among the Singphos also revealed such type of system.

Various religious beliefs and practices are observed by the tribes of Arunachal Pradesh. Available data reveals that a majority of the people are either tribal or Hindu religion. There are certain communities who are partly or wholly Buddhist. The Tangsas have their own religious beliefs and practices, which are mostly animistic. Animal sacrifice is a must in most of their traditional religious festivals and ceremonies. But in course of time, the impact of Hinduism, Buddhism and indigenous tribal faiths are visible among the Tangsas. At present, the Tangsas as a whole are influenced by the *Lord Rang Frah.* In each village, there is a temple of *Rang Frah*, where statue or picture is installed. Regular prayer is performed on every Sunday. But along with this, they continue their traditional religious rites and ceremonies.

The socio-religious life of the Tangsas is revolved round the agricultural calendar. When they were entirely dependent on *jhum* cultivation, the Tangsas performed their ceremonies according to *jhum* calendar. But when they have shifted to wet cultivation, they are to reschedule some of their traditional festivals, ceremonies and rituals which were linked to the cycle of *jhum* cultivation. Some of these have either been dropped or readjusted to the process of wet paddy cultivation. The nomenclature of some of these religious festivals differs on the sub-group level. Each village has its own time schedules and highly systematic mechanism for proper organization and celebration of a festival or other cultural events. In most cases, dates are not fixed once for ever and are normally determined by the village community according to their convenience. The Tangsas in general celebrate *Mah, Mall, Moh Mall* and *Parang* festivals according to their religious calendar. At present the Tangsas believe in a mythological faith and incorporated it in their religion called *Rang Frah* faith and adapted it as their religion called *Rang Fraism* under the *Rang Frah* Faith promotion society.

Now, Lord *Rang Frah* is considered as the traditional God of the Tangsas. He is worshipped and believed to be the creator, destroyer and preserver of this world. The Tangsas celebrate the *Rang Frah* Day in their own village. Earlier the date of celebration was not fixed, but now date is fixed and they celebrate it on the new moon day of November–December. No animal is sacrificed in this celebration. Every Sunday they pray in the temple and the villagers keep fasting until they complete their prayer in the temple.

In the socio-demographic study basic composition of population and the fertility performance is significant. To fulfil this basic necessity few aspects composition and fertility has been incorporated in the study. In demographic study fertility is considered to be an important aspect as it plays a major role in the population size. The age at menarche is considered to be an important parameter in population study as it indicates the age at which girls become physiologically capable to conceive. In this study an effort has been made to understand the reproductive performance of the Lungchang and Muklom sub-groups of the Tangsa women of the area. Attempt is also made to find out the impact of education, age at marriage etc. on fertility.

The frequency of Tangsa women in both the groups was found mainly in the lower age groups than in the higher age group, i.e. from 9–23 years. However, the mean menarcheal age in the two groups show slight variation. Among the Lunchang women the highest mean age at menarche is 13.86 ± 0.09, whereas among the Muklom women it is 14.28 ± 0.13. In the Lunchang groups the range of this age at menarche varies from 10–16 years, whereas among the Mukloms it varies from 12–16 years.

The age at marriage is important in the study of fertility performance as marriage starts the reproductive life cycle. It is found that in Lungchang women the highest mean age at marriage is 22.69 ± 0.37, whilst the Muklom women it is 23.30 ± 0.74.

The Lungchang women start to marry at the age of 16 years, and they usually marry within the age group ranging 16–35 years, whereas the Muklom women start to marry at the age of 16 years, but usually marry within the age group ranging from 16–32 years. A slight variation is observed in the two age groups in this respect. The child-bearing starts shortly after that, i.e. in that age or the immediate next range which is evident from Chapter 7, Table 7.9 in both the groups.

Analysis of pregnancy outcome revealed a trend of less pregnancy towards the smaller age group and the occurrence of live birth also showed almost the same result in both the groups. The average live birth out of 233 Lungchang mothers is 3.80 per cent and out of 182 Muklom mothers it is 4.13 per cent.

The present study reveals that the incidence of spontaneous abortion is much higher in the higher age group in both the Tangsa groups. The incidence of still birth is comparatively lower in the present samples. Sex-wise study of still birth shows that the male still birth has been slightly higher than the female neonates. Further, it has been observed that the higher incidence of foetal wastage is decreasing day by day perhaps due to the impact of medical facilities now available. Now-a-days, with the influence of education and medical facilities the women have become concerned about their health as well as well-being of their children. It was also found that majority of the wastages were due to hard labour done by the pregnant women. In both the group the highest number of women attained their menopause in the age group of 44–49 years. The onset of menopause is comparatively late in both the groups. The highest mean being 46.86 ± 0.27 and 47.10 ± 0.43 among the Lungchang and Muklom women, respectively. However, the present study shows almost 37 years of reproductive life span among them.

The impact of educational status and the age at marriage reveals a similar trend with some other studies done in India as well as in North East India. It was found that the age at marriage is lower among the illiterate group than the literate group. The crude primary sex-ratio and secondary sex-ratio in both the groups show a slight deviation from the ideal 1:1 ratio, which indicates that there is a sexual selection within the both groups of Tangsas of Arunachal Pradesh. The analysis of fertility performance would provide enough scope to interpret the researchers to work in same line in future.

Arunachal Pradesh is marked by an extraordinary range of heterogeneity, in terms of cultural and linguistic traits, within and between the tribal groups. Tangsa is one of the major tribes inhabiting in the Changlang district. At present, changes have been noticed in different spheres of their social life. The society as a whole can be regarded as living organism which moulds itself according to indispensible requirements of the people, but at the same time carried forward traditional features. Traditional and modern forces play the respective role in bringing changes in various spheres. The rate or pace of change varies from society to society, because, man has to organize his ways of life according to his changed environment. The fact that no society remained static for ever or no society totally absorbed the changes. Such universal trend is reflected in the social system of the Tangsas. Although some study has been done among these groups, yet there exists an information gap, as no detailed study has been made so far. The present study among the Lungchangs and the Mukloms, the two sub-tribes of Tangsas have covered certain significant areas of socio-demographic scenario. But still many more remained untouchesd and the researchers hoped that this work will be of immense help to Research Persons who wish to work among the Tangsas in future.

Bibliography

Barua, I. (1992). "The Tai Turungs of Assam: A Study of Socio-Demographic Profile", *Man in India*, Vol. 72.

Barua, I. "Menarche in North East Indian Communities: Some Bio-Social Aspects". *South Asian Anthropologist*, Vol. 17.

Barua, I. (2005). "Socio-Demographic Profile of Tai Phake: Some Observations", *Bulletin of the Department of Anthropology,* Dibrugarh University, Vol. 33.

Barua, S.N. (1991). *Tribes of Indo-Myanmar Border*, New Delhi.

Baruah, S.L. and P.B. Das (1981). "Family type and Fertility among the Khasis of Meghalaya". *Anthropological Perspectives of North East India.* Sp. Vol. Department of Anthropology, X:26-29 Dibrugarh University .

Bhagabati, A.C. (1991). The Tribes as Social Formation: The case of the Tangsas of Arunachal Pradesh, Vol. 19, *Bulletin of the Department of Anthropology,* Dibrugarh University.

Bhendge, A.A. and Kanitkar, T. (2006). *Principles of Population Studes,* Himalaya Publishing House.

Bogue, D. (1959). *Principles of Demography,* New York: John Willey & Sons.

Borodoloi, B.M., G.C. Sharma Thakur and M.C. Saikia (1987). *Tribes of Assam* (Part-I) (Ed.) Guwahati Tribal Research Institute, Assam.

Bhuyan, S.K. (1960). *Assam Burani,* Guwahati.

Chowdhury, J.N. (1973). *Arunachal Panorama*, Calcutta. Published by Mrs. J. Chowdhury.

Choudhury, P.C. (1959). *The History of Civilization of the People of Assam to the Twelfth Century A.D.* Guwahati: Department of Historical and Antiquarian Studies.

Cox, P.R. (1970). *Demography*, Cambridge University Press.

Curjelo, D.F. (1980). "The Reproductive Life of Indian Women". *Indian Journal of Medical Research,* Vol. 8.

Daniel, M. (2008). *Socio-Cultural and Religious Life of Mao Naga Tribe*, New Delhi: Mittal Publications.

Darshan, S. (1998). Conserving a Community Resource: Medicinal Plants. In

A. Katari *et al.* (Ed.) *Communities and Conservation,* UNESCO, New Delhi: Sage Publications.

Das, B.M. (1980). *People of Assam,* New Delhi: Gian Publishing House.

Das, B.M. (1985). "Fertility and Mortality Differentiate among the Khamyang and Turung Populations of Jorhat District, Assam", *Journal of Assam Science Society,* 28.

Das, R. (1995). "Variation in Fertility of two population of Kamrup, Assam", *Bulletin of the Department of Anthropology,* Vol. 23. Dibrugarh University.

Dave, P. and N. Tavkar (1985). "People of a Tribal Child of Panchmahal". *Social Welfare,* 5.

Davis, K. and J. Blake (1956). "Social Structure and Fertility, an Analytic Framework", *Eco. Dev. Cult. Change,* 4.

Deka, R. (1976). "Menarcheal Age among the Kachari Women of Upper Assam". *Bulletin of the Department of Anthropology,* Dibrugarh University, Vol. 5.

Deka and Patojoshi (1977). "Fertility and Fertility Wastage", *Bulletin of Department of Anthropology,* Vol. VI. Dibrugarh University.

Dutta, Das, D. and N. Saikia (2000). "A Study on Fertility of the Tangsa Women: A Tribe in Assam", *Man and Life,* 34.

Dutta, Parul (1959). *The Tangsas,* Shillong: North East Frontier Agency.

Ember, C.R. and M. Ember (1981). *Cultural Anthropology,* New Delhi: Oxford University Press.

Erasmus, Charles, J. (1961). *Man Takes Control.* Minneapolis: University of Minnesota Press.

Erikson, E.H. (1963). *Childhood and Society.* New York: W.W. Norton & Co.

Firth, R. (1941). *Human Types,* London: Thomas Nelson & Sons Ltd.

Firth, R. (1971). *Elements of Social Organization,* London: Tavistock Publication.

Gait, E.A. (1969). *A History of Assam.* Calcutta: Thacker Spink & Co.

Gharami, A.K., *et al.* (2001). A Study on Menarche and Fertility among the Ladiya of Sagar District, Madhya Pradesh, *Jr. of Human Ecology,* Vol. 12, No. 4.

Grierson, G.A. (1966). *Linguistic Survey of India.* Vol. 1. Motilal Banarasi Dass.

Government of India Report (1994). *Ethnobiology in India. A Status.* New Delhi: Ministry of Environment and Forest, Government of India.

Hans Raj (2006). *Fundamentals of Demography,* New Delhi: Surjeet Publications.

Hallowell, A. Irving (1963). "Ojibwa World View and Diseases". In: *Medicine and Anthropology* (Ed.) I. Goldston.

Hauser and Duncan (1959). *The Study of Population: An Inventory and Appraisal.* University of Chicago Press.

Honigmann, J.J. (Ed.) (1973). *Handbook of Social and Cultural Anthropology.* Chicago: R. & Mc Nally College Publishing Company.

Hughes, C. (1963), "Ethnomedicine", *International Encyclopedia of Social Sciences.* New York: Free Press, Macmillan.

Jayapalan, N. (2004). *Social Demography,* Book Enclave.

Junging, Wu, Evsheng, G. and Libao, Z. (2000). Age at Menarche of the Reproductive Women in China, *Reproductive Health, Gender and Development,* (Ed.) Ersheng, G., Delhi: B.R. Publishing Corporation.

Kapadia, K.M. (1956). *Marriage and Family in India*, Bombay: Oxford University Press.

Kaur, Navneet and G.K. Kshatriyas (2007). "Socio-cultural and Demographic Features of Jaunsaris: A Polyandrous Tribes in Central Himalayas". In: Sharma, A.N. (Ed.) *Trends in Anthropological Demography.* New Delhi: Sarup & Sons.

Keesing, R.M. and P.M. Keejing (1971). *New Perspective in Cultural Anthropology,* New Yorki: Ringhart & Winston Publications.

Khatua, N. (2008). "Women's Reproductive and Child Health among the Kumar Tribes". In: Sarkar R.M., *Primitive Tribal Groups in India,* New Delhi: Serial Publications.

Khomrang, K. (2006). A Study of Festivals among the Tangsas of New Changlang Villaae. M.Sc. Dissertation, Department of Anthropology, Dibrugarh University.

Landy, D. (Ed.) (1977). *Culture, Disease and Healing: Studies in Medical Anthropology,* London: Macmillan Publishing Co. Ltd.

Linton, R. (1936). *The Study of Man.* New York: Appleton Century.

Lowie, R. (1953). *Primitive Society.* New York: Bony Liverright.

Mahapatra, S. (1986). *Modernisation and Ritual Identity and Change in Santal Society.* Calcutta: Oxford University Press.

Montague, A. (1957). *Anthropology and Human Nature.* New York: McGraw Hill Book Company.

Murdock, G.P. (1961). *Social Structure*, New York: Macmillan Company.

Mutharayappa, R. (2000). *Tribal Fertility, Mortality and Health Care Practices*, New Delhi: Mittal Publications.

Pandey, D. and B. Tripathy (1997). *A Comprehensive History of Arunachal Pradesh,* Pasighat: Bani Mandir Publications.

Patra, P.K. and Kapoor, A.K. (2006). "A study on mortality among the tribes of India with special reference to Rajis: A primitive tribal group of Central Indian Himalayas". In: *Anthropology of Primitive Tribes in India* (Ed.) Dash Sharma, P., New Delhi: Serial Publications.

Piddington, R. (1952). *An Introduction to Social Anthropology,* London: Oliver & Boyd.

Rao, N.S. (2006). *Tribal Culture, Faith, History and Literature—Tangsas of Arunachal Pradesh,* New Delhi: Mittal Publications.

Saikia, N.D. Dutta Das (2006). *A Study on Fertility of the Tangsa Women of Lido, Tinsukia District. Upper Assam*, Bulletin of the Department of Anthropology, Vol. 34, Dibrugarh University.

Sarkar, A. and S. Dasgupta (2000). *Ethno-Ecology of Indian Tribes, Diversity in Cultural Adaptation*, New Delhi: Rawat Publications.

Sarkar, N. (1993). *Dances of Arunachal Pradesh,* Arunachal Pradesh Research Department.

Sharma, K. (1970). "Fertility and Mortality in Khonds: A Tribal Community of Orissa", *Man in India, 58,* 1:77-88.

Sharma, R.K. (2004). "*Demography and Population Problems*", New Delhi: Atlantic Publishers and Distributors.

Singh, A. and Ram, F. (2004). "Forecasting mortality in India". In: *Population, Health and Development in India: Changing Perspective,* Ed. Roy, T. K. New Delhi: Rawat Publications.

Singh, K.S. (1995). *People of India, Arunachal Pradesh* (Vol. XIV), Anthropological Survey of India, Calcutta: Seaguli Book.

Singh, K.P. (1986). *Correlates of Fertility Behaviour: a Study of Rural Communities in Punjab and Haryana,* New Delhi: Concept Publishing Company.

Sonowal, C.J. (2007). Demographic Transition of Tribal People in Forest Villages of Assam. *Studies of Tribes and Tribals.* Vol. 5(1).

Sonowal, R. and I. Barua (2013). "Indigenous Knowledge and Bio-resource Utilization among the Tai-Khamyangs of Assam, North East India". In: *International Research Journal of Biological Sciences,* (197), 38-43.

Spicer, E.H. (1952). *Human Problems in Technological Change: A Case Book,* New York: Russel Sage Foundation.

Srivastava, M.L. (1969). "Some Aspects of Fertility in a Social Group of India". *Journal of Social Research,* 12.

Srinivasan, K. (1998). "Basic Demographic Techniques and Application": New Delhi: Sage Publications.

Talukdar, S. (1983). "Pattern of fertility and mortality in four caste groups in West Bengal", *Man in India,* 63.

Vidyarthi, L.P. and B.K. Rai (1976). *The Tribal Culture of India.* New Delhi: Concept Publishing Company.

Wadell, L.A. (1901). *The Tribes of Brahmaputra Valley,* New Delhi: Logos Press.

Index